Androids, Humanoids, and Other Science Fiction Monsters

Universal Pictures, 1931. Still courtesy of MOMA film stills archive.

ANDROIDS, HUMANOIDS, AND OTHER SCIENCE FICTION MONSTERS

Science and Soul in
Science Fiction Films

Per Schelde

NEW YORK UNIVERSITY PRESS
New York and London

NEW YORK UNIVERSITY PRESS
New York and London

Library of Congress Cataloging-in-Publication Data
Schelde, Per.
Androids, humanoids, and other science fiction monsters : science
and soul in science fiction films / Per Schelde.
p. cm.
Filmography: p.
Includes bibliographical references and index.
ISBN 0-8147-7930-1 (alk. paper)
1. Science fiction films—History and criticism. I. Title.
PN1995.9.S26S26   1993
791.43'615—dc20   93-274
                CIP

New York University Press books are printed on acid-free paper,
and their binding materials are chosen for strength and durability.

Manufactured in the Unites States of America

10 9 8 7 6 5 4 3 2

Contents

Preface

This book has been a long time in the writing and I owe thanks to the people who have helped, read, and been willing to discuss. First, I need to acknowledge, gratefully, Kitty Moore who originally read my proposal and responded with a contract. I am grateful for the kindness and help I received at the Library of Congress, Motion Picture and Recorded Sound Division in Washington, D.C. Thanks go to the librarians at the 42nd Street Library in New York City and at the Lincoln Center Library for the Performing Arts, who were unfailingly helpful. And I need to thank Dr. Bianca Cody Murphy, who took the time to listen to my largely incoherent speculations about science fiction films, Dr. Barbara Fass Leavy, who was there to discuss or encourage when I needed it and Walter Duncan for his moral and substantive support. Thanks to all of those who read through early versions of chapters or the entire manuscript, especially Dr. Vibeke Rützou Petersen, Rudy Hornish, Dr. Barbara Fass Leavy, and Lois DeWitt. I want to thank my editor, Jason Renker, who was both enthusiastic and critical as needed. But most of all, I must thank Warren Albright, who always listened with interest, always had something intelligent to say, and who put up with me and my computer for the last two years. It hardly needs saying that many of the virtues this book may have were born in the interface with all these people and that any flaws are my responsibility.

Androids, Humanoids, and Other
Science Fiction Monsters

1 ■

Introduction

■ This Is a Book about Science Fiction Film

Although every year sees a new flock of science fiction (sf) movies populate movie screens with aliens, spaceships, androids, cyborgs, and other assorted monsters, the genre has, until lately, largely been neglected by serious film analysts and theorists. And there still is not a book-length study of sf movies that is not a picture book or a picture-book history. The only possible exceptions are *Focus on the Science Fiction Film* (Johnson 1972) and *Alien Zone,* a recent (1990) publication edited by Annette Kuhn. Both are collections of essays, not monographic, unified studies. Both are fine works—the Kuhn book is excellent—but there is still a gap. This book is an attempt to fill that gap.

The science fiction movies genre is important because of its popularity and the huge number of young people who watch these movies. But, with the exception of the above-mentioned volumes and some insightful papers published in scholarly journals, writing about sf movies tends to be limited to "journals devoted to showing and explaining special effects technologies . . . and a steady stream of coffee-table books filled with glossy color stills from science fiction films,"[1] for example, *Mr. Monster's Movie Gold* (Ackerman 1981), *A Pictorial History of Science Fiction Films, Classic Movie Monsters.*

1

My intention in writing this book has been to produce a unified, topical analysis of the sf film, but before outlining the approach and assumptions behind the analysis, let me address another question. Why sf movies and not sf literature? First, science fiction literature has already received a fair amount of scholarly and critical attention.[2] Second, despite appearances, sf movies and sf literature have little in common and appeal to very different audiences. Science fiction literature is, at its best, not afraid of experiments, of intellectual speculation. It asks, as one critic has put it, the question, "What if?"[3] Science fiction literature has a distinct and fairly limited audience—mostly consisting of intellectuals and science buffs.

Sf movies are a very different kettle of fish: the closest relatives of the genre are the horror movie and the action/suspense movie. The audience is not a specialized, intellectual one[4] but, as one student of the genre has said, "merely part of the great mass audience of the cinema generally."[5] And while there may be some audience overlap, I would venture the opinion that the typical sf audience member is not also a reader of science fiction literature. Sf movies assiduously (with a few exceptions) avoid being intellectual and speculative. The focus is not the "what if's" of science, technology, and the future. The sf film focus is on the *effects* of science, on the junction where what science has created (usually a monster) meets people going about living their lives. Sf science does not have to be logical. All that is required is a scary monster. How the monster came to be or where it came from is, if not irrelevant, peripheral.[6]

So, to repeat, this is a book about science fiction *movies*. The overall analysis and the analyses of individual movies are subsumed under a number of theoretical assumptions, the first being that sf films do indeed constitute a distinct genre that can be studied as such. I agree with Kuhn when she says that there is considerable overlap between sf, horror movies, and other types of action flicks. And I agree with her that a fully satisfying definition may be hard to come by. In the second chapter I provide a definition that is, if not satisfactory, operational and, I hope, consistent.

■ Assumptions and Methodology

The folklore and fairy tales of yesterday take up where the mythology of the ancients left off. They are, as Freud said, the run down mythology of former times. Today, a new form has been found. It is represented by the movies, the "funnies" or comic strips, and most recently by the new art of television.[7]

The first and most pervasive assumption behind this book, one that is reflected in the title, is that sf films are a kind of modern folklore. The idea for this book germinated in a footnote to a book about Henrik Ibsen that I co-authored.[8] In that book I argued that folklore, among other things, is a fictional account of the ongoing battle between human beings and the environment, the battle between *nature* and *culture*. Typically, nature is anthropomorphized and is given some kind of human- like—but awful and dangerous—form. Nature in folklore is represented as trolls, monsters, ogres, leprechauns, elves, nixes, and other such creatures whom humans need to befriend or do battle against in order to keep their own distinct domain, that is, culture, intact. The battle is between the raw power of the ogres and trolls and the ingenuity and inventiveness of humans: science and technology.

It is thus understandable that once humans were in a position to explain virtually everything that occurs in nature in scientific terms, the anthropomorphic monsters withered away: traditional folklore monsters seem naive and rather pathetic today. The forests teeming with trolls and dwarfs are gone; the modern scientific worldview has killed them off. There are no longer pockets on Earth that humankind has not invaded, subjected to scientific scrutiny and cataloged down to the level of chemical makeup. Indeed, today we would be hard put to find a person in the industrial west who genuinely would claim to believe in leprechauns or phantasmagorical monsters with two heads and fiery breath. But belief that such monsters did indeed, or at least *could*, exist is the source of folklore and folk tales.

Folklore monsters, the *real* ones that people believed in, inhabited the areas that were outside human control—the forests, the rivers, the mountains, the *wild*. They were metaphorical expressions, shorthand, anthropomorphized "embodiments" of the things humans did not understand in wild nature, the powers, the dangers, the unknown. Today we have new "unknowns" that we would like to explore and subjugate: outer space and far-away planets. We have populated these new unknowns with monsters and ogres that could well be the close relatives of the trolls and ogres of folklore fame. In that sense do I say that sf is modern folklore. Even the most cursory study of the kinds of stories the two genres, folklore and sf, tell reveals that they are remarkably similar—indeed, often identical. And then there is the question of belief: do these monsters, folkloric or from space, exist? Even those of us who are skeptical will admit that our skepticism isn't grounded in concrete knowledge, but rather in the absence of positive proof. There are reputable scientists who consider it very possible that other planets in the universe have developed life forms. But no one has recorded anything remotely resembling proof, although the search goes on.[9] But there are also firm believers, the Whitley Striebers who attest in dire volumes to their one-on-one encounters with aliens from other planets.[10] Just as there were people in the past who firmly believed in the monsters recorded in folklore, there are people today who believe in humanoids from outer space. Sf and the supermarket tabloids are repositories of this belief. Because the tabloids are so full of stories of aliens and their activities on Earth, I occasionally use tabloid headlines to tie sf themes to actual popular "belief" that such things could and do happen. And, as was the case with trolls and leprechauns, those who believe in humanoids are convinced that the monsters/aliens are at least as interested in us as we are in them. There is a whole sf subgenre that deals with these intrusions into the human domain from space aliens (humanoids), from *Invasion of the Body Snatchers* and *I Married a Monster from Outer Space* to *Alien Nation*.

Most sf, however, does not deal with space travel or space aliens; most sf deals with the disasters wrought here on Earth by the very tools humans used to kill the folklore monsters, namely, technology and science. Science grew out of myth and magic,[11] which are, after all, attempts at explaining how the world functions. Science is simply a more efficient, more sophisticated—and testable—model of the world and the way it functions than is magic or myth or, for that matter, religion. But science and technology, like magic, are not just theories about the universe; they are prescriptions for how humans can get the greatest benefit from interacting with nature. And science shares another feature with magic: it has, or seems to have, mysterious and thus potentially dangerous properties. Magic, the "practical" extension of religion/myth, is "a technique that aims at imposing the human will on nature or on human beings by using supersensual powers."[12] Magic is secret knowledge: certain incantations, certain herbs and mixtures or ritualized movements can "tap" into the "mana," the powers of the supernatural, and *direct* them toward specific ends. Magic is knowledge "owned" by a specialist class—magicians, witches, shamans, whatever the term. The same holds for science and its "practical arm" technology; both are the sole property of a class of specialists—scientists—who know the secret "formulas" for harnessing and unleashing the powers lodged in nature.

Science is not "secret" in the sense that magic was, but it is still mysterious and fraught with danger to those of us who are not scientifically trained. Science never reaches us, the ones who have to deal with the effects—good, bad, or indifferent—until it is a *fait accompli*. We are not given a vote on whether or not actually to develop a theory or idea into a product or process. Our vote comes after the fact, if at all, in the stores where the fleshed-out idea is on sale as a product promising to make our lives easier or more pleasant. Science is effects, positive or negative, things happening to the environment, to SCUD missiles, to the ozone layer, to the human body. The processes that trigger the effects are, to most of us, vague and mysterious. Sf movies, from Drs. Frankenstein and Jekyll on, have focused on this element of mystery, of secrecy, of implied danger. In this sense then, the science fiction film, which lionizes this new magic, science, is the structural equivalent of the folktale that recorded the use of magical wands, potions and incantations to harness power.

If the science fiction film is modern folklore, a logical way to approach the genre is to arm oneself with the analytical toolkit of the folklorist/anthropologist. That does not mean, however, that I will not draw upon some of the excellent work that is being done by film theorists.[13]

■ Approaches to Folklore

Folklore—be it fairy tales, folktales, children's rhymes and games, jokes or folk music—did not get written down until it was facing extinction. The great rush to record the humble narratives of common folk, passed orally from generation to generation, did not come until the nineteenth century. That was at a time when traditional oral literature was dying out because of the spread of education and the depopulation of the rural areas. Today, in the Western, industrialized world, traditional folklore is for all intents and purposes extinct.[14] People are no longer telling stories they learned by heart when they were young. There is no reason to; if I want to share a story or narrative with someone, I buy the book— or videotape—and give it to them. Curiously, however, the theoretical and analytical study of folklore is still very much with us. New collections of tales are published every year by major national publishers and university presses, and there is a constant flow of literature about folklore.

Traditional folklore was typically composed in rural settings by poor people. What distinguished folklore from other kinds of literature was that it was oral: composed on the spur of the moment— using received and accepted formulas for composition—it was passed from mouth to ear. It was the literature of the (typically) illiterate. Before the nineteenth century and the sudden interest among literate and academic circles for this "literature of the people," folklore was generally looked down upon. For a person of sophistication and education to listen to, much less repeat, a folk or fairy tale was inconceivable. Folklore belonged to the "common folk" the way comic books, horror movies, and sf movies belong to their modern-day equivalents.

Folklore demands a willingness to suspend, temporarily, reality and logic. The audience needs to *believe*—as is stated in the introductions to many fairy tales. The reward for belief, for suspending critical judgment, is a flight of fantasy. The believer is transported into a separate reality where different rules for behavior are in effect. She will pass through the troll-mirror and be taken on a heady trip down wishful lane and become superwoman for a while.

The fantastical nature of folklore makes it clear that it is wish fulfillment: people can do what is not possible in the waking world of everyday living. That poor and powerless people, typically migrant and seasonal workers who spend their lives toiling to make farmers affluent, have collective dreams in which reality is suspended and the heroes have supernatural powers, helpers, and abilities should come as no surprise. All literature is in some way escapist; it allows the reader to leave his or her own narrow world and problems and to be placed in a separate and often more attractive reality where things are simpler, problems are solvable, and everything is attractively *different*. That a literary genre created by and for the most powerless—those whose lives are constant drudgery—is unflinchingly fantastical and otherworldly is only logical.

Wish fulfillment is also important in sf film. Much sf has the character of a dream where the boundaries of reality have been dissolved to create a new and separate, more interesting "reality." But sf shares another trait with the traditional fairy tale, one that is important for this book: folklore is a symbolic and metaphorical expression of *protest*. Most folktales take their point of departure in the very drudgery and reality of the people who created it. The fact that they are anchored in the reality of the audience makes the impact of the subsequent flights of fancy stand out even more. Anyone who has seen a horror or sf movie will recognize this: these types of films, more than any others, feel the need to anchor themselves and the audience in some kind of recognizable reality. The teenage horror flick invariably starts out by setting the realistic stage upon which the feast of incredible bloodshed is going to take place. For the fantastical to have an effect on us, we have to believe it could happen to us. Both folklore and schlock movies depend on the audience's identifying with the action. In both genres there has to be a hero(ine) with whom we can easily identify—one who comes through it all unscathed and acquires something valuable, usually a treasure (wealth) and/or an attractive partner of the appropriate gender.

The Danish folklore scholar Bengt Holbek, referring specifically to fairy tales (but what he says holds true of most folklore), states flatly that "nearly all the people who tell and listen to these tales belong to the lower or lowest strata of traditional communities."[15]

He finds, as I do, that fairy tales are escapist—vehicles of temporary transportation from lives of toil and want. But more than wish fulfillment, they implicitly engage in social criticism, in indicting a social system that keeps peasants locked in poverty and near slavery. Based on his analysis of a large group of Danish fairy tales, Holbek states that folklore is the specific property of the rural proletariat[16] who in it express a fierce "social aggressiveness."[17] Likewise, Robert Darnton has this to say about fairy tales: "By showing how life was lived *terre à terre*, in the village and on the road, the tales helped orient the peasants. They mapped the ways of the world and demonstrated the folly of expecting anything more than cruelty from a cruel social order."[18]

Holbek is convinced that what he calls "social aggressiveness" is integral to the genre and that it was "washed" out by scholarly and upper-class collectors such as the Grimms before they found it inoffensive enough to print.[19] The form social protest takes in fairy tales is quite direct: in several of Holbek's stories a young boy has problems at home and leaves to make a life for himself. He encounters cruel employers or trolls who own "the means of production." He either makes them respect him by showing his ability to amass wealth or he kills them, in so doing taking over *their* wealth. The protagonist is always desperately poor and alone in the world. He encounters persons in positions of power who abuse that power and threaten to kill him. He has to overcome the powerful and does so by using his skills and physical strength. In the end, he is victorious, marries a princess, and lives happily ever after.[20]

Basic to folktales is the fact that they are protesting a reality which the people who created them have, in effect, no power to influence. The protest is expressed in terms of magic and violence. Folktales are both maps to a cruel reality and statements of protest against a rigid social order "hidden" in the guise of fantastical events and feats.[21] Holbek says that, in the final analysis, most stories, intended as they were mostly for the young, are supposed to teach young men and women to rely on their own wits and strengths—symbolically expressed in the "language" of folklore as magical helpers and tools.[22]

The science fiction film is the same kind of muted "dream"-

protest. The truth of the matter is that ordinary people—the young, the poor, those without access to decision-making—are as powerless vis-à-vis the ongoing "progression" of science and technology as were the users and producers of fairy tales in the past. They have to live with what science does and unleashes upon them. Much sf is a catalog of vague and often irrational fears and complaints about science and technology. That the implicit protest is vague and irrational—which makes scientists and literary sf enthusiasts tend to dismiss it—does not, however, mean that it is unfounded. Sf, like folklore, is first and foremost designed to be entertainment (a point Stephen King emphasizes),[23] but it is also a mirror of the lives and reality of those for whom it is made. The sf film deals with attitudes toward scientists and science and those who control them.

The bulk of this book is dedicated to an examination of this "fear of science." The main argument is that science, as depicted in the movies, threatens not only to destroy the physical world as horror movies such as *Godzilla* suggest, but, more to the point, science and technology are slowly invading our minds and bodies, making us more mechanical, more like machines. Science is robbing us of our humanity, metaphorically expressed as our soul: it threatens to replace the individual, God-given soul with a mechanical, machine-made one.

The organization of the book is as follows. In this chapter I explain in some detail two of my main venues into the interpretation of sf film: the nature/culture schism, and the concept of the soul as it emerges in folklore and as an analytical tool in this book. The next chapter deals with "Dangerous Science" and with scientists as they are depicted in folklore. The main points of the chapter are to establish the folkloric roots of the sf scientists and to deal with strictly disaster movies such as *Godzilla* and *Humanoids from the Deep*. Chapter 2 also introduces the other two *dramatis personae:* "The Hero(ine)" and "The Monster." All of the movies analyzed in this book feature Little People whose lives are rendered chaotic by some kind of encounter with a science-made monster. It is most obvious in the case of movies such as *Godzilla* and *Frankenstein,* but it is true of all of them. In *Death Watch* the monster is a machine/man (cyborg) who intrudes into the life of a dying woman: in *Android*, the monster and the hero are, ultimately, identical: science tries to create a race of humanlike monsters that have no soul or self, no desire other than their masters' whim. But when the "monsters," the androids, kill the scientist, they assert their humanity.

I have tried to structure the book much like a story with a plot. Chapters 2 to 4 introduce themes that go through the book. The "plot" evolves as a story of increasing eradication of the boundary between humans and machines. Each chapter presents a further step in the "dehumanization by science"; also within each chapter, the films analyzed constitute an escalation of that process. An outcome of this is that some films aren't much more than rungs on the ladder, whereas others—the more interesting ones—are given in- depth analyses. Chapter 2 deals with science in general; chapter 3 deals with women in sf; chapter 4 is devoted to creatures from outer space who come and try to destroy, co-opt, or merge with humanity. The result is always the same: human beings, as they are today, will, if the aliens succeed, be phased out. Aliens attacking humans are of course the inversion of the human desire to invade outer space. The idea that aliens might want to invade is, in other words, a scientific bi-product: if science had not found ways to travel into space, we would never have imagined creatures from space coming here. Two of the movies covered in chapter 4 deal explicitly with attempts on the part of alien scientists to take over humans, in the process making them more machinelike, less individually souled beings. The fear being expressed, which crops up again in following chapters, is the fear of forced evolution (evolution is of course itself a scientific theory). What sf protests in these movies is the notion that our fascination with science and with advanced races and organisms may become our demise.

Chapters 5 through 11 constitute the core of the "story": the evolution of the intrusion of science into the lives of "common folk" to the point where humans have become co-opted by science's creation, the machine, and the lines between human and machine have been blurred to the point of eradication. Science becomes in this part of the book the structural equivalent of the aliens who wanted to invade and force evolution upon human-kind.

Chapter 5 introduces "the Machine" as the first encroachment on the human sense of individuality and freedom. Machines that humans have to operate and to which they must adjust their biological rhythms become the first step in the dehumanization associated with the new scientific cosmology, where production and profit are the goals of all things. The folklore troll who owned the means of production and tried to destroy or enslave the hero becomes in these films the Corporation, the President of the Company.

While the machines in chapter 5 do not have consciousness and thus only endanger the human sense of self by making humans adapt to the machines' artificial rhythms, chapter 6 presents computers: machines that not only have a consciousness—however rudimentary—but also volition. Computers in sf are "Disembodied Brains" that, once created, once operating, have no more fervent desire than to wrest power from their creators. Sf computers, like envious aliens, try either to eradicate humans or force them to evolve into more intelligent but emotionless machines like themselves.

Robots, the subject of chapter 7, threaten the human identity even more: they are anthropomorphic thinking machines. Typically, the kinds of robots depicted by sf reflect in their "psychology" the machinelike features in their appearance. Sf robots are either mechanical pets or evil cybernetic races that are out to kill off humanity. The exception is the rebellious Johnny-5 of the *Short Circuit* movies who becomes a "real" human teenager, thus defying the Corporation that constructed him with military purposes in mind.

Chapters 8 and 9 are devoted to other scientific strategies geared toward making humans into docile machinelike slaves. I emphasize again that these films present a scenario in which science invents a method for making humans more machinelike, and the plot then deals with how the Hero(ine) escapes his or her fate by outsmarting The Corporation/Troll. Chapter 8 looks at movies that see the danger of the media (in the broadest possible sense): surveillance, spectacles of violence used as pacifiers, mind- control. Chapter 9 is about "The Dystopia," the police state where humans are enslaved by Corporations/Governments that use fear and intimidation to stay in power and quench opposition.

Chapter 10 begins to merge human and machine. The chapter deals with methods to engineer a new race or change the existing one so it will become more docile. The last part of the chapter examines movies where humans are enhanced by machine parts: biology and technology in symbiosis—cyborgs.

Chapter 11 is where the boundaries are crossed: machines that perfectly mirror humans are constructed to be slaves. Humans have become shadowy forms with no soul to give them substance. Androids, machines, revolt against their human creators/masters and become a new human race. Or conversely, the androids are, as I argue, metaphorical expressions of the human protest against the increasing mechanization of life.

Chapter 12 is a conclusion of sorts where I examine the nature and efficacy of sf as folkloric protest.

■ **The Films**

Although the total data base for the book consists of several hundred movies, I have limited my analysis to sixty five of them. There are three reasons for this. One, it makes the book more manageable for the reader. Two, it allows me to concentrate on movies that are either well known, easily available on video, or have been widely discussed. Three, the truth of the matter is that the sf genre is static: the themes that were introduced in the earliest movies, such as *Frankenstein, Dr. Jekyll and Mr. Hyde,* and *Metropolis,* are repeated over and over with only minimal variations.

■ **Culture vs. Nature: Culture Is Assigning Meaning**

Humans are symbolizing animals. The entire edifice of human culture is built on the ability to communicate, to signify, to assign meaning to. Without symbols, without signifying, there is no culture. Every act by a human being is an act of communication. In our information age the symbolic overload has become so enor-

mous that all acts are not only symbolic but verge on meaningless-
ness because of the cacophony of inherent meanings and the reflection from the media. A movement is no longer a simple movement.
It reflects other movements caught by the fish eye of the camera
lens which gives it multiple contexts. The fictional, *acted*, movement, in its turn, purports to reflect some kind of reality: a movement that at least *could have been real*. Any sense of *real* reality is
an illusion: all acts, movements, thoughts are floating freely, without moorings, in the never-never land of signification like hydro-
foils on puffs of self-emitted air. Any series of events is recast, even
as it takes place, in the mold of the storytelling modes that are
prevalent in our society. Actions are instantly transformed into
scripts that mirror as closely as possible the sitcoms, soap operas,
and news-entertainment programs that have invaded our collective and individual consciousness.[24] But that is our reality today.
The first acts of symbolizing, of assigning meaning, were quite
humble—if revolutionary: humans defined their own segment of
the universe by assigning meanings and significations to the sounds
and actions exchanged among humans. Humans assigned meaning to objects and living things as well as to the vast areas of the
world that were outside culture. Humans assigned meanings, a
role, a "personality" to mighty nature.

Both folklore and sf depend to a large extent on the distinction
between nature and culture. It is of no importance here whether
the distinction is real or desirable; the stories dealt with in this
book assume that it is. The following is a brief outline of an
"archaeology" of the nature/culture schism as a pancultural phenomenon.

To be human is to define. The first act of definition the first true
humans had to attend to was a definition of themselves. For there
to be *culture*, a distinctive human domain, there had to be its
opposite: nature. Culture, in its anthropological sense, is an attempt at creating some kind of order out of relative chaos. Or,
perhaps more precisely, culture is an attempt to carve some kind
of order out of the vast chaos that is nature.

The way humans go about carving out order is to impose it onto
the environment. They arrange themselves and their belongings
in ways that signify—to themselves and to nature—that this is

cultural space. Humans map onto the environment their own theories of the cosmological order. This is true of all human societies —probably of all times. When the !Kung bushmen, until recently hunters and gatherers in southern Africa, set up a camp, however temporary, they invariably arranged it so that it was clearly defined and delimited in the landscape. The camp was set up in concentric circles so that sleeping and cooking were in the innermost circles and waste disposal was relegated to the outermost ones. The idea was of course to make the camp as functional as possible, but also to set it off from the natural, "wild," "uncooked" —to use Lévi-Strauss's term—environment.[25]

■ Nature in the Cultural Script

To early humans, without scientific knowledge and with a very simple technology, nature was a formidable "Other." From the vantage point of early scattered groups of human beings, nature was a vast, mysterious, dangerous, and uncontrollable chaos, which humans, because they cannot live with chaos, anthropomorphized.[26] In other words, humans created a counterintellect to mirror their own. They populated nature with gods, monsters, spirits, trolls, mermen, and other humanlike, but not quite human, creatures.

A hunting and gathering society is likely to see nature, the environment, as essentially benevolent. Hunters and gatherers are dependent on a balance in nature. If they overhunt or deplete an area of natural resources, they cut themselves off from future supplies. More technologically advanced societies, typically agricultural, tend to have a confrontational view of the Other. There are a number of reasons for this. Most importantly, the very basis of agriculture is an act of "violence" where a piece of land is carved from the bosom of nature and transformed into cultural space.[27] So, in agricultural societies nature is seen as something dangerous, as enemy territory. Agricultural societies, such as the European ones that created the folklore and folklore creatures with which we are familiar, populated the noncultural with mysterious trolls, leprechauns, dwarfs, merfolk, Little People, Good

People, fairies, nixes, pixies, and so on. Some are harmless, the majority are malevolent or have to be dealt with carefully.

It was not really until the second half of the nineteenth century that a scientific worldview became dominant. The searchlights of science penetrated the forests, the mountains, the rivers and explained events and processes in its own terms: the terms of physics and chemistry, of weight and measure, of cause and effect. Science cleaned out the supernatural layer between humans' and God's spheres. The power balance between humans and their anthropomorphized environment changed. Humans became more powerful, the environment less so. Even God became more abstract, more distant.

The ongoing battle between humans and supernaturals of any stripe, the Judeo-Christian God included, has been a constant and relentless war of attrition. Humans have used their gifts of ingenuity and their aggressiveness to expand "their" spaces at the expense of nature. Ingenuity has been used to figure out new technological "weapons" to field in the constant warfare. Each of these "weapons"—the plow, the steam engine, and so on—has allowed humans to multiply and to carve out a bigger piece of the cake. The bone of contention has always been *knowledge:* supernaturals and gods had knowledge and powers denied to humans, but humans had intelligence and determination to use it to acquire that knowledge and that power. The oldest human myths deal with this schism: the ancient Greeks told the story of Prometheus who stole fire from the gods and was punished by having his liver picked out by a vulture—in eternity. The root of the conflict is the human desire to become more knowing, more powerful, more *godlike.* As we shall see, many of the movies analyzed in this book feature the scientist who wants to know *too much.*

With the Industrial Revolution (following what has been called the Age of Reason) and the breakthrough of the scientific worldview,[28] humans made another leap forward in the ongoing quest for knowledge and power. God has retained his powers in the areas of beginning and end: he is still ultimately—where the theoretical constructs of evolution and astronomy give up—the Creator, the one who put humans on Earth and the one who determines where we go after our life tenure is over. Everything in between is the property of science and technology, of human intelligence.

Nature, once the all-powerful adversary, has been whittled away. No longer a power to be reckoned with, it has become a victim. Nature has become our collective playground, a gigantic zoo that humans can visit on their day off from the office, a place to visit on Sundays, to be "conquered" once again with our cameras, our four-by-fours, and our AK47s. We even import it: for example, south of Copenhagen there is a "Lion Park," full of exotic, hand-fed animals kept warm by electric heaters. Perhaps this is the saddest and most absurd sight of all, a lion, once the king of the African savanna, standing in the cool Danish summer under a birch tree, staring without comprehension at a carload of day-trippers, clicking away their cameras to take home the proof that they, in person, have once more subjugated and humiliated nature.

Nature has been rendered a powerless victim: its resident monsters have moved to library shelves where they gather dust and to children's lore where they more often than not are depicted as fuzzy and cute. Next, I will turn to a couple of examples of folktales that address the nature/culture schism.

■ Nature, Culture, and Folklore

Since most of the folklore we have today was created after most arable land was under cultivation, we have few stories and tales that actually deal with humans carving land out of nature.[29] But there is an Irish tale about a man who built a house near Derrygonelly, Ireland, and kept on building although he was warned several times not to do so. He was building on the fairies' pass. He was told it was on their pass, but he ignored the warnings. So, the night after he finished he went to sleep and the next day he found the house torn down—not a stone was left upon stone.[30] The man from Derrygonelly had trespassed on the fairies' territory and he was duly punished. The moral is that humans and fairies get along fine as long as humans leave the fairies alone. Whenever a conflict arises, when the paths, for whatever reasons, have crossed, humans have to rely on two things to save themselves and kill or render their supernatural enemies powerless. One of these things is faith, Christianity itself; the other is products of human ingenuity, products of "science" and technology. A Danish tale tells of a hunter who got lost looking for birds and suddenly found himself inside a farm located right in the middle of the forest. He found a girl sitting in a chair, and she told him the people who owned the farm were *tusser* (a type of fairies) and that there was no escape for him. It was the kind of farm humans could not see until they were inside it, and once there, they could never escape. That was what happened to her. He implores her to help him if she can, and she accedes after he has promised to come back and free her after his escape. He can get out by pointing his *gun* at the king of the tusser. The tusser will chase him out and he will be free.[31]

The means of escape is the gun, a piece of human technology. That it is a weapon is important, but more important is the fact that it is made of iron: a product taken from the mountain and transformed, through human ingenuity and inventiveness, into a piece of technology and a *symbol*. The hunter only has to *show* the gun—the girl is emphatic that he mustn't fire at the tusser. Why? Because supernaturals are not killed by gunfire, they are killed by human ingenuity, by having their element transformed into cultural artifacts. The gun is a symbol of human technology and superiority. Other tales give evidence to this. In one Danish tale a woman is stolen by the fairies and her husband manages to free her by throwing a piece of iron into the dust cloud created by the dancing fairies.[32] The iron makes the fairies literally disappear: human science and technology are what killed off nature's anthropomorphic monsters. That iron should be so important is not surprising. Thanks to iron (or metal in general) humans have been able to make enormous inroads into nature's space: plows, axes, and guns have made more land arable, more forests into firewood and houses, more animals into viable hunting objects.[33]

■ The Umbilical Cord: Nature, Culture, and Christianity

So far I have described the relationship between "generic" preindustrial agrarian society and nature. But most of the Western folklore that interests me here was printed in the large national

collections of the nineteenth century and had already been filtered
through a Christian cosmology. The trolls and monsters were assigned positions in the Christian hierarchy.[34] They were forced to
fit on the side of either good or bad: God and his angels, or the
Devil and his horny helpers. Or they were, as we shall see pres-
ently, cast in the role of creations outside the grace of God: soulless creatures with no prospect of salvation.

A type of tale common in Scandinavia and Germany is the
"estranged soul" story: a hunter or traveler comes upon a deer, a
frog, or even a tree that suddenly speaks, asking him not to kill it.
A witch, it explains, has changed it to this inhuman form and it
must stay like this until a human being agrees to do certain things
to free it. Most often the necessary act is fairly innocent, albeit
repulsive: kissing or making love to or *loving* the lost soul. In other
cases, where the soul is trapped in a bloodthirsty wolf, grizzly
bear, or dragon, the act that saves is the killing of the monster.
Once that is done, the human on the inside (always young and
attractive) emerges from the carcass and goes on to marry its
savior and live a life of love and happiness.

In these stories the solution is always to break the spell. The
soul trapped inside the inanimate object, the nocturnal monster,
the ugly frog, has to be set free. Freedom can be obtained through
a sacrifice: someone has to rewire the soul, reconnect it to the
human world. The sacrifice consists in the "savior" giving of her
own soul, a veritable soul transfer: the kiss, the act of lovemaking,
the act of "loving" are uniquely human, as is the ability to sacrifice selflessly. Kissing a frog, having intercourse with a hideous
troll, loving—as you would a handsome person of the opposite
gender—a tree or other inanimate object is a sacrifice and an act
of unselfish love. In folklore this type of kiss or act of love even has
a name, the *fier baiser*, the "strong kiss." In the Christian tradition,
the *fier baiser* is often a symbolic reflection of the selfless act of
love that is the backbone of all Christian salvation: Jesus giving
his life for (Christian) humanity.

I will give a couple of folklore examples, drawn from Scandina-
vian collections because that is the lore I know best. A Danish
ballad tells of a maiden who is wooed by a *lindorm*, a kind of

snakelike dragon. She will, of course, have nothing to do with him, but he forces the issue and sleeps with her. The next day he emerges as a handsome young prince and they live happily ever after.[35] In another ballad a maiden has been bewitched by an evil stepmother/witch who has turned her into a linden tree. Her only escape is to have a prince kiss her roots. He does and they love happily ever after.[36] And there are stories of people in deer, wolf, or bird robes who are saved by love or by having someone kill the animal form.

In Norwegian folklore there is a fascinating creature, half human, half beast, and all fairy: the *huldre*. Often the huldre is described as a beautiful young woman who is fond of human company and loves to go to a dance on Saturday night and bewitch the most handsome young men. There is, however, one problem: she has a tail—usually a cow's tail, sometimes a foxtail—which she tries to hide under her dress. Huldres are attracted to the human sphere; they like to linger outside the warm and cozy house and look longingly through the window at the people. Huldres want to become human because they don't have a soul.[37] One way for a huldre to obtain her wish is to marry a human man. Once she stands in the church, in front of the altar, she loses her tail and becomes fully human.[38]

All of the above themes—the bewitched human, the being who is sad because soulless, the *fier baiser*—are ubiquitous in sf movies. There are new twists—but the connection is undeniable. A couple of examples will show what I mean and help familiarize the reader with my analytical approach. The sf equivalent of the witch who invades a person's mind and changes her into a monster is the evil scientist who uses his mysterious knowledge to obtain control of the mind of another. The movies *Robocop* where a normal man becomes a fierce and deadly machine and *Android* where an innocent and very human android becomes a killing machine as the result of a "brain adjustment," are examples. In some cases the scientist, rather than occupying the mind or body of another, uses his skills to turn himself into an ogre. In folklore, the witch may behave like a perfectly normal human most of the time, but she can change shape and become a black dog, a wolf, or whatever she wants to be. The most obvious sf examples are *Dr. Jekyll and Mr. Hyde* and *Altered States*, where the protagonists become apelike monsters after ingesting secret formulas.[39]

The innocent human who is trapped inside a monstrous form or is inhabited by an evil spirit is common in such 1950s sf epics as *Invasion of the Body Snatchers*, *I Married a Monster from Outer Space*, and *Invaders from Mars*. And the huldre who is sad because she is soulless is reflected in the stories of robots that desperately want to become accepted as human, desperately want to obtain a "soul": the prime examples are the *Short Circuit* movies, where the sweet but metallic *Johnny-5* has no higher wish than to become a normal teenager; *Android*; and, most movingly, *Blade Runner*, where the lovely young replicant Rachel is sad because she discovers she is not human. Like the huldre, she falls in love with a human man who saves her. In all three movies, love—the *fier baiser*—is the source of salvation for the soulless creatures.

■ Sf Soul Defined

For the purposes of this book, I define "soul" as a bundle of things. My definition does not derive from theology, from the Christian concept of soul. Rather, it is an analytical unit that is more often implicit than explicit, yet crucial to an understanding of sf films because of their focus on the fate of "little," ordinary people in a "brave new" world of science and technology. Thus first and foremost, the soul is the umbilical cord, the lifeline that connects the individual to God and to final salvation. It is the key that opens the door to heaven. It is an individual contract between the Supreme Being and those who believe in him.

Put another way, the soul is the locus of individuality, of self. It is what prevents us from being mere statistics, faceless members of a gray human mass. Without soul a human being is open to assault from the outside, can be enslaved, used, co-opted, made into a mindless appendix of a piece of technology. Soul is *free will*.[40]

■ Notes

1. Kuhn 1990:1.
2. Kuhn makes this same point in her book, Kuhn 1990:1.
3. Hodgens 1972: 271. Of the sci-fi movie, Hodgens, apparently an sf literature enthusiast, has this to say: "Science fiction films, with few exceptions, follow different conventions. The premise is always flatly impossible. Any explanations offered are either false analogy or entirely meaningless. The character who protests, 'But that's *incredible, Doctor!*' is always right" (250).
4. That statement needs to be modified, perhaps, in light of the "cult" popularity of such sf epics as *Liquid Sky* and *The Brain That Wouldn't Die.* The "cult" audience tends to be composed of intellectuals and college students. I would contend, however, that such audiences have different motives for seeing these movies than do the mass audiences who are first-run consumers of sf films.
5. Baxter 1970:8.
6. I shall argue in this book that there is an additional difference: sf movies contain, contrary to the case with sf literature, the seed of a rebellion against science and the powers that control science. Since this argument ties in with my analysis of sf movies as a kind of modern folklore, I will ask the reader to be patient and see below. Sf literature is most often so blatantly uncritical of science and technology that it comes across as either inherently reactionary or as science worship. There are of course notable and conscious exceptions; novels such as *The Handmaid's Tale* by Margaret Atwood and *Woman on the Edge of Time* by Marge Piercy (1976) stand out.
7. Grotjahn 1957, quoted in Schechter 1988:1.
8. Jacobsen (Schelde) and Leavy 1988.
9. See, e.g., *Life Magazine* 1989, Golden 1988, Wolkomir 1987, and Broad 1990.
10. Strieber 1987, 1989.
11. See the interesting discussion in Luck 1985, chapter 1 about "Magic." Luck ties myth, magic, and religion together and makes the point that science grew out of this mixture. Examining the Greek and Roman traditions, he finds that in transitional figures such as Pythagoras and Orpheus—whom he calls shamans—magic and religion are combined: Pythagoras was both scientist and shaman. I shall return to this idea in chapter 3 in my discussion of the sf scientist.
12. Luck, 1985:3.
13. I'm referring to scholars such as Kaja Silverman, Laura Mulvey, Constance Penley, Stephen Neale, Vivian Sobchack, and Peter Wolen,

all of whom are cited and referred to throughout this book. See also the bibliography.

14. The exception being the kinds of "urban legends" collected and studied by Jan Harold Brunvand in *The Choking Doberman* and *The Mexican Pet* (Brunvand 1984, 1986).

15. Holbek 1987:405. The same holds for the historian Darnton, who writes: "Thus, whenever one looks behind Perrault [whose collection of Mother Goose tales Darnton is examining] to the peasant versions of Mother Goose, one finds elements of realism—not photographic accounts of life in the barnyard (peasants did not actually have as many children as there are holes in a sieve, and they did not eat them) but a picture that corresponds to everything that social historians have been able to piece together from the archives" (1984:38). The entire chapter, "Peasants Tell Tales," is an attempt to reclaim folklore from the all too "romantic" readings of psychoanalysts such as Fromm and Bettelheim.

16. In modern-day Morocco, the folklore, the oral storytelling tradition, is very much alive and full of political anger—in the major cities. One can speculate that the fact that most of the urban proletariat in Morocco are recent transplants from the rural areas. That they are illiterate and have virtually no access to means by which to better their lives may be the reason for the continued living tradition of oral folklore in Morocco.

17. Holbek 1987:605.

18. Darnton, 1984:38. For Darnton the protest is implied. He says that, in the final analysis, the French tales that are his subject matter are maps to a cruel world that make it obvious that not only is the social order cruel, but the unwary peasant is as likely to be outwitted and cheated by his peers as by those above him in the social order. Thus the better part of valor, since "the world is made of fools and knaves," is that it is "better to be a knave than a fool" (64).

19. Darnton concurs in this, it is one of the main points of his chapter, "Peasants Tell Tales" (1984:9–73). According to Holbek, folklore has, since antiquity, been the property of the proletariat and has always been laced with social anger. First there was myth in simple hunting/ gathering societies. Then, when societies became more complex, the myths followed bifurcating routes. On the one level, they became established religion in the hands of the rich and powerful. On the other, they became, in the hands of poor folk, folklore, full of social aggression. The reason folklore was always held in contempt by the upper classes is exactly because it had this revolutionary tenor. Collectors such as the Grimms made sure they pulled the teeth of aggression before publishing fairy tales.

20. Holbek 1987:458–597.

21. The question arises, of course, if the people who used folklore actually understood the stories they told and listened to. Did they fully realize the protest aspects? It is impossible to say with total confidence that they did, but the uncensored stories are so permeated by anger that we have to assume the protest was perceived as such.
22. Holbek 1987:420.
23. Quoted in Schechter 1988:52.
24. See the interesting article in the *New York Times* by Georgia Dullea about how the ubiquitous camcorder is invading and "scripting" out lives to fit the prevalent stories and storytelling; Dullea 1991.
25. See Levi-Strauss 1983. The information about the !Kung is derived from a number of sources. The best and most complete of these is Lee 1984.
26. This is the idea first put forward by the French sociologist Emile Durkheim, most cogently in his perhaps most famous work, *The Elementary Forms of the Religious Life* (1912).
27. This is expressed also in the verb "to cultivate," to make into part of culture.
28. I realize that this is a simplification: the Industrial Revolution and the scientific worldview presupposed events in the fields of economy, politics, and communication technology that I simply cannot get into here.
29. It is interesting in this connection to note that the folkloric monsters that still have "true believers" are thought to live in deserted mountain areas (Big Foot/the Yeti) or in the dark and murky waters of immensely deep lakes (Loch Ness's Nessie). See the article by Malcolm W. Browne on the search for a "Wildman" in "the wilderness of Shennonjia Forest in central China"; Browne 1990.
30. Glassie 1985:158–59.
31. This story is taken from Christiansen 1964:102–103.
32. See Jacobsen (Schelde) and Leavy 1988, where I give additional examples and a more elaborate discussion.
33. The Freudian overtones are not lost on me: the hunter with his gun who frees the girl who cannot free herself. I will discuss this in a general way in chapter 3, but I can say here that I do think it is important that the male with the gun saves the female who, as it were, lacks one. Many cultures claim that the cultural edifice is the male domain. Men, so the myth goes, *created* culture (perhaps out of womb envy), it is their domain. Women are thus, as far as culture is concerned, marginal. They have to be allowed in. They are more easily lured by nature. Consequently, women have to be the wards of men and let themselves be monitored by them. The gun—certainly a penile object—is, in Lacan's term, the phallic signifier: the phallus (the father) is the one who "pulls" the child into culture, into signifi-

cation. In the Ibsen book I discuss this at great length, and I refer the interested reader to that book (Jacobsen [Schelde] and Leavy 1988, chapter 2 and especially chapter 3).

34. A more detailed discussion and references to sources can be found in Jacobsen (Schelde) and Leavy 1988:42 and note 27.
35. Grundtvig 1853–90, vol. 2, no. 65.
36. Ibid., no. 58.
37. According to another Norwegian tale, "Why huldres are so sad." See Jacobsen (Schelde) and Leavy 1988:107, note 17.
38. Christiansen 1964, esp. part 6, "Legends about spirits of forest and mountain."

   A huldre may, however, retain some of her previous powers. Many Norwegian folktales tell of huldre women married to human men who are grumpy and mistreat them. The woman, after taking the abuse quietly for years, suddenly has enough of it and demonstrates her powers by bending a horseshoe, a rifle, or an iron bar. This act gets the abusive husband's attention and he changes his wicked ways. There are, of course, many ways of interpreting this story, but the female = nature interpretation is probably the most appropriate. Women have "mysterious" natural powers in their ability to pro-create, to regenerate life within themselves. Men, masters of culture, have to allow women into their sphere, but even when women are full members of culture, they have their own "mysteries" locked up in them.

39. In *Frankenhooker* the protagonist, a failed medical student, inserts a drill into his brain in order to hit the centers that govern ethics and morality, and give him the plot's crucial idea: to find the missing body parts to his fiancée's severed head among the prostitutes in Manhattan's Times Square.
40. That the African slaves in the U.S. developed such a fierce sense of soul and salvation was probably, among other things, a means to retaining a core of self, of something the slave owners could not touch, control, sell, or kill.

2 ▪

Dangerous Science

This chapter is designed to do a number of things. I start with a working definition of what an sf movie is, then move on to profile the three most important sf stock characters: the Hero or Honest Joe/Jane, the Scientist, and the Monster. The discussion of sf science, its goals and outcomes, is inserted between the scientist and the monster because science is what the scientist does and because the monster, to an extent, is the outcome of science. But first a definition.

▪ What Is an Sf Movie?

For the purposes of this book an sf movie is defined as a movie that spotlights some kind of "fictional science," by which I mean scientific discoveries or inventions that are (or at least at the time of the movie's creation *were*) purely imaginary. Good examples are such classics as *Frankenstein, Dr. Jekyll and Mr. Hyde, The Invisible Man, Metropolis, "X"—The Man with the X-Ray Eyes*—all movies where the central scientific feat is strictly imaginary. In a few cases, reality has caught up with fiction: movies such as *The First Men in the Moon* have been more than matched by NASA and Soviet space program reality.

Sometimes, the fictional element is in the effects rather than the science. The protagonist of *Incredible Shrinking Man* is the victim of a fairly credible atomic experiment. The effects the experiment has on him are not credible, and neither are the effects of underwater atomic bomb blasts in *Godzilla:* like a grotesque Sleeping Beauty, the giant monster is somehow brought out of a million-year hibernation by the detonation of test bombs. In these movies, the scientific feat is at least acceptable; the effects, unless read as metaphorical, are not.

Movies about space travel are invariably categorized as sf because space travel is predicated on scientific discovery. And very few space movies concentrate on fact as does *The Right Stuff.* Space travel, *actual* space travel, mind-boggling and exciting as it is, is not the stuff of which colorful B-movies are made. It's too technical, too cautious, too *scientific.* Sf movies need plot, Good Guys and Bad Guys, humanoid monsters lurking on exotic planets, spectacular weapons, rocket chases, and blood and gore. So, where action/war movies almost invariably take their point of departure in some dastardly and cowardly act that catapults the hero from inactivity into submachine-gun-wielding maniacal frenzy, the thing that jump-starts most sf movies is a scientific experiment, discovery, or feat.

There are, however, hybrid genres, such as time-travel epics, that take their point of departure in a scientific discovery only to turn into movies that insert characters from the present into a past bathed in a light that is at once tender and ironic, bordering on contemptuous. Movies such as *Back to the Future* are most interesting for being filmic expressions of a common-enough desire, "a primal scene fantasy, the name Freud gave to the fantasy of overhearing or observing parental intercourse, of being on the scene, so to speak, of one's own conception."[1] *Back to the Future* does employ an element of the standard sf vocabulary: the mad scientist who invents the time-travel capsule. But once the sf element has gotten the action going, it disappears for the bulk of the movie only to reappear toward the end when the hero has to get back to his own time. Time-travel movies are apt metaphors for moviemaking itself (machines that produce travels in time and space and dreams for the audience to enter). Christian Metz has said that the cinema represents a kind of enclosure or "reserve" which escapes a fully social life although it is accepted and prescribed by it: going to the cinema is one licit activity among others with its place in the admissible pastimes of the day or the week, and yet that place is a "hole" in the social cloth, a *loophole* opening on to something slightly less approved than what one does the rest of the time.[2]

Movies about the future are by definition sf because they more often than not focus on science and technology.

Often, sf movies mix all of the above: movies that are set in the future, somewhere in outer space (on a far-away planet or a space-ship adrift in the universe), focus on scientific discoveries or their effects. *Battle Beyond the Stars* is set in some timeless future, full of androids, robots, and a few humanlike characters. The central conflict involves a super-powerful weapon that will give those who have it control of the entire universe. *Forbidden Planet* is set in the future in outer space, aboard a rocket that lands on a far-away and "forbidden" planet and focuses on a combination computer/monster that has the potential for destroying mankind.

■ The Sf Hero

Sf movies, like horror movies, depict a kind of bleak universe where people try to muddle by in a world where they have no control of the most important forces impinging on their lives. They never know when their innocent boat trip is going to land them in the middle of a secret atomic experiment or when the honest Bill they just married is going to turn into a glow-in-the-dark space monster on the prowl for Earth-women. The protagonist is almost always a Little Guy/Gal who is trying to live life as normally and happily as possible. But, alas, he or she is interrupted in the midst of a perfectly average life and activities and thrust into the throes of major crisis. Suddenly, our hero(ine) is up against it, and "it" is usually science in one of its manifestations.

The protagonist of *Incredible Shrinking Man*, Robert Scott (a nice, normal name), is vacationing on his wealthy brother's boat. Robert is the archetypical anti-hero, always a couple of steps behind making it, always struggling. From the boat, he sees an atomic explosion in the distance. Moments later he sails right through the atomic clouds. Silvery dust covers him. Six months later, his wife Kitty is preparing his breakfast while Robert is getting dressed to go to work. His pants seem a bit large; irritated, he asks if Kitty got the right pants back from the cleaners. And so it goes. He is shrinking—incredible as it may seem—a result of his exposure (graphically demonstrated by the silvery ashes) to the atomic detonation.

Or take a typical sf heroine, Marge, in *I Married a Monster from Outer Space*. She is a pretty, rather conventional and ordinary girl who lives in tiny Norrisville, somewhere in the heartland. Her whole ambition in life is to marry Bill and live happily ever after.[3] The wedding takes place and the newlyweds take off for their honeymoon. But Bill is acting strange, doesn't know what a thunderstorm is, doesn't know how to behave around an inexperienced and nervous young bride. She's up against it and "it" in her case is that Bill has been co-opted by a space monster who wants to have children by her as soon as the alien scientists find a way to mutate female (human) DNA so "Bill" can impregnate her. What's at stake is the survival of the human race and she's all alone to fight the battle and her way back to her dream: handsome, ordinary Bill, the insurance salesman, and herself merrily busy producing *human* offspring by the station-wagon-load. The sf hero resembles the folklore (or fairy tale) hero, also invariably a perfectly normal person, who suddenly is catapulted into a snake pit of monsters and vicious adversaries who attack him for no other reason than that he's there.

Typically, the sf movie hero does not have much psychological depth. He is "generic," a typical, workaday American. This is, of course, another feature shared with folklore (or at least fairy-tale) heroes. The protagonist has to be normal enough for the audience to identify with; he cannot be so unusual that his quirks become the focus of the movie. The reason is that the protagonist merely is supposed to be *representative*, not psychologically or otherwise interesting. The relative psychological neutrality of the protagonist invites the audience in, sucks them right into the vacuum. The hero is an empty vessel, just waiting to be filled, while everyone around him, typically, is broadly drawn, like the stereotypes we all feel inhabit our lives and worlds. A protagonist who's too colorful, too interesting in himself would take away from the real protagonist: science gone bad.

In movies where the protagonist *is* out of the ordinary, typically the movies where the hero is the scientist, everybody around him (it's almost never a her) is one hundred percent normal and typical. The scientist/protagonist, pursuing his scientific goals, is at the same time destroying his own chances of ever having a normal life, and he is hurting those close to him. Dr. Frankenstein is an unruly genius, his fiancée is an ordinary girl who just wants to get married and settle down. The same holds for the young women in *Dr. Jekyll and Mr. Hyde,* in *The Invisible Man,* in *"X"—The Man with the X-Ray Eyes,* in *The Fly,* and others. They all believe they are married or engaged to perfectly normal men who will allow them to live ordinary, happy lives. They are all wrong, of course.[4]

■ The Scientist as Shaman, Superman, and Romantic Genius

The Little Guy/Gal is an sf stereotype, the way the Angry Father was a stereotype in the Commedia dell'Arte or the Rich Bitch in American soap operas. The second sf stereotype is the Scientist. He shares a number of features with another "owner" of arcane knowledge: the shaman who has secret, mystical, somehow (at least seemingly) supernaturally derived knowledge as his trademark (because shamans usually, but not always, are male, I have chosen to use the male pronoun).[5] As anthropology defines him, the shaman is a religious specialist who through some kind of personal crisis (usually a life-threatening disease) has obtained access to the sphere of the supernaturals. This access, often described as a journey, has given him supernatural helpers and secret knowledge. He is capable of tapping forces belonging to a part of reality that is normally invisible and inaccessible.

The shaman acts as a liaison or conduit between humdrum human reality and the separate reality of extrahuman knowledge. He can, through incantations, magical acts, dances, and other acts transfer these forces—anthropologists like to use the Polynesian term) *mana*—from one sphere to the other. What is more, he is able to apply these imported powers, this mana, to specific ends.

The shaman is a performer. The exact nature of his knowledge and the processes involved in accessing mana are secret. But he does put on a show. He manipulates *symbols* in a way that the audience recognizes and accepts: a child is sick and the shaman is called. He proceeds to perform a ritual. He dances, chants, goes into a trance, and finally, the high point, he "miraculously" extracts a bloody lump of meat that was causing the problem. For layman watching, the process is incomprehensible. But the bloody lump is "proof" that the shaman has performed a cure.

The sf scientist also has access to forces outside normal "reality." He uses secret knowledge to extract the mana from the chemicals or formulas that constitute his magic, and, like the shaman, he is a performer of the first order: surrounded by hissing, boiling, steaming concoctions racing round a test-tube sculpture is the feverishly working scientist, Dr. Jekyll. He is combining chemicals and materials that have never been combined before to obtain the power to undo what God has wrought: the splitting, not of the atom, but of the forces of good and evil in the human soul. This is the sf scientist at work, unlocking "bottled spirits," natural forces. His tools of the trade are his secret knowledge and the "mana" embodying various chemical compounds. The liquids sizzle, churn, and foam to a climax, and Jekyll pours the angry concoction into a glass; the miracle can now take place.

Or take another scientist/shaman. André—in *The Fly* (1958)—has invited his wife Helen to see his latest invention. With much flourish, he places an ashtray in one of two identical glass booths —he calls them "telepods"—and turns on his machinery: a machine that looks like a tape recorder starts spinning, a wall of neon lamps starts blinking off and on, and then smoke forms in one of the "booths," a poof! of an explosion occurs, and the unbelievable has happened: the ashtray has been—as if by magic—"teleported" from one "booth" to the other.

The shaman is usually depicted in his hut with the tools of his trade: herbs and ritual paraphernalia. Likewise, the sf scientist is always presented in a way that shows him in his "natural environment": the lab, the place where he reigns supreme. And always the lab is *mysterious*, a place so different from ordinary spaces as to make it belong almost to another world: a kind of transitory space between the normal, "real" world and the "otherworld" of secret and mysterious forces and powers. The scientist is surrounded by the paraphernalia of his trade, his symbols. He puts on a show where he manipulates the symbols, and we, the audience, accept him and his claim to be a scientist capable of scientific "magic."

The purpose of the test tubes and the bubbling fluids is to instill a sense of awe in the observers (including the movie audience). The processes that are taking place in the tubes or in the entrails of the computers and machines are never explained. They need no explanation because they are a kind of cinematic shorthand for scientist and science—both, by definition, beyond the understanding of the layperson.

So the sf scientist is the modern cousin of the shaman, but he is also the practical cousin of the Great Artist invented by the Romantic movement. The science fiction scientist emerged as a literary figure in the nineteenth century at about the same time as the Romantic artist did. Both the artist and the scientific genius grew out of the Romantic obsession with the individual, the remarkable loner, the genius who single-handedly changes the world and creates mighty works. The emergence of the individualist was tied to the disappearance of the feudal system and the ushering in of the capitalist mode of production. People were no longer locked in a preset pattern, in roles determined by where and to whom they were born. In postfeudal society, each—male, white—person was the author of his own success or failure. The ideal was no longer high birth or ample means, but outstanding abilities and energies. The new hero was the man who was capable of lifting himself out of his social station and catapulting himself into the firmament of stardom by the sheer power of his innate genius.[6]

But being a genius entailed problems. The genius had a calling and a duty. He had to dedicate all of his life and all of his activities, as army advertising has it, to "being all that he could be." The nod of great gifts meant having to make sacrifices. The genius's potential Great Accomplishment could only become fact if he was willing to forsake the mundane and bourgeois happiness of home and wealth and a loving wife. The genius was, like the shaman, not really of this world. He found his inspiration outside the human sphere, constantly tottering on the brink of disaster. To bring off the Big Accomplishment, he had to call in the spirits to which his genius gave him access. But only by being lonely, preferably unhappy, and *outside* could he attract the spiritual help he needed. The man who is destined to become a great writer of love poetry has forever to be separated from the loved one. If he asks her to marry him and she says yes and they settle down and have a houseful of chubby brood, the inspiration will never come. He has to love at a distance and unhappily. The genius has to stay uncontaminated with bourgeois comfort and happiness. Wife, kids, a nine-to-five, and a mortgage are guaranteed to sweep the genius dust from any man's wings.

The sf scientist is cast in this mold. He is the loner, the genius who has the choice of being a happy man, married to a woman who loves him, respected by his peers and family and friends, or of giving it all up and going where his genius leads him. Although Dr. Frankenstein, hero of the 1932 movie of the same name,[7] suffers as he purposely separates himself from his fiancée and family, he *has* to "sacrifice" bourgeois happiness to bring his creation to life. And Dr. Jekyll is painfully aware that he can marry Muriel, his fiancée, and be happy and good, or that he can let his science totally possess him with disastrous results. And he knows that one excludes the other.[8]

Even in *Altered States*, a movie made in 1978, the central choice is between scientific greatness and family/social success. Eddie Jessup is chatting with his visiting friend and colleague, Arthur. Arthur has just learned from his wife that the Jessup marriage is breaking up. Adds the wife, "She's still crazy about him, he's still crazy." Arthur confronts Jessup about the impending divorce, saying he can't see the problem: after all, Jessup is married to a great woman and he is a highly respected scholar and teacher at Harvard. Jessup's retort is both vehement and instructive:

For God's sake Arthur, is that how you imagine me, "a respected and admired figure," a devoted father, a loving husband while I've also published two papers a year for the last seven years—and *not a fundamental piece of work in the lot*. We just sit around the living rooms of other young, married faculty members talking about infantile masturbation and who's sucking up to the head of the department and whose tenure is hanging by a thread. Emily's quite content to go on with this life. She insists she's in love with me—whatever that is. What she means is she prefers the senseless pain we inflict on each other to the pain we would otherwise inflict on ourselves. *But I'm not afraid of that solitary pain. In fact, if I don't strip myself of all this clatter and clutter and ridiculous ritual, I shall go out of my fucking mind.* [Emphases added]

Like so many of his contemporaries, Ibsen devoted much of his own literary energy to trying to ferret out what exactly it was that genius required of its would-be suitor.[9] Virtually all of his late plays are about men who would be great but are not willing to pay the price. Solness in *The Master Builder* believes he is a genius who enlisted from trolls and spirits the help to become successful. But Ibsen says no, Solness sold out. Instead of building churches with steeples that penetrate the heavens, he built villas for the bourgeoisie. And in *When We Dead Awaken*, Rubek is a sculptor of genius who never fulfilled his promise because he became the darling of the bourgeoisie, creating busts of the rich and, in the process, himself becoming a rich, fat cat—minus the genius.

Another side of the sf scientist's Romantic legacy is his status as a kind of Nietzschean *Übermensch*, "superman." The superman is the exceptional human being who by dint of his exceptionality, his extraordinary gifts, has special rights. A literary character, Raskolnikov, the neurotic hero of Dostoyevsky's *Crime and Punishment*, is perhaps the prime example of the genius who claims for himself the right to kill people. Dostoyevsky's novel has much more to offer, I hasten to say, but for my purposes here, Raskolnikov can stand as the prototype of a Romantic anti-hero/superman.

The sf scientist, driven as he often is—like Raskolnikov—by "inner voices" or an inner necessity, feels that he too has special rights. Because he is a genius, he feels he is not responsible to anyone but his own personal gods: science and progress. In most sf movies where the scientist is the protagonist, the moral issue comes up sooner or later and the scientist invariably answers that the doubts and moral hang-ups he is presented with are but "fear of flying": the timid always deny that flying is possible or desirable or worth doing. But he, the scientist, has an obligation to fly, to unfold his wings and see if they will carry him.

Raskolnikov is so poor he is starving. Out of the hallucinations born of starvation comes the crazy idea that he is special, that he has rights no one else has. Likewise in *The Invisible Man*, when Jack Griffith has ingested the potion that makes him invisible, one of the ingredients has the side effect of making him crazy.[10] That, however, is not the way Jack sees it: "The drugs I took seemed to light up my brain. Suddenly, I realized the power I held, the power to rule, to make the world grovel at my feet. Ha, ha! We'll soon put the world right now." He has become superman and has the right to make the world grovel at his feet.

Seth Brundle of the 1986 remake of *The Fly* is just another weird genius until he has the crucial mishap. He becomes a sexual athlete—a match for the most virile porn star. He has enormous energies and appetites: as he says of the "teleportation" he went through, "It purified me, cleansed me!" and later on, "It's like a drug, the power surges inside me." He feels he can do anything. He wants his girlfriend to "go through"; she refuses; he discards her: "You're a fucking drag, you know that? . . . You're afraid to dive into the plasma pool." He goes to a sleazy bar, arm-wrestles a man, breaking his arm so violently that the bone juts out at a jaunty angle, abducts his girlfriend to have sex with her and to try to force her to go through as well. He is convinced that his new energy and lust for life give him the right to do whatever he wants.

And like the Romantic artist, the sf scientist is a *rebel*. He will not accept that there are things he is not supposed to know about, apples that should not be eaten. In Nietzsche's terms, he repudiates mediocrity and a Christian morality that make the average desirable and the end of all human striving. These words, attributed by their author Heinrich Heine to the biblical Adam, could be the anthem of sf scientists:

I shall never miss
the rooms of Paradise;
it was no true Paradise—
there were forbidden trees.

I want my full right to freedom!
If I find but the slightest confinement,
Paradise becomes for me
a Hell and a jail.[11]

The basic opposition is between a traditionalist, Judeo-Christian world-view, a cosmology wherein humans have a preassigned space and allotment of knowledge, and the view expressed by Heine's Adam: that the scientist has the right to discover and invent whatever he is capable of.

Traditional religion fears that science will harm humanity but, perhaps even more, that it will explode the existing order, that science will challenge, attack, or even "kill" God. Gershom Scholem, writing about the Golem, the human-made man of Jewish tradition, notes that "the real and not merely symbolic creation of a golem would bring with it 'the death of God'! the hybris of its creator would turn against God."[12] Some scientists, like Frankenstein, are more than willing to make that challenge. Henry Frankenstein says to Fritz on the night of the great event, "This storm will be magnificent, all the electrical secrets of Heaven, and this time we're ready, eh Fritz?" Frankenstein is not afraid to uncover God's secrets. He scorns the older scientist, his former teacher Dr. Waldman, for being scared of looking beyond the stars. Frankenstein, the scientist, will not be daunted by doubts and fears and moral scruples. He has to fulfill his potential—at any price. In Gialanella's play *Frankenstein*—which distills the issues—the following sequence nutshells the conflict (Frankenstein is, as in Mary Shelley's book, Victor; the friend is Henry):

HENRY: Do you aspire then to be a god?
VICTOR: God?
HENRY: Yes.
VICTOR: That thought had never occurred to me.
HENRY: What of the soul, Victor? The body is but the keeper of the soul and death releases it to heaven.
VICTOR: And proctors of this soul would have knowledge disregarded and truths pronounced miracles. Mysteries were made to be solved, my friend. . . . I am no atheist, no blasphemer, but merely a scientist desiring to understand the secrets of life and perhaps, therefore, of God.
HENRY: Prometheus.
VICTOR: What?
HENRY: Prometheus was punished by the gods for bringing fire down to man.
VICTOR: Prometheus was a fool. The gods were jealous, greedy and possessive.[13]

Victor Frankenstein poised to uncover God's secrets and create life. This is the *shaman* in his technological "otherworld." (Universal Pictures, 1931. Still courtesy of **MOMA** film stills archive.)

The sf movie has a complicated relationship to the sf scientist. In some ways, the scientist is a positive character who tries to further human progress. He is a rebel against mediocrity and stubborn conservatism. He is a "freedom fighter" for the cause and liberation of humanity. He helps humankind distill its potential, helps humans become less like animals and more like gods. But he is also, finally and ironically, the one who threatens to destroy humanity with his lack of respect for the traditional cosmology. Humans, to be humans, need to be contained within that cosmology. They need there to be a God, they need to have a soul inside them that can't be broken down into its chemical constituents and mechanical parts.

The sf point is that science is good and beneficial so long as it "knows its place" and its limitations. The scientist is basically a good man who in a fit of hubris endangers the totality. He encroaches on the territory of God and in so doing refutes his own humanity. The essence of humanity—in sf—is the loving relationship between a man and woman. The scientist always has the antithesis and antidote to his false pride and ambitions in the form of a woman who loves him and is willing to sacrifice herself for him. He always has the choice of giving up his attacks on the eternal truths and be a normal, mediocre, but happy man.

■ The Evolution of the Sf Scientist

While all the above points fit the sf scientist as a genre stock character, there are some subtle ideological and social changes that reflect history.

The "evolution" of the sf scientists follows rather neatly the history of modern science. Bernal, in his *Science in History* (1965), says that after the breakthrough of modern science—tied in, of course, with the onset of the Industrial Revolution and the transition from the feudal to the capitalist mode of production—most scientific research was performed by wealthy individuals who were attracted by the promise of making breakthrough discoveries and having their names etched in the annals of history along with those of Darwin and Pasteur. Later, scientists—in the real world —were likely to be attached to the big universities that could afford to pay them and their increasingly expensive machinery and paraphernalia.[14] The sf reflections of this development are movies like *Altered States* and *Dreamscape*. But it is worth pointing out that, although the outer circumstances change, the sf scientist retains his stock characteristics. He is still, at heart, the shaman/ Romantic genius. The obvious example is Jessup in *Altered States*.

Science became militarized during World War II in a way it had never been before. The war became a race to see who could develop the most devastating weapon fastest. The United States dropped the first nuclear bomb on Hiroshima and Nagasaki and scientists became, for many people, war heroes. Hot war turned to cold, yet scientists were still employed by the government and the military to develop more deadly and efficient nuclear weapons faster than the Russians, and to get Americans on the moon and into space first. When the cold war was at its iciest, belief in the American Way and in American technology and know-how spawned trust in the basic decency of science and scientists. Sf scientists from this period are typically much more socially mainstream than earlier ones: they are neat and do not abandon girlfriends, wives, and children for the supernatural mistress of science. They are of this world, and even when they are most devoted to their work, they worry about their loved ones.

Most of these '50s movies record, not surprisingly, the interactions on Earth or on distant planets between humans and evil extraterrestrials. Much has been written about this,[15] to the effect that all of these movies reflect directly the McCarthy attitude: the Commies are a different species, they are soulless because they don't believe in God. They are envious of what Americans have, and they want to destroy us, change us to be like them, or to steal what we have. Typical movies from this period are *Invasion of the Body Snatchers*, *The Angry Red Planet*, *Invaders from Mars*, *The War of the Worlds*, and *This Island Earth*.

Several of these movies will be discussed in detail in the chapter dealing with aliens (chapter 4), so here I will merely profile Dr. Cal Meacham of *This Island Earth*. He is a brilliant young scientist, high on flying and his work. He is accosted by aliens (masquerading as human scientists representing a huge corporation) who try to convince him to work for them. He does so until he

This Island Earth: Cal Meacham, the scientist-cowboy trapped in the "evil empire" of the Metalunans. Like the "superchildren" of *Village of the Damned* (see illustration p. 129), the Metalunans have peroxide-blond unreal hairdos. (Universal Studios, 1955. Still courtesy of MOMA film stills archive.)

discovers who they are and what they're up to, then he heroically fights back. Cal is an easy-going guy who has a crush on his female colleague Ruth Adams, along with fierce senses of independence and right and wrong. He walks through the movie as a kind of scientist-cowboy, embodying all the '50s male ideals: tough, macho, adventurous, romantic, and brimming over with American ideals. He finally dies for his country and for freedom, with his lover in his arms.

Cal's adversaries are the scientists from the planet Metaluna, which is on the brink of destruction and desperate for some Earth know-how. They are depicted as highly intelligent, but devoid of individuality and emotions (they all look alike). They are robot-like, incapable of individual expression and of creativity. The Metalunans have even created subhuman mutants that do their dirty work (à la *Day the Earth Stood Still* and *Alien Nation*). The ideological reading works perfectly: the dominant view in the United States of people in the Eastern bloc during the cold war was an "evil empire" of people without individuality and creativity, without initiative and devoid of real emotions.

At the same time, besides being useful to the military and the government, science was being "discovered" by the marketplace. In the postwar age of supercapitalism and consumption, the individual with the most effective machines and the best technology had the advantage. Enter the big multinational Corporation as the military's most severe competition for scientific talent. Corporations need to keep pumping new technology and products onto the market and can afford to pay star salaries and maintain top-flight research labs.[16]

The way this development has been reflected in sf films is that the scientist has become a background figure who often is simply absent or shown in super-brief "signaling" clips full of scientific symbolic imagery. So if there is a scientist, he (or, rarely, she) is the stock genius from central casting. But the scientist is no longer responsible for his inventions and creations. The main enemy of the Honest Joe/Jane is the Corporation that employs, owns, or holds the scientist captive. The scientist has become a cog in a large wheel. His inventiveness and inventions are used by ruthless power brokers who have profit or power, not human betterment, as their goal. The scientist may still be the unkempt genius who has no real understanding of the social implications of his work. But he is no longer free to go where his genius takes him. Or rather, his freedom to be a creative genius is at the price of not knowing what his creations are used for.

A couple of examples of "corporation movies" will help make this clearer. In *Robocop* the scientist is hardly even there. The moral center is the "creation," the daunting cyborg (half machine, half left-for-dead cop) who is used by the corporation for its own evil purposes. The Bad Guys are two corporation executives who control the scientists and pit their "monsters" against each other and an unsuspecting Detroit City. *Robocop 2* pits two female scientists against each other. One is caring and interested in the welfare of her cyborg "offspring," but she has no control, no access to the important decisions. The other is the prototypical '80s me-first careerist, who is willing to do the amoral chairman of the board's bidding. Ultimately, however, she too is without control. She becomes the "fall-gal" when the evil cyborg she creates turns homicidal at the wrong time in the wrong place. And in *Short Circuit* two young, crazy, socially awkward, unkempt scientists are holed up in a lab owned by a robotics corporation in the employ of the army. The two scientists are making robots for military use. The corporation and the army are the bad guys here. The scientists are idealists who have only one desire: to create, to do what their genius enables them to do. They are not really aware or concerned with what happens to their inventions once they have created them.

■ Mysterious Science

As noted in chapter 1, sf science is a mystical force that can produce unexplained results. Frazer called magic "primitive science."[17] Sf science has much more in common with magic than with real science. Magic is what the shaman does: the dance, chant, trance, and the lump of bloody flesh add up to "proof" of his skills. The matching sf theatrics are followed by similar "proof": dead tissue suddenly stirs; the monster is alive!

To those of us who are not scientifically trained, real science is not that different. After all, we go to science when we have a problem. Science prescribes a "cure"; we buy the implement and follow the instructions, believing that if we do so, the implement will have the desired effect. Most of us don't really understand the inner workings of, say, the VCR that many of us have hooked up to our TV, but we know what series of ritualized motions will have the desired effects, such as allowing us to record a program or play a rented tape. This, incidentally, also answers a question I assume most readers ask themselves: how could people believe in shamanistic magic when it didn't work? For the same reason that people "believe in" a VCR: it only works when done the right way. If the ritual did not make the patient well, the shaman would say that it was not performed correctly, the objects utilized were contaminated, or the family was not generous enough in paying the shaman. Likewise, if the VCR does not record at the time I wanted it too, it is because (a) it wasn't set right (so I look in the manual again); (b) there is something wrong: the intricate web of wires and lamps that constitute the entrails are not connected correctly. In either case, the user does not have to understand the inner workings of the machine, just to "believe" (a) that the "rituals" prescribed in the manual will work; (b) that the machine can be made to work by taking it to a mechanical "shaman" who, using his "magical" wands, pokes around until he finally pulls out the offending piece of wire with a flourish.

To most of us science and its products and "inner workings" (the theoretical knowledge necessary to imagine and construct a VCR) are as mysterious as the knowledge and rituals of the shaman is to his audience. All that is required is a general agreement on the way the world works. The truth is, if I don't believe that something like a VCR *can* work, if I think the theoretical framework behind it is ludicrous, I'm not likely to buy one. And *magic* sometimes works too, which does not mean that if I watch a shaman extract a lump of bloody *something* from a patient's body and then see the patient "miraculously" get up, I will start believing in shamanism. I have to be, on a fundamental level, in agreement with the person who performs the magic to be able to believe in it: I have to share in his cosmology.

■ Sf Science Goals

In a certain sense, sf science is real science seen through a troll mirror. "Real" science has a reputation for being emotionally restrained, dignified, serious, and respectable. Sf science shows the "true" face of science, that it is potentially dangerous, that it is about egos and fame and fortune, and that it is a threat to the Ordinary Joes/Janes of this world. Real science tries to solve scientific quandaries and make humans increasingly masters of their environment. The goals are always stated in the noblest terms. But what are the goals of sf science? "I'm working on an invention that will change the world as we know it." The quotation is from the 1986 *Fly* but could be the motto of every sf movie scientist.

Although sf science is almost invariably disastrous, the intentions are usually the best. The sf scientist is given to declaring how his invention is going to do wondrous things: talking about the two sides of "man," the Good and the Bad Dr. Jekyll says: "Now if these two selves could be separated from each other, how much freer the good in us would be, what heights it might scale! . . . In my experiments I have found that certain chemicals have the power. . . ." André declares *(The Fly* 1958): "I've been lucky enough to make the most important discovery since man sawed off the end of a tree trunk and found a wheel . . . humanity will never want or fear again." Seth Brundle *(Fly* 1986): "I'm working on something that will change the world as we know it." In *Honey, I Shrunk the Kids,* Wayne Solensky, typical scientist, explains to his colleagues at a scientific conference that his invention will be immensely useful to the space program because he can shrink physical mass. In *Humanoids from the Deep,* Dr. Susan Drake has been experimenting with genetically engineered salmon that will be bigger, grow faster, and thus make it possible to open a canning factory in the little fishing village the protagonists call home. In the classic *Forbidden Planet,* the near godlike race, the Krell, have constructed the ultimate repository of scientific and ethical knowledge, a super-"computer" that contains what amounts to their collective psyche. It is supposed to be a synthesis of knowledge and of all that is good and moral and wonderful.[18]

And when the intention isn't strictly to make the world a better place to live in, it is to advance human knowledge, to *discover*, to make an effort that will at once give a place in history to the scientist and advance humanity en bloc toward a new scientific plateau. To Dr. Waldman's worried comments about his "creature," Dr. Frankenstein says: "Where would we be if no one tried to find out what lies beyond? Have you never wanted to look beyond the clouds or the stars, or to know what causes the trees to bud and what changes darkness into light? And if you talk like that, people call you crazy—but if I could discover just one of those things, what eternity is, for instance, I wouldn't care if they *did* think I was crazy."

When Dr. Jekyll's stodgy sidekick, Dr. Lanyon, pooh-pooh's experiments, the retort contains this tirade: "I tell you, there are no boundaries, Lanyon. Look at that gas lamp. But for some man's curiosity we shouldn't have had it and London would still be lighted by linkboys. And wait, one day London will glow with incandescence. It will be so beautiful that even you will be moved by it." In *The Invisible Man*, Jack Griffith's answer to his colleague Kemp's question, "But why? Why do it, Griffith?" is: "It was a scientific experiment at first, that's all. To do something that no man in the world had done." Emily, fiancée and wife-to-be of the protagonist Eddie Jessup *(Altered States)* says to him the night she proposes: ". . . and you're a Faust-freak, Eddie. You'll sell your soul to find the 'great truth.' "

But whatever the intentions, the result is invariably disastrous: Dr. Jekyll creates, instead of Pure Good, the evil Mr. Hyde who is fond of brutalizing people, especially women. André *(The Fly* 1958) becomes a miserable, increasingly inhuman "fly-oid" and dies in his own metal press. Seth Brundle becomes a giant fly and has to be killed to protect the world. Wayne Solensky's invention shrinks his own children and those of his neighbor exposing them to all manner of dangers. Susan Drake's genetic experiments result in the virtual destruction of the village by mutants. The Krell were killed off by the "monster in their machine." Frankenstein's creature presents a real danger to a small Alpine town. *The Invisible Man* is a megalomaniac with mass murder on his mind. Eddie

Jessup kills some sheep and a guard, and his experiment threatens to suck the universe back into the pre-Big Bang void.

It is not only in movies with "mad scientist" protagonists that science is disastrous. *The Day After, On the Beach, Soylent Green, The Terminator, Godzilla, Maximum Overdrive* (and many more) all show the disastrous effects of inventions that are usually perceived as beneficial and positive: atomic power in *Godzilla, The Day After,* and *On the Beach*; technology in general in *The Terminator*; industry (including chemical wastes and pollutants) in *Soylent Green*; and trucks in *Maximum Overdrive.*

Thus, the first paradox is that sf movies tend to portray science as having the best of intentions with the worst possible consequences. Perhaps those science fiction buffs who claim that sf is inherently inimical to science are right. Perhaps, but I don't think so. It is not science per se that sf opposes, it is a certain *kind* of science—science that crosses unseen boundaries, science that trespasses where humans have no business entering.

■ **Scientific Transgressions in Sf Films**

To understand the nature of the transgressions, I have to go into some detail. Since there is little real thematic variation, I will present three longer analyses, two of 1930s movies, *Frankenstein* and *Dr. Jekyll and Mr. Hyde,* and a more recent one, *Altered States,* followed by several shorter analyses.

In *Frankenstein,* Henry F. has decided that he wants to do what no other man has done: he wants to create Life. His areas of expertise are "chemical galvanism" and "electrobiology" (whatever those are)[19] and he has found a color beyond ultraviolet in the spectrum, "the great ray that first brought life into the world." A machine, containing (or producing) the ray is to be powered by the electrical supercharges of lightning "caught" on the roof of the abandoned watchtower he calls his lab. He has stitched and sown a human form together from parts of dead bodies he has stolen from graves, the gallows, and even from the lecture hall of his former teacher, Dr. Waldman.

Dr. Frankenstein makes it clear what's at stake when Waldman shows up in the company of a onetime student colleague, Victor, and Frankenstein's fiancée, Elizabeth: "That body is not dead—it has never lived. *I* created it. I made it with my own hands from the bodies I took from graves, from the gallows—anywhere." Frankenstein wants to undo death, or, conversely, he wants to create life—from scratch. He wants to do God one better.

The reason the experiment fails is instructive: the crucial element seems to be the brain. Frankenstein sends his half-wit helper, Fritz (whose moral turpitude is inscribed on his body: he is a hunchback), to get a perfectly normal brain, but Fritz drops it on the floor and steals a criminal brain instead. Fritz never tells his master about the switch, and Frankenstein places the criminal brain in his creature-to-be (the word "creature," from "create," is especially apt and eerie in this connection) and jump-starts him with a lightning jolt. It is not clear if we are to assume that if a normal brain had been inserted in the relevant cavity, the creature would have been more benign. But Frankenstein makes light of the problem when it is called to his attention: "Oh, well, after all it's only a piece of dead tissue."[20] Whatever the case, the creature turns into a monster: it kills Fritz the half-wit (who hated and teased it) and—it is suggested—rapes and kills a little girl whom it encounters after escaping the watchtower.

Assuming, for a moment, that the creature becomes a monster because the wrong brain was inserted, it becomes obvious that the scientist failed to control every part of his creation (as we are told God controls every aspect of *his*). But I think the nature of the brain is irrelevant here. The central issue is that Frankenstein transgressed on God's turf. The reason Frankenstein's experiment *had* to go wrong is that he wanted to tap the very knowledge and energy of God: the ray that science had not been able to discover. To obtain the desired effect, Frankenstein tapped divine energy: lightning. Lightning is a staple in sf movies where dead tissue or inorganic materials become imbued with life. Lightning is of course associated with king deities in many religions. Zeus was the wielder of lightning, the advent of the biblical God was often announced by lightning.[21] The movie never says so, but we can assume divine interference made the experiment go wrong.

In the end Frankenstein has two choices. He can try again or he can kill the monster and destroy his notes. If he chooses the former, he will—for a while—be a kind of perverse and flawed God who has created monstrous life. But he will surely cause rampant death and destruction, including his own and that of Elizabeth. A man who tries to create a Golem risks his life: "Golem-making is dangerous; like all major creation it endangers life of the creator—the source of danger . . . lies in the tension which the creative process arouses in the creator himself. Mistakes in carrying out the directions do not impair the golem, they destroy its creator."[22] In scenario number two, which he chooses, Frankenstein will be a privileged and highly regarded *human* man who has to create life the old-fashioned way: by marrying and having children with Elizabeth.

The sf Frankenstein chooses to be human and know only what a human man should know. On the other hand, his literary forebear, created by Mary Shelley, perishes in his scientific madness, as does his entire family and his fiancée. But then, Shelley's work is a Gothic novel, James Whale's movie is an sf film, "made in Hollywood." Movies have a very different audience from novels. The Hollywood audience expects, indeed demands, a happy end; the novelist is free to experiment with different kinds of closure.

Dr. Harry Jekyll's story is in many ways similar. Jekyll is devoted to three things: his fiancée Muriel Carew, his science, and his charity patients. His basic choice is made even clearer than in *Frankenstein:* early on he begs Muriel and her father, a stubborn-mule of a general, to allow an early wedding rather than making the young lovers wait.

The urgency in Jekyll's voice stems from his knowledge that if he does not marry soon, he will lose himself in his current experiment. On some level he realizes that he has the same choice as the one described above for Frankenstein: he can become lost in his experimentation, which involves trying to obtain forbidden knowledge, or he can marry and be redeemed by Muriel, using her as his anchor to humanity. She will be his moral compass, his unbreakable link to Christian values. Muriel can do this because she is a woman and because marriage is a religious ceremony

taking place in a church, before the face of God.[23] Jekyll can be saved because the divinely endorsed chain of marriage joining him to Muriel, by extension, will join him to down-home values and can keep his high-flying ideas from sundering his ties to humanity. Marriage and Muriel can prevent him from floating freely in the liminal space between the human and the would-be divine spheres.[24]

What is it that Jekyll does that is so dangerous and *verboten?* He thinks he has found a means to split, not the atom, but its spiritual counterpart, the human soul. What he proposes to do is take a drug that will separate the Bad instincts and intentions (meaning roughly sex and the "good old *ultraviolence"*) from the Good ones, love of a virginal woman (exclusively), and general Goodness.[25] Love of this kind is, presumably, accompanied by a moderate and not too passionate amount of intramarital sexual activity with procreation as its main or only goal.

Jekyll wants to split Good and Bad and hold on to Good while letting Bad run its course and self-destroy. The outcome, however, is that Good disappears—as long as the drug is active—and Bad takes over. The aristocratic Jekyll becomes apelike—with kinky hair, a flat and flaring nose—and hirsute, a feature signaled by recurrent close-ups of his long, elegant fingers curling up and turning into hairy claws when the drug kicks in. He also becomes shorter and more compact, and he becomes violent and sexually supercharged.[26] Jekyll becomes the aptly named Mr. Hyde: a man who lives and does his deeds, hidden by darkness and slinking along buildings, preferring locales frequented by the lower classes to the lecture halls and dining halls of decent people.

So Jekyll's transgression is to tamper with the soul—that part of the human entity that is the property of God—to be returned and judged by the proprietor at the end of the loan period. God did not create humans to be all Good, he created them morally ambivalent. He had a reason for this. He wanted each human

In his attempt to separate good and bad in the human soul, Dr. Jekyll has become a concentrate of base instincts and a throwback to a more primitive stage in evolution. I especially love the hairy "claws." (Paramount Productions, 1932. Still courtesy of MOMA film stills archive.)

being to choose to be good, to overcome the baser instincts through prayer and living a good and righteous life. Jekyll's experiment attempts scientifically to usurp a divine prerogative; in Christianity, God wipes away sins and evil from the individual soul and lets those he has rendered without sin enter the Heavenly Kingdom. If Jekyll had been successful, he would have become God. It is thus obvious that his experiment had to fail.

The results of Jekyll's playing God are (1) the creation of a monster (Hyde), who is a concentrate of base instincts and possibly a throwback to a more primitive state (which is exactly what "anthropologists" claimed blacks, Italians, and others who were short and dark were); (2) his own death; (3) the breaking of Muriel's innocent heart.

The movie maps out the transgression—the crossing from the natural to the unnatural—quite explicitly. To get from Jekyll's exquisitely handsome and cultured living quarters to his subterranean, dark, and messy lab with the test tubes and even a witches' cauldron constantly bubbling over with an ominous and sticky-looking liquid, he has to cross a little bridge. Whenever he crosses that bridge, Jekyll enters a forbidden world. The bridge looks out of place in the movie. It is a folkloric reminder: the narrow and dangerous bridge that young men and women have to cross before they can marry and be fully part of culture. Young women who slip are the victims of mermen, nixes (river trolls), and other natural monsters. Young men become the victims of their own base characteristics.[27]

The bridge between house and lab in *Dr. Jekyll and Mr. Hyde* connects Jekyll, the Good doctor and husband-to-be, and Jekyll, who is experimenting with the forbidden and who is Hyde. Jekyll must choose between the two, and he is drawn to the danger of the lab. That is why he so desperately wants to have an early wedding. Muriel will tie him to the Good side of the bridge. When his prayers are not heard—Muriel and the general take off for a month-long trip to Bath—the temptation becomes insurmountable, and Jekyll takes one "trip" too many and is trapped on the wrong side of the bridge.

The lab—the "wrong" side of the bridge—is also where the law and decency (the police and boring, unimaginative doctor-sidekick

Lanyon, respectively) finally catch up with Jekyll (or Hyde), and he is killed. The last image of the movie is the final transformation from Hyde to Jekyll. Dr. Jekyll expires on the floor of his lab, having been shot in mid-monkey swing—as Hyde—from the rafters by a police bullet. Society and propriety have gotten their man once again and order is restored. In the terms of folklore, the "trapped" soul is released as the monster is killed. When the dying Hyde becomes, for the last time, Jekyll, his soul is "saved." He dies as himself. That Jekyll has to die has to do with the fact that he, the scientist, is both witch and monster: he was the one who transgressed, and he has been punished for his hubris. The punishment is graphically obvious (both for Jekyll, Edward Jessup, discussed below, and, for that matter, *Frankenstein*): for stepping over the line that separates humans from gods, he is thrown back, reversed to an earlier evolutionary stage. He becomes, instead of a sophisticated scientist, a hairy and "primitive" ape-man.

Dr. Edward Jessup in *Altered States* (the reincarnation of Harry Jekyll—thus the similarity of name) is a somewhat more consciously philosophical man than his 1932 forebear. He is convinced that each and every human mind contains the sum of human experience (or evolution, if you will) and that a code can be found that can unlock the bound knowledge. Says he, speaking of what he calls "the original self":

We've localized it, . . . We know where the self is—in the human mind. It's a form of human energy. Our atoms are six billion years old. We've got six billion years' worth of memory in our mind. Memory is energy, it doesn't disappear. There's a physiological pathway to our earlier consciousness and I tell you it's in the goddamn lumbic system! [Jessup is a hip, modern scientist who says "goddamn" and "fucking" and "infantile masturbation"].

The science is shaky but sounds seductively "real." We all know that human fetal development largely mirrors evolution; we know that there are areas of the human mind that need further study and that there is a lumbar system. Put them all together and you have something that sounds half convincing. Jessup proposes to find the "pathway" by floating in an isolation tank (submerged in water, sort of a "return" to the primeval soup or womb) while popping Mexican Indian mushrooms.

Jessup addresses the religious issue head on. His intellectual and dream life since the death of his father has been a struggle with God. He has settled for being an atheist, but not a happy one: "Ever since we dispensed with God we've got nothing but ourselves to explain this meaningless horror of life."[28] Being a good nineteenth-century scientist, Jessup is on the trace of the *Ur*-something. In his case it is the *Urselbst*, the primal self: "I think that that true self, that original self, that first self is a real, measurable, qualifiable, tangible and incarnate entity and I'm gonna *find* the fucker."

What he is trying to do is to make his soul (not *mind*, but *soul*) return to the first soul. To do this he travels to Mexico and meets a fictional version of Carlos Castaneda's Indian medicine man (Don Juan)—all wrinkled and wise—who advertises the mushroom soup Jessup is about to ingest in the following terms: "It's unborn *stuff* [as translated by Jessup's Hispanic companion from Spanish materia]. Then you will go into a void, you'll see a spot becomes a crack—this is the crack between the nothing. Out of this nothing will come your unborn soul." Jessup, himself an adept slinger of nonsensical hogwash, is game and goes on to do and see as directed. The upshot is that Jessup eventually finds not only the void but also the crack, and he is about to be sucked, along with the entire universe, into the crack to be absorbed by the void. In other words, his experiment verges on reversing not only evolution but also the creation of the universe out of nothing.

En route, Jessup has visited the primeval steppe incarnating one of the first humanoid creatures. After several visits to the steppe and the humanoid ancestor's mind, the effect "solidifies" and he emerges from the immersion tank transformed into or reincarnated by—or perhaps both—a small bipedal primate. The primate creates havoc in the lab, the university security system, and the local zoo. Dr. Jessup/Mr. Primate looks amazingly like Lucy of archaeological fame: small, hairy, bipedal and with a face that has both primate and human features.[29] The humanoid acts according to its base instincts: has thought only for hunt and food, the primal needs. Returned to his 20th century gestalt, the cerebral Jessup is exhilarated to have had this very basic experience.

Whether Jessup's transgression is against the divine principle is not as clear as in the cases of *Frankenstein* and *Dr. Jekyll and Mr. Hyde*. He announces that he lost his faith at a critical time in his life, but his entire dream world is populated with burning crosses and Bibles and other religious symbolic paraphernalia, including devil imagery. His discourse is couched in religious iconology and phraseology. He arrives, for example, at the idea of the *Urselbst* via the absence of gods in Buddhism. But if there is a god at the core of Jessup's scientific disaster, it is a more remote, more modern, and more abstract one than the Old Testament father who punished Drs. Frankenstein and Jekyll for their transgressions. Still, I would tend to suggest that the cause of Jessup's problems is that he violates a "sacred" entity, the soul, by taking it apart (just as Dr. Jekyll did). And Jessup meddles with another divine exclusive: the creation and evolution of humanity. Jessup is punished in the standard way: for interfering with the macrocosm, he is hit closest to home, in his own microcosm. He and Emily are about to vanish into the void. Whether the retribution is divine or not, he is punished for poking his meddlesome brain into things that are none of his business.

Without going into detail, I submit that the same analysis holds for movies like *Invisible Man*, *"X"—The Man with the X-Ray Eyes*, *The Brain that Wouldn't Die*, *The Fly* (sequels, remakes, and all), *Frankenhooker*, *Flatliners*, and others of this type. Each one of these scientists transgresses by tampering with fundamental processes or issues and/or by trying to become petty gods.

A quick survey. In *The Invisible Man*, Jack Griffin discovers a way to render objects and people invisible. In and of itself, that does not seem to be a major sin. But the movie makes it clear that Jack transgresses in several ways: he conducts his scientific experiments in secret. Kemp, his dull colleague and nemesis (and rival for Flora's heart), is emphatic on this point: reputable scientists work openly. And at one point Kemp says to Flora—not knowing what Griffin is up to—that he "meddled in things men should leave alone." Griffin is also suffering from hubris, downright me-galomania. He sees himself as a god who can see without being seen, who can take life without ostensible cause, who, because he is invisible and a genius, has a right to rule the world. He is a flawed and perverse god. This "god" visits himself upon a village full of broadly drawn innocents going about their silly but normal lives. He is like an evil Second Coming: a mysterious apparition—wrapped in bandages—who comes out of the dark and rainy night, settles at the inn, and refuses all attention. He punishes and kills arbitrarily and relishes his powers: "I realized the power I held, the power to rule, to make the world cower at my feet. . . . We'll begin a reign of terror, a few murders here and there. Murders of great men, murders of little men—just to show we make no dis-tinction. We might even wreck a train or two." Like Jekyll, Griffin is his own monster: a creature radically different from the man who "created" it. Like God, he kills and causes disasters seemingly at random and inexplicably.

In *"X"—The Man with the X-Ray Eyes,* Dr. James Xavier wants to help humanity, at least initially, and he experiments with com-pounds that will make his vision more acute. Xavier is successful; his solution allows him to see "any one infinitesimal part of the universe." In other words, he has become God or is en route to becoming him. He wants to "explore all mysteries of creation. Knowledge is power." In religious terms he sees too much. He knows what no human should know and that becomes his final insight: in the film's last scene, having wandered into a religious revival tent, Xavier gores his own eyes out after hearing the preacher proclaiming that "if your eyes offend you—pluck them out!"[30]

In *The Brain That Wouldn't Die,* the doctor/scientist wants to attach a new body to his fiancée's severed head. He has a Franken-steinian monster locked up in a closet (the monster kills Kurt, the half-wit assistant) and is generally up to following in Franken-stein's footsteps by reviving dead tissue and so forth. There are numerous transgressions in *Brain*—not the least being against good taste—but the most serious one is that the doctor wants to be a god of sorts who decides between life and death. To get the desired body for his fiancée, he is willing to kill a hapless young woman, and he refuses the "head's" wish to be allowed to die.

More interesting is the remake, or send-up, *Frankenhooker*. Jeff Franken has already been kicked out of several med schools for tampering with the forbidden. He is fascinated with creating living things out of "scrap" body parts. As is the case in *Brain*, his fiancée is killed in an accident (with a lawn mower) and the only whole part left of her is the head. Jeff decides to reconstruct her by killing several prostitutes to get the perfect parts for the perfect body for his beloved. The movie is an excellent, and a conscious, example of what Mulvey has called the "fragmented body."[31] Not only is Jeff an amoral murderer, he is also the ultimate male chauvinist. His punishment for both transgressions is that he is killed and revived with a woman's body attached to his own head and mind.[32]

The "crimes" of André and Seth in the *Fly* movies (1958 and 1986) are slightly less obvious. Both have the best of intentions but end up as ugly apparitions, monsters full of bloodthirsty and primitive urges. Their transgression seems to lie in the nature of the experiment itself. It is clearer in the '86 version than in the original: the problem is that the novel transportation system[33] involves taking creatures, including human beings, "apart," disintegrating them into their constituent atoms and then reconstituting them. In other words, the process involves, however momentarily, undoing creation, disintegrating what God hath wrought and then—this is the real sin—reassembling. It is worth noting here that the "telepod" became a recurrent feature as the "transporter" in *Star Trek:* "Beam me up, Scotty!"

The point of the transgression in the *Fly* movies is that humans are not cars or machines. Humans are *creations*, not constructions. Taking them apart is the prerogative of the one who created them and he'll do it in due time. If humans insert themselves into the process and take the human form apart, they do so at the peril of not being able to reassemble it correctly. One of God's smaller creatures gets mixed up with the transmission by accidentally being disintegrated and reintegrated along with the human form. The atoms become scrambled, a new and dreadful mutant is the result, and evolution is reversed (at least in this one case).

In *Flatliners*, a group of med students plays dangerous games with life and death. All die for brief periods to experience what's on the other side. Initially, they claim to have experienced things that confirmed the existence of a "benevolent presence." But what they really find are buried moral transgressions against others. The posters for the movie state, as a kind of subtitle, that "some lines shouldn't be crossed." The reason is that once the protagonists are revived, people from their past come back with them as evil leprechauns that haunt them and hurt them. The movie is interesting for directly addressing the issue of whether there is a god or not. As it turns out, the only thing the travelers find is purgatory and eventually atonement and one-on-one forgiveness for their sins. The whole development becomes psychotherapy on a grand scale. Instead of God, they find Freud.

In all of these movies the protagonists are scientists who work on their own, in secrecy. Scientists are loners who perceive themselves as having—by virtue of their genius—special rights, and they end up crossing the ultimate boundary: they put the group in danger because of an insane ambition to create something no one else has even dared to imagine.

■ A Monster Is Born

Regardless of whether a lone Scientist/Madman or the Corporation is responsible for the invention or discovery, the result is the same: a monster is created that threatens to destroy the world. Along with The Hero and The Scientist, the Monster is one of the three sf stock characters—and synonymous with science gone bad.

By interfering with nature, science dredges up sleeping monsters that go on rampages in the city, the bastion of culture. The perfect example is *Godzilla*, where the Sleeping Monster is awakened by an H-bomb detonated under the sea. Godzilla attacks Tokyo and destroys it. The movie has spawned a virtual subgenre of films that feature monsters emerging from the sea: the monsters of *Slime People, Humanoids from the Deep,* and *The Terror Within* all look like smaller Godzillas but with more fish features. And like Godzilla, they are scientific by-products, unforeseen effects of human attempts to control the natural environment. Each and every monster is brought on by human hubris. Humanity has been placed within what could be called a capsule, a defined space—

Godzilla: an unforeseen effect of the human attempt to control the environment
goes on a rampage in the bastion of human culture, the city. The toy-train drib-
bling from his mouth is especially unimpressive. (Toho Productions, 1956. Still
courtesy of MOMA film stills archive.)

physically, intellectually, and morally. Inside the capsule, humans have free will, have the right to know and manipulate and do as they please. But they can break out of the capsule only at the risk of disaster. They cannot bite into the apple that contains forbidden knowledge.

Once the capsule is broken and humans obtain and utilize illegal knowledge, they stand a very good chance of reversing the order that kept everything in place. Evolution may become undone or reversed. Godzilla was not meant to wake up millions of years after his evolutionary creation. The prehistoric fish of *Humanoids from the Deep* were never meant to feed on DNA5, but once they have, they are catapulted into rapid evolution, starting out as tadpoles and becoming "humanoid in the last stages." And because they want to get on with evolution, they have to find human mates. The creatures of *The Terror Within* are mutants created by an unknown scientific mishap. Those of *Slime People* are a subterranean race forced out of their natural habitat by subterranean explosions. All of them can be seen as metaphoric expressions of nature reemerging, folklore monsters reborn of the human-created apocalypse.[34]

"Shrinking" movies—*Incredible Shrinking Man, Honey, I Shrunk the Kids*—are the inverse of monster movies. In *Godzilla* the monster is awakened, huge and dangerous, by the scientific transgression. In *Incredible Shrinking Man*, the atomic cloud triggers a human to be "cut down to size" so that ordinarily harmless little animals like cats and insects suddenly become huge and dangerous monsters. The outcome, however, is the same: nature reemerges as a dangerous force. This is true even in fairly realistic movies, such as *On the Beach* and *The Day After*, where humans are reduced to cowering creatures at the mercy of the air they have poisoned or, as in *On the Beach,* a huge tidal wave.

If the folklore monsters of the past symbolized the powers of untamed nature, the monsters of sf epics symbolize the dangers inherent in trying to dominate nature. While being the primary tool in the human ascent to absolute power in the world, science may also ultimately be the tool of our destruction. Science is the monster. In its bosom hide the Godzillas, the Slime People, the Humanoid Fish on the evolutionary fast-track.

A scientific mishap causes a human to shrink in *The Incredible Shrinking Man*, and suddenly a harmless, little animal like a cat is a huge monster. The trick-photography is not great: both cat and man seem to be responding to stimuli absent from the picture. (Universal Productions, 1957. Still courtesy of MOMA film stills archive.)

What sf movies that focus on science keep hammering out is a warning: we humans have reached a plateau at which we have to make some crucial choices. We have acquired enough knowledge not only to control the environment, but to destroy it. Indeed, we can destroy ourselves many times over. We have reached a point where we have the potential for going beyond being creations among creations. We can bust the world wide open. But, warns sf, we don't really know what we're going to find once we move to the other side of the line between being creatures and creators. We may find that we have reached the point in the loop where we are knocked back to square one, where the universe will look a lot like the world of our earliest forebears: we will once again be reduced to being small and weak creatures in a world populated and dominated by towering, ferocious, and threatening monsters.

In this chapter, I have introduced the protagonists of the sf film and of the "plot" of this book: the folklore Hero, the Scientist, and the Monster that, in sf, is Science anthropomorphized. But sf is not just about science, it reflects societal attitudes in general.

■ Notes

1. Penley 1990:120.
2. Quoted in Elkins 1980:280.
3. The movie was made in 1958, when it was assumed that this is what women want.
4. In Ibsen's *The Master Builder*, the protagonist Halvard Solness thinks he owes his worldly success not only to "spirits" who helped him but also to the fact that his success as an artist has been at the expense of his wife, Aline. Aline lost her children in a fire, which Halvard sees as crucial and as the starting point of his climb to success. The whole concept is steeped in what could be called "the Romantic ethos": the idea that artistic (and scientific) success is at the expense of happiness, normalcy, living a productive but uncreative bourgeois life.
5. Actually, the sf scientist has much in common also with the Witch, the Magician and the Alchemist, but for reasons of economy with words, I will here let the shaman represent all of them.
6. Innate ability is of course another kind of preordained marker for success or failure—just as was the feudal class system. All the various versions of social Darwinism, under whatever name—recent entrants are Jensenism and the Culture of Poverty—are attempts at locking

society into its present shape. Those who are on top are so because they are innately superior, those who are below are so because they are innately inferior. Since people's social success is determined by innate abilities, there is no guilt for the powerful and no reason to change the status quo.

7. All my references are only to the 1931 version of *Frankenstein* and the 1932 version of *Dr. Jekyll and Mr. Hyde*. See filmography for details.
8. I will discuss both of these movies in greater detail below.
9. Jacobsen (Schelde) and Leavy 1988.
10. The drug is called "monocane" in the movie; when injected into a dog, the animal went "raving mad."
11. My translation. In the original, these two last stanzas of the poem, "Adam der Erste" (Heine 1956:501), are:

Vermissen werde ich nimmermehr
die paradiesischen Räume;
das war kein wares Paradies—
es gab dort verbotene Bäume

Ich will mein volles Freiheitsrecht!
Find ich die gringste Beschränkniss,
verwandle sich mir das Paradies
in Hölle und Gefängnis

12. Scholem 1969:181.
13. Gialanella 1982:20.
14. Bernal 1965, vol. 1:33–35.
15. See, e.g., Laura 1972.
16. Bernal 1965, vol. 1:1–35.
17. Frazer 1963:55, 824–825.
18. The reader may have already made this connection, but *Forbidden Planet* is essentially an outer space/computer version of the Dr. Jekyll/Mr. Hyde theme, just as *Altered States* is a '60s LSD trip version.
19. In *Frankenhooker*, the protagonist, Jeff Franken's fiancée, Elizabeth, explains to a girlfriend what her boyfriend does, "He calls himself a bio-electrical technician, whatever that is." Jeff is obviously Frankenstein incarnate and does something equally unreal.
20. In *Robocop 2* the "criminal brain" issue is raised again. The cyborg-cop that is supposed to replace the original (which has been destroyed by criminals) is given the brain of a dying drug addict cum unscrupulous criminal, with, of course, disastrous effects. In this movie it is made clear that the nature of the brain inserted into the technological crust is crucial.
21. I am indebted to an anonymous reader for reminding me of this. Lightning is a recurrent "life force" (to use the term of the alchemists,

"male fire")—it shows up again and again in sf, e.g., in *Short Circuit* and *Frankenhooker.*

22. Scholem 1969:190–91.
23. I remind the reader of the Norwegian huldre who lost her tail and became fully human under the same circumstances: marriage in a church.
24. I will discuss in the next chapter why it is that women can be such anchors. For now, I ask the reader's indulgence in taking my word for it: sf women have this capacity.

    In folklore it is a bit different, because pre-Romantic patriarchal ideology conceptualized women as being closer to nature than men (the logical opposite, culture, thus being a male domain). Women were the more likely victims of temptation from nature's seducers, slick-haired mermen, trolls in the (temporary) shape of handsome young princes, and so on. The Romantics stood this on its head. Nature became something good and wonderful and healthy, culture became a stodgy but necessary middle ground; the ones who were endangered were the geniuses, the males whose lack of a viable link to "ground-control" put them at a peril of ending up weightlessly and endlessly orbiting the rest of humanity.
25. Sort of an early example of "mirror image" chemistry: "Many chemicals important to life are combinations of mirror-image twins, in which one partner may cure disease, quell headaches or smell good, while its mirror-reversed counterpart may be poisonous, smell repugnant or simply be inert. Scientists are investigating the chemistry of thousands of such pairs, learning to make pure forms of the desirable twins, and thereby creating many new products" (Browne 1991a:C1.).
26. The physical changes could be taken out of one of the (now) infamous tracts of physical anthropology that were the ideological manuals and excuses for colonialism, slavery, and contempt for later waves of immigrants from the southern parts of Europe to the United States: low intelligence and high sensuousness (both undesirable by contemporary standards) were mapped onto the physique as short stature, dark hair (the kinkier the worse), dark skin, extensive body hair (the darker the worse), short limbs (I don't know if this extends to reproductive organs, since the few treatises on penis size extant from the time claim that Anglos have the largest penes), short, muscular necks (an especially bad sign, redolent of sexuality and a high score on the animal-nature test), flat noses, heavy eyebrows, and so forth. Whoever designed the makeup for Mr. March's Hyde must have copied directly from one of these works of "anthropology."
27. The best example I can think of is the Danish folk ballad, "Ebbe Skammelsøn." Ebbe crosses a bridge and becomes "lost," and he kills and maims. This passage from unmarried classificatory child to adult

is called a "rite of passage" in anthropology. The term was coined in the early twentieth century by Dutch anthropologist Arnold van Gennep. The period when the individual is between stages, neither adult nor child, has been dubbed the "liminal" by van Gennep and Victor Turner. See van Gennep 1960 and Turner 1967, especially chapter 4, "Betwixt and between: The liminal period in *Rites de Passage.*"

28. This line, in all its pretentious nihilism and hollow-sounding *Weltschmerz,* is tough to take.

29. See Johanson, 1990.

30. The religious imagery is interesting: the goring of the eyes after listening to the preacher in the revival tent reads; Xavier, realizing that he has been competing with God—and having his own belief in God revived—demonstrates to God his remorse and willingness to relinquish his status as unworthy god.

   Shades also of Oedipus, who gouged his eyes that had seen what no man should see: his mother as the mother of his children.

31. Mulvey 1975.

32. In this movie, all the male chauvinists get their just desserts: the pimp of the prostitutes—who have conveniently exploded after smoking Jeff's "super-crack"—is dragged into a chest where the loose body parts have come to life after being charged by lightning. We can assume he is killed, smothered to death by the Picassoesque constructions of body parts that once were his livelihood when they were whole prostitutes.

33. "Teleportation" is the solid-object equivalent of TV—as André keeps repeating in the 1958 movie: objects and organisms are transported from one "telepod" to another.

34. Movies such as *The Road Warrior* are different expressions of the same thing: after the atomic war, the survivors will have to start over, living lives that are short, nasty, and brutish—to paraphrase Hobbes.

3 ■

Meanwhile, Back in the Kitchen; or, Women and Science

■ **Female "Nature"**

In her nature lies the healing power which replaces that which has been used up, the beneficial rest in which everything immoderate confines itself, the eternal Same, by which the excessive and the surplus regulate themselves. In her the future generation dreams. Woman is more closely related to Nature than man and in all her essentials she remains ever herself. Culture is with her always something external, a something which does not touch the kernel that is eternally faithful to nature.[1]

Here Nietzsche intends to praise woman for her constancy, her healing, life-giving, but basically uncreative "nature." This image of woman as being rooted in nature, with culture being just a varnish, is ingrained in the Judeo-Christian tradition. Woman the life giver, the Earth Mother, is one of our cultural icons. Her natural opposite is volatile man. Where women are rooted in the eternal and traditional, men are creative and given to excesses. Ibsen, in his last play, *When We Dead Awaken*, arranges it neatly. The woman is the model, whose inner strength and earthiness inspires the artist to create his masterpiece, "The Day of Resurrection," a sculpture group of a young woman, an Earth Mother, surrounded by her "creations"—animals, children, and so on.

It is interesting here to note that it is not only the Western tradition that subscribes to this sharp division between female "naturalness" as opposed to male "culture." I have touched on this before, but it is essential to understanding gender differences in sf film, so I will briefly outline it again.

Since women have what could be called "natural" creativity— they are procreation "machines"—men had to come up with something that was exclusively their field of creativity. Enter *culture*. The majority of human societies have constructed some version of the "woman equals nature, man equals culture" paradigm. The cultural sphere—politics, the arts, philosophy, religion—are male concerns; the rest—child bearing, nursing, nurturing, socialization, cooking—belong in the domain of women. I emphasize that this is a construct, but a self-fulfilling one. If a society perceives women as capable only of things that pertain to cultural *maintenance*, it is obvious that a woman who strives to enter the areas of politics or hunting is going to be met with ridicule and suspicion—whether she has the ability to do what she aspires to or not.

Our cultural "ideal" is the restless, slightly crazed male who roams and wanders, who explores and philosophizes, who destroys and creates, takes apart and reassembles. Conversely, the female "ideal" is The One Who Is Always There, by the fireplace, in the kitchen. The rock, the one to come home to, the one to join once the peregrinations are over.[2]

In this chapter, I shall look at how sf perceives and portrays women. First I look at women and science, real and sf, then at how women influence and interact with the male sf scientists I discussed in the previous chapter. This is followed by a number of condensations of the sf stereotypes of women. The second part of the chapter is devoted to more contemporary sf images of women —films that present more positive, or at least more nuanced, female characters. I want to emphasize that this chapter is not intended as the discussion of women and gender in sf. On the contrary, it sets the parameters for my discussions in chapters to follow.

Before the nineteenth century (before Victorianism), women were perceived as less sexually continent than men. A woman who was not under male control, so the fiction went, would have unbridled sex with anything male (folklore is full of women mating with donkeys, horses, bears—the bigger, the better). To "control" rampant female sexuality and to make sure a man supported only children he was the biological father of, women had to be under constant male supervision. In the nineteenth century, with the Romantic movement, this idea was stood on its head. Female sexuality "evaporated." Women were just (more or less) patient vessels for male sexuality, itself only geared toward procreation. Instead of being sexually incontinent and in need of supervision, women became sexually empty, paragons of a culturally defined ideology. Both woman-the-voracious and woman-the-asexual are male inventions designed to control female sexuality.

But even the Victorian "asexual" woman was tied to nature in a way men were not. Culture was still foreign territory for her. Victorian women were children in the male construction of culture. They had to learn culture. Where men were allowed aggressive and creative outlets, women were forced into a cultural straitjacket. I don't have to argue at length that boys are perceived and encouraged to be much more creative and aggressive than girls, who in turn are perceived and encouraged to be pliant, obedient, pleasing—because we all know it is a cultural fact. The other side of that coin is that women, because of their role as "children," are allowed to be much more "colorful," playful, and unbalanced. Women, but not men, are shown in advertising, jumping, off balance, leaning on, looking up to men, and so forth.[3] Ballet is considered a very acceptable female career, whereas male ballet dancers are sexually suspect. And this despite the fact that ballet reinforces three-dimensionally the patriarchal order by having women be "airborne," the ones who are supported, carried, thrown around by men.

■ **Gendered Science**

In a provocative article, the French philosopher and feminist, Luce Irigaray, asks, "Is the subject of science sexed?" Trying to come to terms with the language of science, how scientific theory and discourse are expressed, she asks this further question: "Is a woman scientist wholly a man? A generic aberration? A monstrosity? A bisexual human being? A woman cowed into submission, or not yet subdued? Or?"[4] An answer to Irigaray's question is provided by the American scientist and philosopher of science, Evelyn Fox Keller, who says that science is gendered, couched as it is in male terminology:

When we dub the objective sciences "hard" as opposed to the softer (that is, more subjective) branches of knowledge, we implicitly invoke a sexual metaphor, in which "hard" is of course masculine and "soft" feminine. Quite generally, facts are "hard," feelings "soft." "Feminization" has become synonymous with sentimentalization. A woman thinking scientifically or objectively is thinking "like a man"; conversely, a man pursuing a nonrational, nonscientific argument is arguing "like a woman."[5]

Women are still few and far between in the "hard" sciences and they are certainly not found in the sf science labs. Even as society in general has become more open to the idea of female scientists and creativity, the sf genre is locked in the old patterns. In sf the scientist is always a man, or, if she is a woman, she is either a freak (sexually and socially isolated) or just nominally a scientist while really being an embodiment of every male stereotype of femininity.

■ Woman the Polluter

Basically, sf movies of the type discussed in the previous chapter perceive women as inimical to science and its goals. Science is abstract, future oriented. Sf women are focused on the concrete and the private. While Henry Frankenstein is busy "re-creating" humanity, his fiancée is interested only in Henry, the future husband. "I'm worried about Henry. Why has he left the university? He seemed to be doing so well and he was so happy about his work." She has no quarrel with his being a scientist, nor does she have any interest in what exactly he is doing. He can do whatever he wants to as long as it doesn't interfere with their relationship and with the upcoming wedding arrangements. When she does find out what he's doing, her first reaction is concern for him. She does not give a thought to the creature, to Fritz who is killed, to the historical implications of what he has done. She fears for his physical and mental well-being and wants to take him home so she can nurse him. When Henry says that he has to be alone and she has to go away so he can finish his work, her answer is, "Wait a minute, I understand, I believe you—but I can't leave you tonight!" She is satisfied to sit by his side and let him wreak all the scientific havoc he can think of. In the amusing *Frankenhooker*, this issue is the stuff of comedy. Jeff Franken is trying to tell his mother that he is afraid of his own desire to do amoral science: "I seem to be disassociating myself from reality. I'm antisocial. I'm becoming dangerously amoral. I've lost the ability to distinguish right from wrong. I'm falling into a void of utter madness." Her retort is: "You wanna sandwich?" He shakes his head no, she continues: "Just promise me one thing."—"What?"—"That you won't stay up all night."

The subject is the romantic notion that genius and family life do not mix. Mental exertion drains all the creative and physical juices from a man. He cannot simultaneously be a genius and a lover and husband. The nineteenth century subscribed to a notion that the essence of humanity, that which makes humans distinct from animals, is the human brain. But for the brain to be working at its peak, all physical energy had to be channeled from the body to the brain.[6] Add to this the fact that the Victorians tended to agree that men should curtail sexual expenditure. Each ejaculation of semen was drawn against the accounts of mental and physical health. The masturbator would invariably become a slobbering idiot, of course, but even the married man who indulged in the pleasures of the body for nonreproductive reasons had a price to pay. The man who impregnated his wife over and over was making a sacrifice to society: he was risking his health and faculties for the continuation of the race.

We are faced with a circumscript version of the old "pollution" theory. In certain Papua New Guinea societies, the fear of sex and female pollution is so intense that men prefer to spend most of their time in male lodges and in the company of other males (there isn't much homosexual activity, either; like the Victorians, these people have a highly developed fear of sexual expenditure in general). Men marry late in life and have sexual relations only hesitantly and only for procreative purposes. The rest of the time they sit around the campfire and delight in having their creative juices intact and unspent.[7] Something akin to this underlies the relations between scientists in sf and the women who love and pursue them. Henry Frankenstein is quite blunt: when Elizabeth turns up on his big night and demands to be allowed in, he says, "You'll *ruin* everything! My experiment is *almost* completed." He can't have her there; she'll "contaminate" his experiment with her femininity.

The other side of that coin is of course that women are restful and "heavenly" beings, "angelic" redeemers who can make a man forget about science and mental exertion. Henry Frankenstein's choice is simple: either he thinks about science exclusively or he settles down with Elizabeth and forgets about science. His work or his home: these are different worlds, different cosmoses, mutually exclusive and inherently inimical.

Frankenstein is the movie in which woman-the-polluter is most clearly drawn, but in all the movies the issue shows up somewhere. Jessup *(Altered States)*, in a passage already quoted, invokes marriage and the "meaningless pain we inflict on each other" as the reason he is unable to do breakthrough science. Early in the movie, he has been established as the Genius, a man totally wrapped up in his scientific pursuits. But meeting Emily, herself an anthropological whiz kid, he lets himself be sidetracked by sex and marriage. The film quite clearly contrasts Jessup to other scientists (like Emily) who are not destined to do great work and can handle their pedestrian science quite well while being married and having children. But the genius has to use all his creativity for his work. Jessup and Emily break up so he can go to Mexico and eat mushroom stew and try to find the path back to the primeval mind and time's initial moment. She goes to Africa to do basic research about chimp language—with their two kids.

In the 1958 *Fly*, the married scientist is separated from his woman when he works. Helene spends almost all her time in the kitchen, cooking, playing with their son Philippe, and happily innocent of what André is doing in his lab. That's his world and it has little to do with her. When he does invite her down to his "netherworld" to see what he has wrought, she is shocked, dismayed, and unhappy, but only for a brief moment. When it turns

Woman the *nurturer*: when Helene's scientist husband is becoming a mutation between a man and a fly, she is the one who has to make the ultimate sacrifice of operating one of his machines and destroying him. The *shaman* perishes by the technological tools of his secret and mysterious trade. (*The Fly*, 20th Century-Fox Productions, 1958. Still courtesy of MOMA film stills archive.)

out that his machine is not quite what he thought it was, she cheerily troops back up the stairs to her world.

In the 1986 version, the scientist has lived as a recluse while perfecting his scientific feat. Seth Brundle does not meet Veronica until he is ready to present his innovative "telepod" transportation system to the world. And in the others, *Dr. Jekyll and Mr. Hyde, The Invisible Man, "X"—The Man with the X-Ray Eyes, Altered States*, the same pattern holds: the woman is never part of the scientist's work. He isolates himself and will not let her see him while he is working.

The problem is the artificial separation between the private and the public, between mutually opposed—and gendered—worlds. Henry Jekyll is a moral and even a good man. Dr. Jekyll, the scientist, marches to a different moral beat. The scientist has different values and rights that Henry Jekyll, the private citizen, does not have. The same holds for each one of the sf scientists I have discussed so far; they are different men with different values depending on whether they are in the "home" world or the "science" world. Klaus Theweleit has shown that this is not just a problem for sf scientists. It's a problem in our Western culture. Theweleit's *Male Fantasies* (1987–89) shows the perverted and separate world of the Nazi brass,[8] men who lived in a world of power and sick ideology. In their male world the killing of men, women, and children was acceptable if they were Jewish, Gypsies, or otherwise "lower races." The same men were good husbands and fathers and friends. But they had built a watertight wall between their "power" worlds and "home" worlds.[9]

■ Stereotypes

I have distilled the image of woman in sf as five stereotypes: women as *nurturers, producers of children, sex objects, earthy and homebound beings,* and *socializers.*

The first sf stereotype is that women are *nurturing:* the image of Elizabeth nursing Henry Frankenstein after his nervous and exhausted breakdown is typical. An even stranger one can be found in the 1958 *Fly* movie: Helene is introduced by André to a hamster he is going to "transmit"—that is, disintegrate and reassemble. She is horrified: "I won't allow it!" But he does it anyway, of course, and it's a success. He wants to keep the hamster around to see if there are ill aftereffects. Helene asks, "May I look after him?" And later, after the "accident," when André has the head and right front limb of a fly, she desperately wants to take care of him. When Seth Brundle of the 1986 version is in the same predicament, the one who mothers him—despite his hostile attitude—is Veronica, the journalist who is his lover and confidante.

The contrast between the women in the two *Fly* movies is obvious, Helene is a wife and mother and no more. She is scared of science, she wants nothing to do with André's world, but she loves her man unconditionally. Veronica, on the other hand, is an independent woman, she wants to define herself and her space (a subplot shows her claiming her independence vis-à-vis her one-time lover who is still her editor). She is a science writer, no less. She is a person unto herself, until she meets her male destiny, Seth. Then she becomes an appendix to him. She is supposed to write about his experiment and about him. In the final analysis, she is not the one who creates; like Helene, she is just a mirror (in her case literally) for her man and what he does. Seth and Veronica become lovers. After his "accident" she becomes the nurturer who takes care of him. Thirty years between the two movies have changed some formal things: she is not "just" a homemaker, she has a job and a career, but she is still defined by relationships, not by her own choices and ambitions.

In *The Invisible Man*, when Flora and her father, Jack's one-time employer, finally catch up with Jack, all bandaged up for visibility, she entreats him to come back and work with her father, "then we'll have those lovely, peaceful days again, out under the trees, after your work in the evening." She wants to get him home so she can nurse him well again and put him back in line to succeed her father. She is not concerned with what he has done or intends to do; she is concerned with him and with their relationship. Even the totally silly *Honey, I Shrunk the Kids* is virtually a textbook example of showing man, the scientist, and woman, the nurturer. The Solenskys have two children: a boy and a girl. The boy is younger, bespectacled, and a genius and inventor in the embryonic stages. The girl is older, motherly, nurturing. When the two and the dumb neighbor's two boys are shrunk and have to fight a hostile environment, she is the one who mothers everybody. In *Frankenhooker*, the mother of Jeff Franken is only interested in seeing him well nourished, rested, and married; whatever else he does is of no concern to her. She is the nurturer turned absurd monster.

The second stereotype is that the primary goal in the life of women is the *production of children: Frankenstein*, for example, is all about juxtaposed ways of reproduction. Old Baron von Frankenstein makes it quite clear that he expects Elizabeth to produce heirs to the name. His entire function in the movie is to talk incessantly about future and past generations of sexually reproduced Frankensteins. He is the extension of the natural father/god whose function is to be an alternative to his unnatural usurper-god son. When he is not talking about reproduction, he is shown leering at the young, pretty maids at the castle. The women of *Fly* 1958, of *Honey, I Shrunk the Kids*, and of *Altered States* see the mother role as central in their lives. All are shown nursing, playing with, nurturing children. Even in the 1986 *Fly* the problem of motherhood comes up as Veronica discovers she is pregnant with Seth's child. She wants an abortion so as not to bring a monster into the world. But she is torn because she also wants to have his child.

Stereotype number three is that women are *sex objects*. The most obvious examples are *The Brain That Wouldn't Die* (1959) and *Frankenhooker* (1990). In the former, the doctor's fiancée is crushed in a car accident and all that survives is her severed head. Her fiancé, the doctor/scientist who is sort of a latter-day Dr. Frankenstein, decides to find a suitably sexy body to go with the severed head. He takes to the task with enthusiasm, hooks the head to machinery to keep her alive, and heads for the hookers and the strippers to find the perfect little sex toy to bring home and attach to the good girl. This is perhaps the textbook example of what Laura Mulvey calls the "fragmented body,"[10] the notion that the female body can be cut into eroticized, objectified parts for male scopophilic pleasure. The movie legitimizes the male tendency to fragment when the doctor goes off to find a body to go with the severed head. We, the presumed male audience, and he can both (with the camera) delight in seeing female forms chopped into eroticized parts. In the same article, Mulvey points out that a frequent feature is the objectification and eroticization of the woman until the male hero becomes romantically involved with her. Then she loses the "glamor" and becomes the sole erotic property of her husband/fiancé. The gaze no longer fragments and eroticizes. The doctor in *Brain* wants to have his cake and eat it too: he wants a virtuous girl with a stripper's body. What Victorian man could ask for more? When they're out, the sinful body will be discreetly covered up and she will look virtuous for all to see. Then, back home, he can enjoy the sinful and gorgeous body of a fallen woman. The question posed by Thomas Mann in his story "The Transposed Heads" never surfaces: which one is she, the head or the body? In Mann's story, the woman the two men want decides that she is married to the body, not the head. In *Brain* there is never any doubt: the new entity will be the virtuous girlfriend. She becomes a biological Stepford Wife: at once a good girl and a prostitute. It is never, however, a question of her identity, it is about his desires. In Mulvey's terms, his gaze is the one that sees her and fragments her, making her into the perfect object of desire.

In *Frankenhooker*, the question does arise: once Jeff Franken has created his sex-object collage, the fiancée initially identifies with her composite of prostitute body parts and stalks off to ply her trade.[11] Jeff retrieves her and gives her a dose of his electrical juice and she is jolted back into being "herself."

Sf stereotype number four is that women are earthy, *anchored to home and hearth*. They are "fearful of flying." Their primary concern is to get their man tied to them in marriage and to nest. The fly they catch their man with is *love*. The woman will profess to love the man, and once he has reciprocated, the next logical step is toward the altar. Now it's all over, his flight is stopped, she has him, the breeding and nesting can start. When Emily *(Altered States)* meets Eddie Jessup, she falls in love with him immediately. How could she not—he is so handsome, so crazy, so brilliant, so aware of his own preciousness: "I'm telling you now, so you'll know what kind of a nut you may get mixed up with." Emily's problem is that Eddie won't reciprocate, he won't say he loves her. Sex, yes, but not those three little words. She has to do both the proposing and the saying yes for both of them: "We're born in doubt, we spend our lives trying to persuade ourselves we're alive. One of the ways we do that is we *love* each other like I love you. I can't imagine living without you. So, let's get married."

Every single one of them—Elizabeth, Muriel, Emily, Helene, Veronica (1986 *Fly*), Dr. Xavier's woman friend—wants to make her man jump through the love and marriage hoop so he will be hers forever; he need just go to the lab to bring home the bacon and not do things that are too brilliant and dangerous. Even in movies where there is no central scientist/fiancée conflict, the nesting issue is central. In *Humanoids from the Deep*—where the scientist is a woman—the protagonists are the very conventional household of Jim and Carol. An early scene shows the cozy home life of these two attractive young people: the young child is playing on the floor with the dog, Jim is talking to a visitor, Carol is serving drinks and snacks. This is the idyll, the image of perfection that the subsequent events threaten to destroy. This is normalcy, order—the way things are supposed to be. Everything that follows threatens that order.

The fifth and final sf stereotype is that women are *socializers*. It may seem paradoxical that in a culture that considers women to be cultural outsiders, perennial semichildren, the task of enculturating the young is entrusted to women. There are reasons for this, of course. Being cultural "outsiders," women themselves have to *learn* culture like a lesson. They have to stick much more to the cultural norms than men. Men are allowed to play with the rules, stretch them, manipulate them, for, after all, they're *their* rules. The truth is, of course, that women—in our society—tend to be more traditional minded, more rule-bound than men, more afraid of violating established codes (not, I hasten to say, because women are genetically more afraid of cultural flight than men—no matter what Freud and the sociobiologists say—but because they are taught to be that way). Because they are so rule-bound and afraid to violate the accepted, women are the ideal socializers. Men, with their flights of fancy, might confuse and upset the impressionable minds of the darling young.

In the following chapters, we will encounter some strange instances of woman-the-socializer. In all cases the socializee is a male being and pretty badly in need of some basic training. Johnny-5 of *Short Circuit* (the original) is taught how to behave by a crazy but nurturing, mothering, sexy lady; the awkward lab robot, Ulysses, in *Making Mr. Right*—an extension of his asocial and obnoxious male "maker"—is socialized for the marriage market, rather than as planned for the space market, by a foxy PR lady who is getting tired of males of the human variety; *E.T.* is taught about human (= American) culture by a child who is teaching as he himself learns from Mom, and so on.

■ Women from the Future and Androgynes

Sf was until recently a male genre—movies made by and for men. This has changed over the last twenty years. As women have become interested in sf because the genre lends itself to producing alternative social models, films have begun to appear that reflect a more diversified image of both women and gender. Below I discuss four such movies, *Liquid Sky* (1982), *Alien* (1979), *Brainstorm* (1983), and *Millennium* (1989). All four films are directed by men, but they are all imbued with sensitivities that reflect the feminist movement and changing gender roles.

Brainstorm is interesting for featuring a female scientist, Lillian Reynolds (played by Natalie Wood). Lillian is brilliant and tough, a scientist who has much in common with the ones discussed in the previous chapter. She is a workaholic who practically lives in her lab. She is a rebellious genius who will not allow anyone to co-opt her invention. She is especially passionate about not wanting the military to take over her work and turn it into a new superweapon. The invention that Lillian and her primary co-worker, Michael Brace (Christopher Walken), are so determined to protect is a machine that can record thoughts, feelings, and even sensory perceptions.

Lillian conforms to the standard genius stereotype; she virtually has no life outside her work. There is a suggested love affair with the younger Mike Brace, but it is much more like an affectionate mother-son relationship—a feature reinforced by her dominance and charge-taking when they are in the company of their boss or outsiders. Several times in the film, he protests against her treatment of him as an inferior, a minor who has to shut up when "the adults talk." And Mike's real infatuation is with Karen, his wife, from whom he, at the outset, is about to separate. Lillian Reynolds is slightly masculine; she wears no makeup, her hair is hanging down flat and unattractive, she walks like a man. Karen, on the other hand, is very feminine and attractive. She too is involved with the project, but as the designer whose job is to streamline the heavy helmet that records and transmits thoughts into an elegant headset much like that for a Walkman. Lillian dies in the middle of the movie from a heart attack, a fact that has less to do with choice than with what had to be: Natalie Wood's tragic boat accident took place during the shooting of the film.

As it stands, *Brainstorm* is most interesting for having a female scientist, but much of the effect is obfuscated by her being so masculine (the same holds for the female scientist in *The Andromeda Strain* (1971)). Making women into men is not terribly interesting and certainly not what the feminist movement envisions as the future in gender relations. But in sf, that is what most often happens. In *Aliens*, the protagonist, Ripley (Sigourney Weaver), is the science officer aboard a space cargo ship, months away from Earth. Ripley is hardly gendered at all, apparently a conscious choice on the part of the screenwriter, Dan O'Bannon, and Ridley Scott, the director: "Dan O'Bannon's treatment for the first film *Alien* was unique in writing each role to be played by either a man or a woman."[12] Both *Alien* and the sequel, *Aliens*, are less about sexuality than about gender, or, more to the point, about natural versus scientific reproduction and about *gender roles*.

Currently there is much interest among scholarly film critics in Freudian approaches to analyzing movies. The focus is on the changing gender patterns and how they are reflected in the interaction dynamics of the nuclear family and represented on the screen. Traditional views of gender and the family are under attack and being transformed in our society, and it is no suprise that some of the visceral energy involved in such crucial changes is reflected in the colorful mirror that is popular culture. Mainstream movies have tried, in a feeble fashion, to deal with changing gender roles and family patterns since the late '60s, but sf, always a distinctly male-oriented genre, resisted the onslaught of modernity for a long time. That films dealing with the new realities did emerge may be related to the fact that sf, precisely because it always has been a corner of the movie industry where heresies could at least be suggested, has become popular with a segment of the feminist movement. Sf literature has been rescued from the science buffs and adventure aficionados by a virtual invasion of women writers who have seen the opportunities for imagining different worlds inherent in the genre. A favorite of mine that can stand as representative of this is Marge Piercy's *Woman on the Edge of Time* (1976).[13] In this brilliant novel, Piercy confronts the dismal present-time reality of a Latino woman and mother with two diametrically opposed, but equally logical, future outcomes of that present. We can either continue on the route toward the patriarchal/scientific dictatorship, or we can "feminize" our values by putting people, emotions, and science for the people at the center. I doubt that Hollywood will be ready to make a film of Piercy's book any time soon. It is depiction of our own society is too angrily realistic and bleak, its feminized future too happily revolutionary. But still, some of the intellectual fervor has reached the screen in movies such as *Brainstorm*, in the *Alien*-movies, and in two other movies, *Liquid Sky* and *Millennium*.

I discuss the *Alien* movies in chapter 4 and include a discussion of the mothering/reproduction imagery, so here I will only quote Penley. Having established that *Alien* is unique in essentially eradicating sexual differences, she goes on to say about *Aliens:*

Aliens reintroduces the issue of sexual difference, but not in order to offer a newer, more modern configuration of that difference. Rather, by focusing on Ripley alone (Hicks [her male colleague] is awkwardly "disappeared" from the film in the closing moments), the question of the couple is supplanted by the problem of the woman as mother. What we get finally is a conservative model lesson about maternity, futuristic or otherwise: mothers will be mothers, and they will *always* be women.[14]

In *Millennium,* based on John Varley' story "Air Raid," the subject of time travel helps introduce the novel idea of a society where there are no sex differences and no sex, juxtaposed with our own patriarchal and gendered world. In this film we are introduced to a future America where wars and pollution have taken their toll. People are dying and infertile. In order to maintain a population and to introduce people who are reproductively viable, squads of soldiers are sent back into the past to abduct people who are about to die in airplane crashes. The squad leader is a young woman who, via plot twists, meets, has sexual intercourse, and falls in love with a man from the 1980s—an air-crash investigator, played by Kris Kristofferson.[15]

The love affair is played out in an interesting way: the woman from the future, Louise Baltimore, does not know how to be seductive and feminine. In her own world she is known to be a brash and fearless soldier, not necessarily masculine, just ungendered and matter of fact. Steve Neale has argued that "narrative cinema works towards a systematic regulation of desire, position and identification in terms of sexual difference. Sexual difference itself is specified primarily in terms of the gender of the characters who perform its narrative functions and actions."[16] In *Millennium* the issue of sexual differentiation is given a twist: Louise has no female gender specifics. She is instructed (via teleprompting) by her computer companion in how to wiggle her behind and how to generally fit the *fin de siècle* model of seductive womanhood. That she is not totally successful and comes across as eccentric and "foreign" is what makes her endearing and attractive to Bill, the investigator. He has never met a woman quite like her. She is direct, voracious in her appetites for foods not available in her world, and, once she discovers it, for sex. While the film is not totally successful because of some rather obvious problems with the script, it is instructive in several respects. That Louise has to learn, before the audience's eyes, to become gendered, to become a woman instead of a neuter, shows how *unnatural* the seductive and submissive behavior of women in patriarchy is. And it is the behavior of women that is unnatural, not that of men. If Louise resembles either gender in her own time, she resembles a man. She is almost the male ideal: direct, frank, courageous. So male behavior, the movie suggests, is not gendered, it is neutral, natural. Female behavior has to be learned, it is an overlay on top of the natural. Women, as Freud suggests, in order to appeal to men have to become gendered by being different. Women have to pull men out of their gender neutrality by behavior that marks them as sexual, as objects for male pleasure. All of this is reinforced by the fact that there are no instances in the movie where a biological male from the future has to learn to fit the male-gendered role. All of the men from the future remain sexually neutral. And interestingly, Louise's personal robot, who acts like a combination subconscious-conscience-teacher-engagement calendar, comes across as slightly effeminate, a "gay" robot who would like to be in Louise's place.

That Bill accepts and falls in love with this future Louise is equally instructive. He is attracted to her not so much because of her seductive behavior but because of her "otherness," her lack of gender characteristics. He sees, in a sense, himself, the brash and effective workaholic, mirrored in her, and he likes what he sees. The problem with the film, as I see it, is that the base against which all behavior is measured is the male—almost a military, robotlike male. But only almost: Louise is not just an Amazon warrior from the future, she is depicted as caring and a savior of lives rather than as the taker of lives. And it is refreshing to see a film where it is made clear that the submissive, erotic female is a cultural construct.

Margaret in *Liquid Sky* is a logical opposite to Louise Baltimore: she has been brought up in rural Connecticut to become the perfect housewife, the ultimately gendered woman who can seduce a lawyer or doctor into marrying her and supporting her. But she has rejected that role, is not willing to pay the price of being the perfect hostess and lover. She has moved to New York, to the Village, and has become a model/actress and lives with a lesbian lover. Margaret wants desperately to find someone to be. She doesn't want to be what she was brought up to be, the bride and mother, she wants to be *herself*. *Liquid Sky* is interesting for being a first feature by a Russian immigrant, Slava Tsukerman, and for

having an alien creature that is never seen, although the audience
from time to time gets to see through the eyes of the alien.

Margaret, typically for someone who is in search of identity,
has taken acting classes and has discovered that the problem with
being an actor is that she cannot escape the female role that way.
She had to "be nice" to her teacher, to her agent, to directors, and
others. And the punk subculture and living with a woman does
not solve the problem either. As Vibeke Rützou Petersen and I
have put it, "then when you are fed up with being 'nice' to all
those men, you become androgynous, a free woman, a lesbian,
and, instead of men walking all over you, women do."[17]

For all its insistence on alternative life styles and androgyny,
Liquid Sky is about finding "Mr. Right." Margaret's quest takes
her from polite society, via the "alternative" world of the theater,
in the move embodied in the person of her acting teacher, a '60s-
type dopehead who likes to talk about freedom—and mostly means
his own freedom to sexually exploit women. But "as it turns out,
the alien is Margaret's prince." She thinks he loves her for herself
and she wants to supply him with what he needs, a drug produced
in the brain during orgasm. Put another way, when Margaret, at
the end of the film, removes her make-up and punk persona and
puts on an old-fashioned wedding dress to "marry" the alien, she
reverts to the role she has spent the entire movie trying to escape:

In the end Margaret becomes one with her own bourgeois background
and accepts its values. She still believes in bourgeois happiness: finding a
strong, decisive man who loves you unselfishly. *Liquid Sky* is so over-
stuffed with contradictory symbols and images that they all finally cancel
each other out and all we are left with is an escapist wallowing in punk
esthetics with a little social criticism thrown in for good measure. *Liquid
Sky* ultimately becomes a metaphor for itself. The world is just images, a
flickering of light and darkness across the retina. Margaret who has been
sectioned up and voyeuristically ogled by the camera all the way through
the movie is also the only person in the movie who *tries* to become a
whole, real person in a whole, real world. But she ends up being a
projection, a bit of footage played too fast. She disappears at the turn of
the switch that gave her ephemeral "life."[18]

Liquid Sky is most interesting for its depiction of the model/ punk worlds where traditional gender roles and characteristics are rejected. Margaret and Jimmy, a gay model played by the same actress, Anne Carlisle, are both androgynous to a fault. As Janet Bergstrom has pointed out, this demonstrates "how classical sex role expectations in our society have become unreliable. *Liquid Sky* represents changing social conventions embedded within a more conservative framework that is *itself* unstable." [19]

At its most provocative, sf points to other possibilities in terms of gender and roles than the ones we are accustomed to. In *Alien*, gender is absent, in *Millennium* its artificiality and culture-specificity is demonstrated, and *Liquid Sky* demonstrates the unreliability of fixed gender behaviors. The problem with all these movies, as with most sf (and for that matter, most folklore), is that the inherent protest ultimately is abrogated: in *Aliens* gender crops up and women are reduced to the traditional roles as mothers, socializers, in *Millennium*, the "otherness" (foreignness) of women vis-à-vis males and patriarchal culture, is emphasized by having the male role be the unlearned, the natural role. And in *Liquid Sky*, which in many ways is the most "revolutionary" of these movies, the heroine settles in the end for a white wedding and the "male principle" as her Mr. Right.

■ Notes

1. Nietzsche, from "The Greek Women," quoted in Lloyd 1984:2.
2. Again Ibsen provides an example; in his *The Lady from the Sea*, the young would-be artist Lyngstrand woos the lovely Bolette, trying to make her pledge herself to wait for him while he is abroad becoming a great sculptor. He feels he will be more creative if he knows she's there waiting for him. Ibsen, a master of irony, has Lyngstrand say next that he of course will not marry her once he comes back, rich and famous—she'll be too old then!
3. Goffman has written quite persuasively about this in Goffman 1979.
4. Irigaray 1985.
5. Keller 1985:77.
6. See Russett (1989:196) for discussion of the notion of "the depletion of bodily resources through intellectual activity." And Marcus (1974,

esp. 1–33) makes the point quite clearly that male sexual expenditure was drawn against the account of mental and productive (work) activity. Dr. Vibeke Rützou Petersen has pointed out to me that also yoga teaches that the brain can work only at its peak if all physical energy is channeled to it from the body—via meditation.

7. See Meggitt 1977.
8. Theweleit 1987–89.
9. Ibid. The brief discussion in the text is, as Dr. Vibeke R. Petersen has called to my attention, a gross simplification. Theweleit's thesis has to do with subject formation in male groups. But the simplification will do for my present purposes.
10. Mulvey 1975.
11. She is a bit wobbly and the sutures are still visible, but she manages to find customers. She turns out to be a "poison damsel" who kills her customers when she climaxes. *Frankenhooker* is obviously a send-up of many movies, the cult classic *Liquid Sky* among them. *Liquid Sky* is discussed later in this chapter.
12. Penley 1990:77.
13. Piercy 1976.
14. Penley 1990:77.
15. I am grateful to one of the publisher's anonymous readers for calling this movie to my attention.
16. Neale 1986:125.
17. Petersen and Schelde 1986:10.
18. Ibid., 18.
19. Bergstrom 1986:60.

4 ■

Humanoids in the Toolshed

■ Need Space, Will Travel

Today, because of continued economic and technological growth, we stand on the threshold of space. Although it may be easy for some to dismiss the dreams and designs to colonize space as mere extensions of Western imperialism or of technological thinking gone wild, we maintain that the urge to expand into space is basic to our human character. We are the exploring animal who, having spread over our natal planet, now seeks to settle other worlds.[1]

The quote from Finney and Jones makes the genocide of 25 million Native Americans[2] and of thousands of Aboriginal Australians not only acceptable but also inevitable. Humans are "exploring animals" who cover continents and planets only to move on and settle new ones. We can't help it, it's our nature. Actually, the book containing the above quotation is rather thoughtful. But the authors do take it for granted that human "imperialism" and technology are like cancer: you can't stop them. They have to grow, evolve, take over. This is the attitude behind an obsession new to the twentieth century, the obsession with traveling in space and encountering alien organisms that invariably, or almost invariably, turn out to be hostile. But space travel is—at least potentially—a two-way street. If we could evolve on this planet to the point where we're ready and able to move out and on, why shouldn't beings out there in space be able to do the same? And who says we're the first and the most capable; maybe someone's already at it, maybe they are on their way, maybe they're already here.

The notion of space travel owes a lot, of course, to our image of ourselves as born explorers, to Columbus and Magellan who went out, discovered "new" worlds, and spearheaded European invasions. And stories about space travel owe a lot to folklore: the anthropomorphic monsters of yore have become the space monsters of today. As already noted in chapter 1, space is the new "wild" nature humans would like to explore, invade, and, perhaps, settle.

Some of our earliest written sources deal with humans exploring the "wild" and recounting their meetings with strange tribes and unusual animals. Herodotus, who traveled widely in the then known world, could report that "in Ethiopia, near the Egyptian border a tribe called the Troglodytes live underground. They eat snakes and lizards, and their language resembles the screeching of bats."[3] In the Middle Ages, travelers (and even those who did not travel) gave reports about humanoid monsters. There was a whole literature devoted to *Homo monstrosus*, "monstrous man,"[4] a creature that resembles humans in some traits, but has others that make it more animal or freak. *Homo monstrosus* is invariably reported to live in remote areas of distant lands. This creature can take many forms: *cynocephali*, dog-headed people, goose-headed people, people with but one enormous foot, and so on.[5] In this chapter, we shall look at some of the stories sf has to tell about monstrous creatures from outer space. I have chosen to concentrate on alien organisms—humanoids—encountered here on Earth.

■ Living Things from Outer Space

UFO sightings, by now a common enough phenomenon, are probably a case of life imitating art. Jacques Vallee says that the first reference to "a blackout caused by a UFO" was in Arthur Koestler's 1933 play, *Twilight Bar*. Actual sightings of UFOs and their effects on electricity come after this.[6] Vallee finds the "coincidence between these works of imagination and the actual details of the reports that came from the public a remarkable one," and a thought-provoking one. But whether the idea of UFOs is a fictional one or not, we have since been inundated with newspaper articles and books about experiences with aliens and even "scientific" volumes listing hundreds of encounters all over the world.[7]

I am not interested here in trying to evaluate whether or not there are, have been, or will be UFOs, but what the literature about UFOs reminds me most of are the recorded tales of encounters with trolls and witches and other creatures of the folkloric past. A layer of scientific discourse has been added, but the aliens of today seem to behave in ways that are remarkably similar to their folklore forebears. They seem to prefer darkness, they mostly appear in isolated locales, and they are given to abducting their victims to their own separate "world." In folklore that world was a netherworld under the ground or water or inside the mountain. Aliens take their victims to the "overworld"—to coin a term—of flying apparatuses and subject them to scientific scrutiny or implant fetuses in them.[8]

Later in this chapter I discuss a number of movies that show alien monsters as attackers, brought on by our fascination with science. The evil aliens are extensions of science and scientism: the idea that all life is a Darwinian struggle where the fittest will always survive. The evil, soulless aliens show that human concerns with free will and soul ultimately are backward, evolution must go on, even if it means our demise. The second half of the chapter reverses the image; the aliens are Messiahs from outer space who *warn* humans about the evil effects of science.

■ Organismus Monstrosus

Actually, the first movie I will discuss is not about a UFO, but about monstrous life from outer space. *The Andromeda Strain* details rather realistically—by sf standards—the scientific battle to isolate, analyze, and destroy an organism, brought back by a space probe, that proves deadly to humans.

A satellite returns to Earth and lands in Piedmont, a remote town in New Mexico. The satellite contains a capsule, which in its turn contains a space probe. The town doctor takes the capsule to his office and opens it. By the time the team tracking the satellite

arrives on the scene, all the inhabitants of the town except two—
an old, alcoholic man and a baby—are dead. The van with the
tracking team enters the village and the two men in it die as they
are reporting their discovery. Quickly, the military assemble the
team of scientists that has been designated to deal with just such
an emergency. The scientists, plus one M.D., are whisked to a
desert lab and research center, hiding under a Department of
Agriculture research station. The subterranean lab has the code
name "Wildfire," the satellite program that brought back the probe
is "Scoop." Both are top secret. Not even the scientists know
exactly what is going on. The bulk of the movie details the collab-
oration and squabbles of the scientists over a period of four days
as they try to identify the killer organism. The goals are to de-
scribe it physically and chemically and to exterminate it.

The Andromeda Strain is perhaps, after all, a space movie of
sorts: the scientists are locked in a "building" that goes five stories
into the ground, a virtual "rocket." They are made as "ritually
clean" (= sterile) as possible as they pass down through the various layers to the most "sacred" one. They eat food specially
designed for use in outer space. They are more or less isolated
from the rest of the world.

The organism turns out to be a tiny piece of rock with "pista-
chio green spots." The spots are "alive," they expand, the individual cells divide and mutate. The chemical makeup is much like
that of life on Earth—except that there are no amino acids. All
organic life contains amino acids. That is the difference; the space
organism is a crystal. It's "the ultimate chemical weapon," it is
"perfect for existence in space—consumes everything, wastes
nothing." The scientists also find that there is one flaw: the crystal
can exist only within a very narrow spectrum of salinity. A
supercolony of Andromeda Strain, moving along the U.S. coast, is
seeded from above and forced into the ocean and an innocuous
demise.

The Andromeda Strain is virtually unique for being a movie
showing science and scientists in a positive light. The Bad Guys
are the politicians who see the scientists as alarmist and refuse to
believe them or act on their advice. The military is not portrayed
sympathetically, either. They may, with the politicians, have or-

chestrated the whole thing for spurious purposes. Says Dutton, the oldest of the scientists: "The purpose of Scoop was to find new biological weapons in outer space and then use Wildfire to develop them." There is even a hint of suspicion that Stone, the head of the scientific team, knew and was part of the chemical weapon scam. That theme is not developed. But the scientists, besides being difficult prima donnas, are the heroes of the movie. They put their lives on the line, examining and combating a deadly organism and knowing that if it escapes the isolation tanks, all of them will have to be destroyed by a nuclear bomb built into Wildfire as a fail-safe device.

But even this movie is a folklore-protest because the real villain is Science—not the individual scientists—as the puppet of the politicians and the military. Science provided the know-how that sent the satellite into outer space, science designed the instruments used to "scoop" the organism into the capsule. Science was given the assignment of developing the organism as a secret weapon. The Little Guys are represented in the movie by the old alcoholic and the baby from the village of Piedmont. Only by chemical accident did they escape the scientific monster in the capsule. They are innocents who did not know about the satellite and the military applications, victims of secret scientific feats about which they had no say.

A major theme in *The Andromeda Strain* is secrecy: the credits are shown over shuffling documents stamped Top Secret and the like. Secrecy is exactly what makes science and those who control it suspect. Richard Hall asks in his book about UFOs and cover-ups: "Is the Government concealing important—perhaps vitally significant—information about UFOs? My answer would be an unequivocal 'yes!' The indications of secrecy are overwhelmingly strong, including 'leaked' information about spectacular military cases withheld from the public and cases forced into the open through Freedom of Information Act (FOIA) lawsuits."[9]

There's paranoia here, but perhaps understandable, since most people have a sneaking suspicion that there are hundreds of things they should know that are being kept secret. And because people know there are important things that are never revealed, they imagine the worst. Governments and those in power treat their populations as children who cannot be told about the really important things that determine the future and welfare of everybody in the family. Maybe one of the reasons for the stubbornly recurring reports of UFO sightings and alien contacts is simply a reaction to this knowledge that not everything is being revealed.

The tabloids especially are full of stories about encounters and "leaked" reports from scientists and government officials about aliens and scientific feats and their effects on ordinary "moms" and "dads," to use the tabloid terms (people are not just "people" or "men" and "women," they are their social roles). I refer to the supermarket tabloids here because they are repositories of modern folklore, they offer "indisputable proof that, far from having been wiped out by modern mass culture, folk literature . . . has simply taken on new and different forms."[10] One such tabloid headline declared: "Medical expert explains why we sometimes feel tired and worn out: Tiny space aliens zap our energy!"[11] The article goes on to tell how a named Belgian "virologist discovered the invisible life forms in a two-year study of fatigue and low-energy syndrome." He claimed, "They merely enter the body, siphon off enough energy to meet their demands and leave." That certainly brings to mind the organism in *The Andromeda Strain*. The question arises, of course, if the ubiquitous aliens appear in tabloid headlines, does that mean those who read these publications believe they are reading the truth? Probably not; more likely, some believe or would like to believe some of it, and most people just read it because it's fun to think it might be true. So it is quite possible that tabloid and sf stories about alien encounters tap into a repository of belief that such things can or could happen, and on that level they are "true."

The tiny aliens siphoning energy (space gnats or space deer ticks) seem to have a kind of intentionality, but not so the organism in *The Andromeda Strain*. It seems to have only one purpose— and not a conscious one: to survive and multiply. It is suggested by one of the scientists that the organism is a kind of "message" to tell humans that there is indeed life in space. The originator of the message, then, would not know that the message could have deadly results for humans. But that theory is just posed, never followed up.

Just as efficient, and much more willfully complex, is the organism in *Alien*. The space cargo ship *Nostromo* is about ten months away from Earth—the distant mother—and members of the crew are checking a planet from which they have received weak life signals. The space-suited and heavily armed crew members enter a giant, womblike cave (maybe the carcass of a living thing) and come upon some huge, brown, leathery "eggs." A crew member touches one and it begins to hatch. As they watch in horror, a crablike creature with long tentacles erupts and affixes itself to the face of the crew member. With due haste the others hustle him back to the ship. But the security officer will not let the victim and his attacker in. The rules exclude bringing alien organisms aboard, for obvious reasons having to do with contamination. But the science officer, Ash, takes it upon himself to let the man be carried in.

Portrait of an alien organism: the Alien seems to begin as a self-fertilizing "egg." Once the egg is hatched—which seems to be triggered by the presence of another living organism—the "neonate" attaches itself to the intake cavity (the mouth) of a host organism, where it has to mature further as it enters the organism —presumably for the purpose of living off it as a parasite. The next step is that it breaks out and is ready to live on its own, hunting and absorbing all the living organisms it can get its fangs into. It grows rapidly, becoming very large. Its "blood" acts like a superacid on Earth materials. The Alien lives—like a virus in the blood vessels—in the ducts of the *Nostromo*, infecting and attacking everybody who comes within its reach.

Alien is interesting for its ubiquitous "mothering" and procreation imagery: "Ripley's foe is a primal mother defined solely by her devouring jaws and her prolific egg-production . . . the monster's femininity is confirmed by the vulva and labia."[12] The battle for life and death is on between a huge, alien, totally instinctual *vagina dentata* and the male creatures swarming from the penile piece of human technology, the spaceship. The irony is that the one representative of male procreation, Ash, the robot, is also the one who wants to keep the Alien alive at all costs. Ash is destroyed by Ripley, and in the end Ripley destroys the creature as she— like a protective mother—cradles the ship's cat. In a review of the sequel *Aliens*, Bundtzen interprets the central imagery:

The Alien other, I believe, quite literally embodies woman's reproductive powers. She arouses primal anxieties about woman's sexual organs and in her combination of multiple tentacles and oozing jaws is the phallic mother of nightmare. The band of marines who enter her vagina, then her womb (which is also a catacomb cluttered with bony human refuse), with all their fire power and ejaculatory short bursts of guns, are ineffectual and insignificant male gametes.[13]

In both *Alien* and the sequel, the outcome is that technology is victorious over monstrous motherhood: Ripley flushes the alien into "the vacuum of space"[14] in the first film and blows it to smithereens in the second.[15]

Alien is also a "corporation movie." The *Nostromo* is owned by the Corporation, which sets the rules and the parameters and employs the entire crew. The Corporation is interested in finding and analyzing alien life forms—especially if they hold the promise of military applications. Thus Ash, the science officer, makes all final decisions relevant to science issues—including decisions about alien organisms and how to deal with them. He is within his rights, or so he claims, when he overrides the orders of Ripley, the security officer, and allows the alien organism and its victim to be carried aboard. And he is "willing to sacrifice the crew for the sake of science," as per Special Order 937, which is "for the science officer's eyes only." Order 937 is laconic and succinct: "Most important thing is to get organism back for analysis—crew is expendable." In this book's terms, that means that in a male-created, technological cosmos where Science is god, ultimate power over human life is placed in the hands of an android, a piece of technology. The lives of men and women are not as important in the scientific cosmos as are potential new technologies for death and destruction.

Ripley (especially if the sequel is taken into consideration) represents human natural reproduction. She fights the monstrous mother and her offspring while protecting Newt, the human child. Ash and the Alien represent male, technological, procreation and the monstrous forms of life it detects and generates, and the fact that Ash is a robot/android begins to explain why he is the perfect "corporation man" and why he admires the alien as a "perfect organism—no conscience or delusions of morality." Ash, the robot, is of course the mirror image of his masters, the high officers of the Corporation. He reflects their views, he is the Corporation. To quote Tony Safford: "The android-scientist is a functionary of the Company, itself a metonym for capitalism." [16] Expressed slightly differently by Jeff Gould, "In the system of the narrative, the Alien is the double, we might say the *biological analogue*, of the Company." [17]

The *Alien* movies pit male and female procreation against each other, but are also examples of something I mentioned in chapter 1: the technological excursion into "virgin" territory to be colonized and exploited economically by humans has potentially disastrous results. Along with the mineral cargo, the ship nearly brings home a "natural" monster that might destroy the human edifice of culture. "The creature is, in fact, an embodiment of nature as perceived by corporate capitalism, and by an evolutionary science whose emphasis on competition is a manifestation of capitalist ideology." [18] The alien other is nature—metaphorically expressed as female sexual capacity—once again battling the onslaught of human (= male) culture and technology. Once again culture—but mediated by the natural woman/mother, Ripley—is victorious, but only after a long and deadly battle against a creature determined to survive and proliferate.

The alien who is a stubborn survivor shows up again with a vengeance in *The Thing*. The 1951 version, directed by Christian Nyby, alias Howard Hawks, is most interesting because the monster is "a vegetable." A group of American scientists and military types find a huge, circular indentation in the inland ice on Greenland and determine that a flying saucer crashed there. Inside the saucer, in a "sarcophagus," is an eight-foot-tall "man." As it turns out, it's a "super carrot" that feeds on human blood and is superior to humans because it has no emotions and sexuality. Emo-

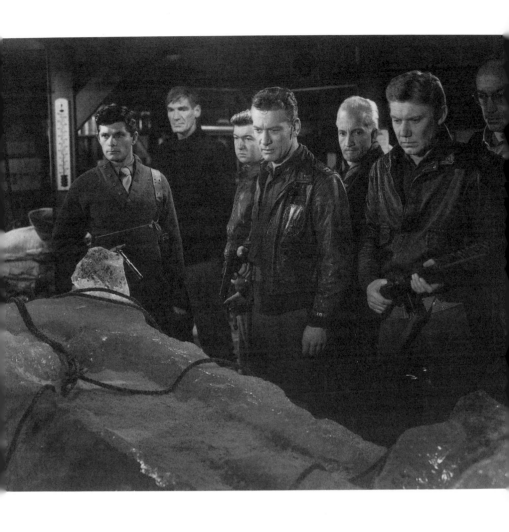

A team of American scientists in *The Thing* watch the chunk of inland ice containing an unadulterated folklore monster: an eight foot, mobile meat-eating plant.
(RKO Productions, 1951. Still courtesy of MOMA stills archive.)

tionless and intelligent creatures that want to kill or feed on humans are a staple of sf, but this '51 Thing is one of only a few herbaceous monsters in sf history.

This is a '50s movie, made when portraying the military in heroic terms was still the norm; the villains are the scientists who care more for the Thing than for their fellow humans. "Knowledge is more important than life, Captain. We owe it to our species to stand here and die." The Thing is a pure, unadulterated, folklore monster, sort of an evil Green Giant: a mobile meat-eating plant. It is almost as if Mother Nature, the victim of science and technology, had concentrated all her powers and made one last attempt to regain control by reversing roles: giant carrots feeding on humans—culture reduced to its protein value. But in the end the emotionless monster is no match for humans. They roast it over a fast fire—as it turns out, the only way to kill it is to burn it.[19]

The 1986 version, directed by John Carpenter, is more interesting from the point of view of this book. The Thing makes its appearance as a wolflike dog being pursued and shot at by a mad Norwegian in a helicopter. The movie is set in Antarctica at Section 4, U.S. National Science Institute. The protagonists are the personnel, scientists, and technicians at the camp. The first scenes establish for the audience a sense of strained normalcy: ping-pong, jazz, cards, pool, booze, and minor personality conflicts. We are, after all, in Antarctica, surrounded by nothing but ice and bitter cold. And all the personnel are men. But one gets a feeling of camaraderie and alcohol-induced mellowness. There is, in other words, an equilibrium of sorts. The advent of the dog, pursued by the trigger-happy Norwegian, spells the end to the equilibrium.

The chain of events that led up to the incident with the dog is subsequently reconstructed. A Norwegian research chopper came upon a vast circular indentation in the inland ice. They checked it out and discovered what turns out to be a space ship—from the position in the ice, the Americans later determine that the ship must have been there at least 100,000 years. Inside the ship was at least one "Being," frozen in place. The Norwegians carved out a block of ice containing the Being and transported it back to base. After thawing, the Being turned out to be alive and homicidal. It killed off the Norwegians—except one—took the shape of the dog, and fled, and then is set to repeat the pattern with the Americans. Presumably, what it ultimately wants to do is spread all over the Earth and "take over" all known life forms. For that is what the alien Thing does: it mimics organisms—perfectly.

The Thing is a common-enough alien: a life form that is capable of adapting to any physical environment and that can mimic any living organism. All it needs is some time alone with a victim and it slowly takes over. The process seems to be that it "sprays" its victim to enter, then it slowly becomes the organism, taking over its organs and their natural functions. Then, in the last phase, it erupts into its own form like an evil meat-pod opening; out of the pod come tentacles and a slimy, ugly organism.

The Thing has some interesting properties, such as the ability to change shape (the technical term is a "shapeshifter"), a capacity it shares with the witches and trolls of folklore. Witches can change form and become any animal they want to imitate, they can fly, they "enter" their victims and "consume" them from the inside. And the Thing is not just one organism—it is thousands. When it mimics a human, every cell, every drop of blood, is one "individual animal with desire to protect itself." This, ultimately, becomes the Thing's demise as the humans devise a method for finding out who among them are still human and who are Things. Each one must submit to having blood drawn into a lab dish; then the blood is singed. Since Things are endangered only by fire (exorcism), the "hidden" animals erupt and try to escape. The surviving Things—inhabiting human forms—finally decide to burn the camp down and thus kill off the surviving real humans who could warn the world. The Things are perfectly happy to be frozen down again to await a new chance.

The movie's main image system is fire and ice: extremes on a spectrum. The whole plot is about extremes: men in an extreme environment, living under extreme circumstances, and being attacked by the ultimate and extreme disaster. There are ubiquitous images of fire and ice and of life and death—two other extremes —as the human protagonists face still another image system: monstrous life. Ordinary, cozy, and lovable organisms—humans and dogs—are invaded by evil, and they explode into disgusting, tentacled creatures.

The Thing could be given all manner of psychological interpretations—humans *in extremis* who play out their personal and psychological conflicts as a battle to the death against the hostile situation and environment in which they are placed. Such metaphors would work, but the conflict that interests me is the one between a human outpost in an uninhabitable area and the monsters coming out of Antarctica's inland ice—one of the last uninhabited places on Earth. The fact is that, space alien or not, the monster has—for 100,000 years—inhabited the inland ice: it is carved out of the ice, it is "the troll" inhabiting this last unexplored area of Earth. The movie is, in other words, more a traditional folktale about humans transgressing on the "fairies' pass" than it is about space travel or visiting UFOs. The humans have to overcome the environmental monster, like the first humans, by (re)inventing fire.

An interesting issue that is never developed in the movie is the state of consciousness of an invaded human: is he a human who unwittingly harbors the alien organism (as is the case in *Alien*), or is he an alien masquerading as a human, but with an alien "self?" Thus the issue of "who" the invaded are is never explored.

■ Invaded Minds

The alien organisms encountered so far have invaded the bodies of their hosts to feed on them; they are fancy parasites. A Thing or an Alien may mimic or germinate in humans, but it invariably discards the host organism once it has taken what it needs and emerges as "itself," a monstrous, unconscious animal guided only by almighty instinct.

The aliens of *Invasion of the Body Snatchers*—both the 1955 and 1978 versions—are more complex. They arrive on Earth after having drifted through space for millennia. They are seeds with only one purpose: to find an organic home anywhere life exists. In the 1955 movie, the pods are just suddenly there; in the 1978 remake, they are seen seeding rain clouds and coming down inside the rain, ready to glom onto plant organisms. They enter organic

5504-26D

The alien life form in *Invasion of the Body Snatchers* is programmed to mimic any life form: notice how the body on the table is an exact replica of the man on the left. (Allied Artists Productions, 1956. Still courtesy of MOMA film stills archive.)

life on Earth via plants, the simpler life forms, and quickly begin to take over the most complex ones—human beings.

Seeds invading slowly and insidiously with the potential for destroying the cultural artifice are evocative. Alien organisms spreading like wildfire suggest infectious disease: alien microbes or viruses entering the human body and breaking down the resistance to other natural disorders. The movies can be read as metaphors—in retrospect—for AIDS and other contagious and/or venereal diseases.[20] Nature, in its most subtle and invisible forms, is always there; ready to attack and destroy humans and their artificial constructs. Nature may seem defeated, but even the smallest crack in the human defense systems can become the cause of the demise of culture. Ruins of past empires grown over and practically obliterated by grass and moss are there to remind us. Nature is resilient and patient: a coconut can drift for months on the ocean before landing on distant shores and seeding itself. In Florida, horticulturists had imported a beautiful and resistant tree from Australia, the *Melaleuca leucadendra*;[21] now, twenty years later, the tree has spread everywhere and poses a threat to much of the natural vegetation because it spreads rapidly and is virtually impossible to kill. The alien seeds from outer space can easily be seen as metaphors for the lingering fear we have for that alien "Other," nature.

Both Invasion movies are love stories in an alienated world. Becky and Miles in the 1955 movie are both recovering from stranded marriages. They are suspicious of new involvements, yet they have their antennas tuned to eligible others. Both are back from the microcosm of a relationship to the macrocosm of society at large. And they have trouble recognizing the world they knew before they married. When we meet them, they have both just returned to the small town they grew up in. Becky has come from England where her marriage had taken her, and Miles is back from a medical conference. Things have changed in Santa Mara, California. Miles's office is besieged by people who claim that their close relatives have changed. Aliens are taking over, one individual at a time.

Programmed to mimic any organic life form, the aliens invade their hosts cell by cell, becoming the host. But only up to a point. The invaded person is aware of being invaded; she knows she is an alien, she has the memories and knowledge of the human host intact. All that is lost is emotion, love, hatred, empathy. As far as the "converts" are concerned, the changes are for the better. One of them, a psychiatrist, says to Miles:

Miles, you and I are scientific men. You can understand the *wonder* of what's happening. A month ago, Santa Mara was like any other town, people with nothing but problems. Then, out of the sky, came a solution —seeds drifting through space for years took roots in a farmer's field. From the seeds come pods which have the power to reproduce themselves in the exact likeness of any form of life . . . they'll absorb your memories, your minds, and you'll be born into an untroubled world.

Miles answers, bitterly, "Where everyone is the same?"—"Exactly!" Human beings will still look like they always have, they will still eat and drink and work, but they will be soulless, mechanical survival machines, victims of a scientific world order where the only purpose of life is the continuation of life. Miles, by now in love with Becky, asks if they will still feel the same about each other when they have "changed." The alien psychiatrist answers that love is superfluous, as are all emotions: "You've been in love before, it didn't last. It never does. Love, desire, ambition, *faith*—without them life is so simple, believe me."

Danny, the psychiatrist-alien, has just declared the death of God and with him of any notion of a personal, individual soul; but for that, the aliens could be Moonies or members of some other religious sect: brainwashed, invaded, cut off from the relationships and emotions that governed their lives before. That the alien spokesman is a psychiatrist is, perhaps, not so strange. Psychiatry is the new science of the "soul," not the Christian soul, but a new, scientific, mechanical one. The new soul is geared toward functioning, but not toward loving and being happy.

On one level this movie about aliens invading the everyday world is about alienation in a rapidly changing world where life is becoming increasingly mechanical and fragmented. The traditional reading is that *Invasion of the Body Snatchers,* the 1956 version, as so many other '50s alien-invasion epics, is about the fear of "communism which gradually takes possession of a normal person, leaving him outwardly unchanged but transformed within."[22] Another interpretation is suggested by David Wingrove, writing about the production of *Invasion:* "As a historical footnote, this was the time of McCarthyism in America, of sameness and blind conformity to an alarming degree."[23] The truth of the matter, of course, is that there is not much to choose between the fascism of McCarthy and the communism of Stalin. Wingrove suggests, incidentally, one further interpretation, namely that "small-town conformity is a kind of living death."[24] But both movies can also be seen as warnings against the more generalized danger of scientism: a world where science is getting ready (1956) to invade outer space is also one where outer space might invade us. When Becky asks Miles what the seedpods can be, he says, "So much has been discovered the past few years. They may be the result of atomic radiation [i.e., mutations] or weird alien organisms."

The 1978 movie is clearer on this point. The image systems are infection, contagion,[25] seduction, conspiracy. Both of the protagonists work for the Public Health Department. Matthew is a health inspector and spends much of his time checking restaurant kitchens and trash cans. In the opening sequence, the infestation/contamination imagery is introduced with his discovery of rat droppings in a restaurant's food. Elizabeth works as a chemist, analyzing specimens brought in by inspectors. She also has an interest in plants that attach themselves to other plants and organisms and live off them. Disease metaphors are obvious: nature trying to destroy civilization at its most vulnerable level, the level of biology. Nature can do nothing against the mechanical and metallic constructions that are taking over its territory, but human beings are still organisms, biological entities, subject to AIDS, cancer, viruses.

The remake is set in San Francisco, essentially chronicling the further spread of the Body Snatchers that started in tiny Santa Mara. The original begins with the image of Miles, by now the only "survivor," on the highway outside Santa Mara, running up to cars and trying to convince them of the danger. In the sequel, he, or someone like him, has made it to San Francisco and still no one believes him. Matthew and Elizabeth are walking along the street when they suddenly see a man throwing himself onto the hood of a passing car, screaming, "Help, help, they're coming and you're next—they're already here."

The way the aliens introduce themselves into the chain of organic life on Earth is consistent with the parasitic infestation imagery. They come down with the rain and attach themselves to plants to produce pods that can infest human beings and make them into automatons.

Again I think the movie ultimately is about living in a world where science every day is redefining what it is to be human. Old values and old definitions of humanity are being fazed out as evolution is taking another turn. One character in the movie, who, ironically, is given to playing classical music for the benefit of her plants, states that she firmly believes humans evolved from the mating of apes and visiting space aliens. The effect the Body Snatchers have is that they are "screwing up the genes—like DNA —recombining us, changing us." The aliens are the harbingers of a next step in the evolutionary process where humans become mechanized: more efficient, more intelligent, more content, but emotionless and dead inside.

The essence of what it is to be human, in both movies, is love, the kind of love that makes a man and a woman feel as if they are all alone in the world, the kind of love that isolates, that stresses individuality and free will.

The same kind of reading could be applied to *I Married a Monster from Outer Space*. The subtext of this movie is that you never know the person you marry. The movie is from 1958 when that was especially true: cohabitation was not yet an accepted custom. And the truth is, of course, that you never really know someone until you have lived with him or her. Once the magic dust of infatuation settles, you get a chance to meet the real person. And many have discovered that the Bill or Jane they are married to is a totally different person from the one they courted.

I have already briefly discussed *I Married*, but let me quickly recapitulate. Marge lives in Norrisville somewhere in the heartland; she's engaged to be married to the handsome and ordinary

insurance salesman, Bill. The wedding takes place but Bill is acting strange: he doesn't know that he has to turn on the car's lights
at night, he's angry, he forgets his bride in the car when they
arrive at the honeymoon hotel, he doesn't know what thunder is—
in short, he acts is if he is from another planet, which, it turns out,
is the case. Bill belongs to a species that has come "halfway across
the universe. We come from a planet in the Andromeda Constella-
tion. Our Sun became unstable so we built some spaceships, enough
to get all our people away before our Sun exploded. But it took
time to build those ships and in that time, as our Sun's rays
became more intense, our women died. But we went on anyway, a
race doomed to extinction." A story about a doomed race on Earth
to find women, about monsters-stealing-our-women. It reminds
me most of all of a Danish folk ballad, in which a young woman
goes to a dance and meets a handsome young prince who whisks
her away and takes her to his home under the sea. During the ride
he and his followers unmask themselves and show their real troll-
natures. The young woman is lost forever—her screams can be
heard all over the parish.[26] Folklore is full of such stories about
young, marriageable women who are abducted by trolls who
"marry" them and have children by them. Bill, and several of his
race, have married Earth women, mimicking their real husbands
—with the express purpose of procreation. Marge follows Bill to
the space ship and sees him change into a horrible Monster. Later
she confronts him and he tells her the truth. She says, "Your race
has no women, you can have no children—eventually you'll die
out."—"Eventually we'll have children with you."—"What kind
of children?"—"Our kind." They are waiting for their scientists to
"mutate human female chromosomes so we can have children
with them."

The way the monsters "mimic" their hosts is that they abduct
them and keep them in the ship as unconscious transmission
sources. "Electrical impulses from the *real* human body must give
form and shape, even memories" to the masquerading monsters.
These signals from the human forms are received by the monsters,
who use them to become almost perfect replicas of their victims.
But there is obviously some kind of "static noise" in the transmis-

sion, since the monsters aren't quite convincing as human husbands.

Once Marge has convinced the authorities that there is a ship full of alien monsters in the woods (which is where the folklore monsters lived too), a posse heads out there to see what they can do. They find the human men hung in a neat row inside the alien ship—like Grandma and Little Red Riding Hood in the wolf's stomach. And, as was the case in folklore, once the "spell" is broken—once the "copies" are destroyed—the trapped humans are free to leave and go back to the women who love them. As in folklore, the man who was trapped—in the form of a monster—is freed by an act of love and courage on the part of the woman who loves him. Marge single-handedly faces the Monster and the ridicule and disbelief of her fellow humans, and her persistence leads to the final scene where the "hunter" comes and kills the "wolf."

The aliens can be seen as metaphors for the reality of the chasm between men and women in a society where gender differences had been taken to a ridiculous extreme. In the '50s, men and women were perceived to be natural opposites and forced to act—by social stereotyping—as if they did not belong to the same species. Men were tough, unemotional, logical, world oriented. Women were their opposites: soft, emotional, instinctive, home oriented.

Many Native American tribes have tales about Star Husbands who come to Earth and abduct young marriageable women. The woman is forced to live in a strange world with a strange husband for a number of years before she finally is able to escape and return to Earth and her own society. Such stories are usually interpreted as metaphoric rites of passage, and Barbara Leavy[27] suggests that the women may be protesting their future role in a harshly patriarchal culture by creating fictional flights. The Star Husbands are always insistent that the women bear them children. The similarities to *I Married* are obvious. All the women in the movie marry men who turn out to be aliens. They are, in other words, going from being unmarried and on the film's terms presexual to being adult women whose future function is to produce children and take care of their husbands. By making the husbands so alien, by *Verfremdung*, the absurdity of the situation becomes visible: from being individual human beings, these young women are changed into reproduction machines for a patriarchal society that is created for the benefit of men.

The movie can also be read as a warning against science and the ways it is slowly robbing us of our humanity. The alien scientists, reacting to a natural disaster, came up with a plan whereby they could go and take over another species—without asking, transforming the host and the offspring into soulless, logical, superior beings who do not know how to live and love. The film makes it clear that the aliens represent a technologically and intellectually superior race of beings. Though they may look like monsters to human eyes and though they may smell like "wild things" to dogs—who growl and attack them as if they were wild animals—they are more advanced than humans, perhaps the next step in evolution.

Returning for a moment to the tabloids, the disseminators of modern folklore, an alternative reading suggests itself: the movie could reflect reality—as the following headline from the *National Examiner* implies: "I've Been Married to Space Alien for 12 Years." The article tells the story of "goddess Irena I" who has been married to an invisible alien god for twelve years.[28] Or this *Weekly World News* headline: "A space alien made me pregnant—then stole my baby!" The story—which could have been Marge's— goes that Christine Florenz of New York was abducted by three-foot aliens who "used strange medical instruments to impregnate her aboard their spaceship."[29] Constance Penley has suggested, in a discussion of "Science Fiction and Sexual Difference," that these kinds of stories can be interpreted as referring to a desire to locate an evaporating sexual differentiation.

Aliens that abduct human women and put fetuses in them—that's not quite what happens in *Village of the Damned*, but almost. Something strange takes place one day in the tiny, rural village of Midwich in England. Everybody suddenly falls down unconscious in the midst of whatever they are doing: humans, animals, everybody. The movie camera records scenes like the ones we know from Pompeii and Herculaneum. Life is temporarily frozen—literally too: as the military comes in they feel cold—and then

I Married a Monster from Outer Space: the story of a space-age "troll," mimicking a human, who marries an Earth woman with the express purpose of procreation. Here they both look perfectly human and normal — but true to fifties gender-patterns when men and women inhabited different worlds: notice the expression on her face as she looks at him. (Paramount Productions, 1958. Still courtesy of MOMA film stills archive.)

everybody wakes up again, having, apparently, suffered no harm and no ill effects, except that all women of childbearing age suddenly are pregnant. The women all have normal, if fast, pregnancies and give birth to normal, beautiful babies. Except the babies all look the same, and not like their "parents," and they are all astoundingly fast learners—miniature Einsteins in the making. Very soon the children opt for independence, refusing the love and attention of their "mothers" and preferring each other's company. They travel together, a pack of golden-haired, cold-blooded super-children.

One of the children, David, is born to the scientist Gordon Zellaby and his wife Altea, and Gordon takes it upon himself to study the children. He discovers that David's hair and nails are not normal; the chemical makeup is different. He also discovers that the children have unusual powers: they can manipulate objects and people with their minds, they can direct electrical and other energy out into space, they share knowledge—if one learns something, they all know it. They have a "shared" mind. And they can read human thought. The last is the worst because it turns out that the "aliens" are unwilling to submit to human laws and morality.

Village of the Damned is a taut little gem of a movie that presents its story realistically. There are no scary three-fingered monsters, no clumsy space ships, just very normal people and some children who look normal but are not. It is especially frightening that the aliens are children who have germinated in human women and who grow up—as strange "cuckoos"[30]—in the "nests" of humans.[31] In folklore terms, these children are "changelings—the offspring of elves or other supernatural beings left to be raised by humans."[32] Changelings are always eventually recognized as "alien" because of their rapid development, their physical strength and their inability to laugh—the children in *Village of the Damned* are always terrifyingly serious and intense.

Village of the Damned is a warning about the kind of scientific progress that would change human beings into emotionless automatons: a conversation between Gordon, the scientist, and a general who wants to destroy the children will demonstrate what I mean. Gordon says, "What we're dealing with is a mass mind,

In *Village of the Damned* a pack of gold-haired, cold-blooded miniature Einsteins turn out to be aliens, unwilling to submit to human laws and morality. Notice the eyes and the smug and serious superiority, uncanny! (Metro-Goldwyn-Mayer Productions, 1960. Still courtesy of MOMA film stills archive.)

an entirely new development, like a colony of ants or bees. These children all want to dress alike and what one does, they all do. They are one mind to the 12th pi. Now just think what it would mean if we could guide it. We could leap forward in science a hundred years." The general answers, "At the risk of being destroyed." Gordon: "The age old fear of the unknown."

Gordon is the extension of Drs. Frankenstein and Jekyll, the scientist who wants progress, scientific progress, at any cost. He believes humans should evolve, should try to climb—by whatever means—up to the next evolutionary step. The alien children represent that next step. They even tell him as much: "If you didn't *suffer from* emotions and feelings you could be as powerful as we are" (italics my emphasis). The problem with humans is that they allow emotions to overrule logic and technology. Gordon, at least for a while, agrees. For him evolution and scientific "progress" are inevitable and desirable.

In the following chapters we shall meet other scientists who subscribe to those tenets of faith, scientists who use technology to obtain power over people's minds, to override the emotions, to eclipse love, to further the evolutionary process. But first a look at some encounters of a kinder, gentler sort.

■ Alien Gods [33]

Like other supernaturals or folklore creatures, aliens are not necessarily all evil or enemies of humanity. They all seem to share certain features, such as the ability to enter into the minds of humans, and they have innate powers, mana, that allow them to manipulate physical objects, make the Earth tremble, or control electricity and all kinds of machinery. Just as folklore monsters embodied the raw power of nature, aliens seem to embody the magic—science—that causes mechanical toys or electronic gadgets to work.

The movies discussed here present an alien, who is central to our culture—the Messiah who comes to Earth to save humankind or warn us against our mistakes.

A central myth in our culture is the myth of the Messiah, the savior from the heavens above. Science fiction, a genre that has helped transform traditional folkloric myths into modern ones about science and outer space, has created several twists on the Christ myth. Two of these are by Steven Spielberg and are among the most interesting and personal entrants in the alien-movie lineup. This chapter derives its title from his 1982 *E.T.: The Extraterrestrial*, where the alien takes refuge in a toolshed. Elliot, the protagonist, Spielberg's and E.T.'s alter ego, hears noises from the shed, throws a ball in there—and *something* throws it back to him.

E.T. is a conscious fairy tale about a little boy who solves some very real emotional and existential problems by creating a "magical" friend. E.T. is EllioT, as the names suggest, and Elliot is a healthy child in a world of trouble. His father, whom he adored, has left. He is the middle-child of three, with a dominant older brother and a younger sister. He has trouble asserting himself—the middle child syndrome.

Elliot has no friends of his own and is too little for his brother and his friends to play with. When the older kids play Masters of the Universe, Elliot is sent off to pick up pizza. But Elliot finds something that makes him the center of his siblings' attention and gives him, as he makes his brother Mike admit, "absolute power." Elliot finds a real live alien (or elf or leprechaun or goblin). In the movie, the alien is real, but metaphorically he is of course the ability to create stories, fictional characters. Elliot becomes an artist to overcome his problem. He fills the emotional void left by his father's absence with a creature of his own invention that "cures" him—physically and psychologically.

E.T. becomes a stand-in for the father in Mexico, he "wears the absent terrestrial father's clothing, drinks beer, reads the paper and watches TV."[34] E.T. helps Elliot let go of his father and, eventually, of E.T. himself. Elliot comes out stronger, more full of love, richer because he will always "believe" in E.T. He will always have E.T. in his heart, he will always have the ability to create fantasies that can help him and others cope. In one scene Mary, the mother, is reading a story to Elliot's younger sister, Gertie; E.T. and Elliot secretly listen in Elliot's huge walk-in closet: "She says she thinks she could be well again if children believed in fairy-tales." E.T. is a fairy tale helper with magical abilities, and he is a projection of Elliot and his problem. After all, E.T., like Elliot, has been abandoned; his spaceship took off without him and he is left in a strange and frightening world.

The scare, for both Elliot and E.T., is the adult, scientific world of disbelief and taking life too seriously. The teacher in the school wants Elliot and his classmates to chloroform and dissect living frogs so they can "notice the heart and notice how it's still beating." The scientists who have been pursuing E.T. since the alien spaceship took off want to study him as if he were a frog or scientific specimen, as Elliot says when E.T., presumed dead, is frozen—just as the frogs were chloroformed: "They're just gonna cut him all up."

The adult, serious world has its values all screwed up. Innocent frogs are cut up by children who learn disrespect for life and lack of compassion—in other words, they learn to become adults. But Elliot, "tuned" to E.T., sets the frogs free and "makes love" instead, kissing the pretty little blonde girl he has only dared admire from a distance before. Elliot feels E.T.'s feelings and thinks his thoughts—because they are, of course, one—and he assists E.T. in creating a kind of phone to call "home." One of Elliot's problems is the schism between his own world of fantasy and the adult "real" world of science and seriousness. He has to choose. Choosing his own world to the exclusion of reality would make him a mental case. Choosing the adult world exclusively would kill his ability to create magic. Elliot chooses both, as all artists must: he bids his magical helper adieu, but he retains him, as E.T. promises him by pointing his "wand"—a finger with a "light" in it—at his forehead, "I'll be right here." Elliot/Spielberg can live in the adult world, but he will retain the ability to dream and create magical beings.

The movie really has three levels. On one level it is about a boy whose father has left and how he learns to work his way through the pain and the separation and come out wiser and warmer on the other side.

On a second level, it is about UFOs and space aliens. This is the least interesting level because the movie, the title notwithstanding, isn't *about* extraterrestrials. Spielberg's story is a fairy tale, but a modern one where the fairies are from outer space.

On the third level, it is a Christ parable of sorts: a story about faith in supernatural and magical beings who can help. E.T. is an alien—in the gnostic sense—god who can heal by laying on hands, and who can help the lonely and the frightened if they believe in him. He can move objects, can make plants grow magically. He can, like Jesus, enter the minds and hearts of those who believe. And like the biblical Jesus, this one has to face an establishment, a set of experts (scientists) who think they know all the answers and want to study him. The scientists, like the biblical owners of the faith, want "proof." They want to cut E.T. up and see what he is made of. The scientists represent a bumbling, clownish, and clumsy culture, the establishment that clings so desperately to its own theories and convictions that its members have no access to their emotions. They could be metaphors for psychiatrists who are so busy categorizing and fitting the boy and his experience to their theories that they have no time to listen to his cry for help.[35]

Like the other Jesus, E.T. dies and is resurrected by the faith and love of Elliot and by his distant "father," the spaceship. When E.T. is declared dead and when Elliot no longer can feel him, the boy stands by his dead friend and says solemnly, "I'll believe in you all my life, every day, E.T. I love you." He closes the lid to the "coffin" and sees some potted flowers E.T. earlier "resurrected" suddenly bursting with color and life. E.T. awakens and say "E.T, E.T. phone home." Elliot asks, "Does that mean they're coming?" It does. E.T. has been called home by his heavenly "father" and has been given life by the love and faith of Elliot. Elves, gods, and goblins only exist if children believe in them.

Close Encounters of the Third Kind, which was made in 1977, shares a number of features with *E.T.* The protagonists are a boy-man and a little boy. The boy-man, Roy, cannot handle being an adult, doesn't want to be one. Barry is an adorable and totally trusting child. The bulk of the movie records the effects a group of aliens have on people and objects and the chase the scientific and military establishment stage to catch up with them.

The aliens are Little People of the extraterrestrial kind: small, playful—even mischievous—and vaguely godlike beings who enter into the minds of those who believe, those, like Roy and Barry, who are not too closed and cloaked in seriousness to bounce off signals from other worlds. The "believers" are invited to an encounter with the aliens—all have the image of a particular mountain in Wyoming implanted, to the point of obsession—in their minds. The visit—encounter—is a joyous feast of sight and sound, humans and aliens exchange light signals and stage a veritable concert. Then Roy walks aboard the ship and it takes off, becoming, to the tunes of "When You Wish Upon a Star," a bright and shining "city of the gods."[36] Vivian Sobchack has argued convincingly that *Close Encounters* addresses the failure of patriarchy. The traditional *pater familias* is becoming an anachronism. Into the patriarchal vacuum moves the innocent child/alien. [37]

These aliens are like visiting angels—clips of the aliens are interspersed with clips from a church service where the minister says, "God has given you his angels to watch over you." The aliens/angels watch over Barry and all who believe, and they take Roy back with them, rewarding him for his tenacity and his faith and making him, perhaps, one of them—an angel. Fitting has expressed it with admirable clarity: "*Close Encounters* renews this metaphysical rewriting of human history by focusing on our contemporary sense of anxiety and alienation and then offering a religious solution. The answers to our current troubles and dilemmas do not lie in human activity or understanding, the film tells us, but outside and beyond us, in the heavens."[38]

One of the protagonists in *The Day the Earth Stood Still* is also a fatherless boy who becomes the first to accept the alien "god"— on faith. The movie tells the story of a spaceship that arrives in broad daylight and lands in Washington, D.C. There are only two "beings" aboard—a man, Klaatu, and an eight-foot robot, Gort. They are emissaries from distant worlds with a warning for humans. The movie is an assault on human—read male—aggression, pride, and competitiveness.

Predictably, the alien emissary runs afoul of male aggression and competitiveness, and in the end there is a near confrontation between humans and Gort, the giant robot. Gort, the space "cop" whose "job" is to demolish any aggressive race in the universe, is a metaphor for soulless science in the service of aggression—the

Klaatu, the alien "god" who came to warn and save humans, has been killed by them and is about, in Christ-like fashion, to be awakened briefly by the technological angel, Gort, before his final ascension. Note the technological halo above the robot/angel's head. (*The Day the Earth Stood Still*. Twentieth Century Fox Productions, 1951. Still courtesy of MOMA film stills archive.)

atomic bomb. He is science as monster: impossible to kill, determined to kill us if we do not change our ways. Science is a straitjacket we are strapping ourselves into.[39]

If Gort represents the danger of the kind of science that has brought us the atomic bomb, Klaatu is another Christ figure, another "alien god" who has come to earth to save us.[40] He—and his human extensions, Helen and Bobby—represents the core of humanity. Like Christ, he is a symbolic expression of the most treasured human ideals: compassion, willingness to sacrifice, love for all living things. Like Jesus (and E.T.), Klaatu dies for humanity and is resurrected to give a final speech to the nations and ascend to the heavens. But Klaatu is also the Old Testament god, stern and just, without mercy for the morally errant. He makes it clear that if humans persist in their evil ways, he will destroy them:

I'm leaving soon. You'll forgive me if I speak bluntly. The universe grows smaller every day and the threat of aggression by one group anywhere can no longer be tolerated. There must be security for all or no one is secure. That does not mean giving up freedom, except the freedom to act irresponsibly. Your ancestors knew this when they made laws to govern themselves and hired policemen to enforce them. We of the other planets have long accepted this principle. We have an organization for the mutual protection of all planets and for the complete elimination of aggression. The test of any such higher authority is of course the police force that supports it. For our policemen, we've created a race of robots. Their function is to patrol the planets in spaceships like this one and preserve peace. In matters of aggression, we have given them complete power over us. This power cannot be revoked. At the first sign of violence, they act automatically against the aggressor. The penalty for provoking their action is too terrible to risk. The result is that we live in peace without arms and armies, secure in the knowledge that we are free from aggression and war. Free to pursue more profitable enterprises. We do not pretend to have achieved perfection, but we do have a system and it works. I came here to give you these facts. It's no concern of ours how you run your own planet, but if you threaten to extend your own violence, this Earth of yours will be reduced to a burned-out cinder. Your choice is simple, join us and live in peace or pursue your present course and face obliteration. We shall be waiting for your answer. The decision rests with you.

The aliens encountered in this chapter exemplify two kinds of myths, one folkloric, the other religious. The invaders and Things that try to kill off humans or replace them are really reincarnations of folklore's angry monsters who wanted to destroy the "wall" separating the human construct, culture, from the environment. If the trolls had won the war, humans would have sunk back down into the morass of unconscious and soulless nature, reduced, once again, to being slaves of instinct, creatures without free will. The alien trolls differ from those of folklore in that they are, like the children in *Village of the Damned* and the seedpods of *Invasion of the Body Snatchers*, intellectually superior to humans. The implication is that we might become like them, as smart and effective as machines, but also as soulless and joyless as creatures whose only goal in life is to reproduce. In a certain sense, these kinds of movies are rejections of scientism, of the idea of the necessity of evolution. Indeed, the real villain in these movies—without ever being named—is evolution, the fear that we will one day evolve to become mentally superior to the human beings we are today, but morally and emotionally as vacuous as carrots. Which leads to the other myth, the one central to Christian cultures—the myth of the Messiah who will save our souls, not only from onslaughts from the old-fashioned devil, but also from the scientific one of scientism, of force-fed evolution.

■ Notes

1. Finney and Jones 1985:21.
2. Todorov 1982.
3. Malefijt 1968:113.
4. Malefijt says that when Linné published his famous list of living organisms, he included a section on *Homo monstrosus*.
5. Malefijt, 1968:113.
6. Vallee 1966:162.
7. A couple of examples: Bowen 1969, and Hall 1988.
8. Recently, of course, two books by Whitley Strieber have told us about his "experiences" with aliens (Strieber 1987, 1989). Strieber, claiming to have been abducted and examined by creatures that look suspiciously like "little people," records the horror not only of being coopted by aliens but also of being harassed, pursued, and hounded by the FBI and nonbelievers. At least he can find consolation, one would think, in the fact that *Communion* was a best-seller and was

made into a movie, and he has at least been able to profit from the experience.

9. Hall 1988:165.
10. Schechter 1988:120.
11. *Weekly World News*, 17 May 1988, 11.
12. Bundtzen 1987:12. My discussion of the "feminist" aspects of this movie is more or less a paraphrasing of Bundtzen.
13. Ibid., 14.
14. Ibid., 16.
15. For several interesting discussions of *Alien*—coming to the task of interpretation from widely different angles—see Kuhn 1990. See also the "Symposium on *Alien*" edited by Charles Elkins (Elkins 1980).
16. Safford 1980:297.
17. Gould 1980:283. In the same vein is Peter Fitting's comment that "the monster figures as the repressed psyche of late capitalism"; Fitting 1980:286.
18. Ruppersberg 1990:40.
19. For the sf enthusiast who wants to know more about this movie, I suggest the long article in von Gunden and Stock 1982:26–37. Most of the article is production notes and plot outline, but there is a brief, if not very penetrating, attempt at locating what the movie means. Von Gunden and Stock find that complex antiscience sentiments are expressed.
20. Another interesting use of AIDS and viral disorders as metaphors is currently popular in the debate about computer "viruses" and computer hackers. I quote from an interesting article by Andrew Ross:

> In fact, the media commentary on the virus scare has run not so much tongue-in-cheek as hand-in-glove with the rhetoric of the AIDS hysteria—the common use of terms like killer virus and epidemic; the focus on hi-risk personal contact (virus infection, for the most part, is spread on personal computers, not mainframes); the obsession with defense, security and immunity; and the climate of suspicion generated around communitarian acts of sharing. The underlying moral imperative being this: you can't trust your best friend's software any more than you can trust his or her bodily fluids—safe software or no software at all. (Ross 1991:3)

21. See Watkins and Sheehan 1975:292.
22. Laura 1972:71. Laura goes on to call that kind of thinking simple-minded, but says it "corresponds to the average American's views as they have been shaped by television and a wide range of periodicals" (71–72). Fitting says about *Invasion of the Body Snatchers:* "This film is an allegory for the McCarthy period and the difficulties encountered in uncovering the Communists at work in our midst"; Fitting 1980:287.

23. Wingrove 1985:125.
24. Ibid.
25. At one point in the movie a character says, "Kippner [the psychiatrist] is talking about a hallucinatory flu going around."—"Is it contagious?"
26. Jacobsen (Schelde) and Leavy 1988:57–59. The ballad is called "The Deceit of the Nix."
27. Quoted in ibid., 81–82.
28. *National Examiner*, 25 October 1988, 1, 27.
29. *Weekly World News*, 12 April 1988, 12.
30. The title of the book by John Wyndham on which the movie is based is *The Midwich Cuckoos* (1962).
31. Barbara Leavy has pointed out to me that the story of *Village of the Damned* is very similar to that of *Rosemary's Baby*.
32. Von Gunden and Stock 1982:156.
33. This is a reference to the gnostic religion, one of whose tenets is that God is a cosmic alien who is the first life, who is God, who is ultimately the one who saves and throws light upon the world. See Jonas 1958, esp. pp. 51–55. A somewhat similar, if thin, treatment of the Messianic aliens can be found in Ruppersberg 1990 ("The Alien Messiah"). In addition to the movies dealt with here, he discusses *Star Wars* and *Terminator*, which I give a similar interpretation in chapter 11.
34. Sobchack 1986:5.
35. I realize that they could also be the all-too-intrusive and dissecting critics who won't leave stories alone and have to look for levels and meaning—but I'm ignoring that.
36. Sobchack (1986) discusses this movie interestingly in a paper that analyzes the ubiquity of children who are alien/alienated paternal figures.
37. Sobchack 1986:19–21. Sobchack's argument about *Close Encounters* is sound; the rest of the article, however, is confused, full of psychobabble and loose ends.
38. Fitting 1980:291.
39. Gort is a precursor of Colossus, the supercomputer that is handed the right of life and military defense in the movie of the same name. See chapter 6.
40. According to von Gunden and Stock, "*Day* is a modern retelling of the Christ story and, as such, has enormous appeal for a troubled world. In this manifestation the alien is a Messiah, not an invader" (1982:43).

5 ■

In the Belly of the Beast

■ **The Mechanical Landscape:** *Technologie Moralisée*

Fictional science and genius scientists are important ingredients of sf. But at the core is the interplay between science's most profitable invention, the machine, and the human beings who have to operate them, program them, or be them. My discussion will deal with machines versus humans in terms of power play: Will machines conquer us, will they eventually dominate us? But what's really at stake is the sense of self, or "soul." Can humans remain human in a world where more and more of our time is spent interacting with machines and technology? This is the chapter where the "plot" really gets going: the fight to the death between human beings and their creations, the machines. The sf machines discussed in this chapter begin the gradual process of dehumanization by forcing humans to adapt to their choppy, mechanical rhythms and demands.

Technology and machines are ubiquitous in sf. In *Metropolis*, the drudgery of the working classes in the fictional oligarchy, headed by Joh Feddersen, is demonstrated by their descent into the bowels of the Earth to toil in a virtual *landscape* of complex and ominous-looking machines that totally dwarf them. Space epics, such as the *Star Wars* trilogy, *The Last Starfighter*, and *Bat-*

tlestar Galactica are composed almost exclusively of images of frail human characters against the cold, hard technological backdrop of metallic walls, gigantic computers, and machinery that opens doors, makes food, and fires death and destruction.

In *The Terminator*, the last scenes are the culmination of the chase that has been the subject of the entire movie: Sarah Connor, the protagonist, and her back-from-the-future lover Kyle Reese are fleeing Schwarzenegger's Terminator. The Terminator is driving an extra-long double-rig truck: expanses of silvery metal, towering and menacing. And inside the huge machine is the robot/cyborg, the flesh already partially blown off its face, showing metal underneath. The rig crushes the small truck from which the two humans have leaped to safety only seconds before. Kyle stuffs a dynamite stick into the exhaust of the rig; fire engulfs rig and driver. Out of the smoldering remains emerges a red-eyed, clanging, metal skeleton, hell-bent on fulfilling its mission of killing Sarah.[1] The two humans flee into a factory with the unstoppable machine-devil in pursuit, metallic limbs clanging and rattling. The next scene is set in the factory. The humans slam a huge metal door shut in the face of their pursuer and switch the machinery on. The final showdown between human and inhuman can begin, a scene played out against the backdrop of the empty factory with machines chugging and chomping and grinding vacuously.

The cyborg bursts through the iron gate and the human lovers climb a metal staircase to a narrow metal bridge, high above the ground. The noise and movement of the machinery keeps the robot temporarily occupied, but soon the Terminator clangs—metal against metal—up the stairs to finish its mission. Heroic and unselfish, Kyle throws the last stick of dynamite at the Terminator from close quarters: Kyle dies but the dynamite hits its mark, the cyborg is hit. Sarah is finally safe? No, the torso of the robot comes crawling toward her, relentless. She too has to crawl because she was wounded in the explosion. She barely manages to get under the flat steel slab of a giant metal press as the metal fingers grab at her feet. She slides off the metal expanse and pulls a grille shut behind her. With the mechanical claws grasping at her through the grille, she manages to reach the button that activates the metal press. Inexorably, the two metal plates come together, squeezing the electric "life" out of the robot; blue sparks emanate —extinguishing the bright red and evil light of the eyes.[2]

The scene, although extreme, is typical. The final showdown between Good and Evil—not only in sf movies—is often set against technological "landscapes." Machines—huge, hard, and impersonal—are not only backdrops in sf, they enter the action, becoming, as in the scene from *The Terminator*, virtually the *deus ex machina*.[3]

Visually, machines are the perfect backdrop for the human figure because they are so rigid, so large, so dangerous. Moving across the "landscape" of machinery, the trope of the human form seems small, frail, unpredictable. Machines and humans are logical opposites. But that still does not explain the love affair between sf and technology. To understand the juxtaposition of the human form and machines better, I shall turn my attention to another movie genre: the Western. In Westerns such as *Rio Grande* and *The Searchers*, the action is played out against the enormity of the American landscape. The landscape is a bona fide character: huge, immovable, distant mountains stand like monuments to the eternity and incorruptibility of the land. The vast prairies, the mighty rivers are dangerous and powerful but also symbolic of a kind of natural and eternal morality. The French term for this phenomenon is *paysage moralisé:* a landscape with a built-in morality.[4] The actions of men and women played out against the Western landscape are also, in a sense, measured morally against it. The landscape destroys or mutilates those who do not measure up. The evil or weak are swallowed by the roaring river, fall off the precipice, are killed by poisonous snakes. The good may have to struggle against the land, may have to prove that they are worthy of it— but they almost invariably persevere and come out victorious in the end having conquered not only evil but also the land.

The Western heroes and villains move across the enormity of the American continent in pursuit of happiness and, if not wealth, an honest livelihood. The land is an adversary that once conquered, once it has stamped its approval on someone by letting her survive and settle on it, becomes a source of wealth and happiness. The mountains provide coal and iron ore, the forests timber for housing and heating, the animals skins to clothe and protect, the land sprouts grains and grass to feed the domestic animals.

The sf equivalent of the Western landscape is the factory hall full of sophisticated machinery and technology. A "missing link" of sorts between the Western and the sf is *Maximum Overdrive*. In this movie, written and directed by Stephen King, machines (mostly large trucks) attack and surround people holed up in a diner in a remote area. This recalls the Western image of settlers having to defend themselves against a noisy force of Indian attackers that ride around the wagon circle. In the end, the trucks go back to being docile tools, but only after having brought out the true natures of the beleaguered: the evil and cowardly have been exposed and killed and the good have learned important things about themselves. Technology, although created by humans, shares qualities with the Western landscape: it is huge, dangerous, impartial, incorruptible—a modern *paysage moralisé*. Good and Bad are matched against the enormity, the power, and the moral superiority of technology. Machines are vacuous in terms of desire. They, unlike humans, do not lust, are not greedy, do not cheat. They are *there:* they have innate properties and powers but no consciousness.[5] And like the Western landscape, technology has the ability to bestow power, unlimited and enormous, on the one who controls it.

■ Sexy Weapons

Before turning my attention to Willful Machines, I want to focus briefly on another kind of ubiquitous technology in the sf film: weapons. At the core of the vast majority of sf movies are means of destruction: guns, rifles, laser swords, machine guns—sf heroes don't care to be seen without them. Arnold Schwarzenegger, himself a product of fantasy and sf movies, is the prime example. His popularity as an sf actor can to a large extent be ascribed to the fact that he himself is a magnificent man/machine/weapon. I want the reader who is familiar with the sf genre to visualize Schwarzenegger in *The Terminator*, in *Predator*, in *Running Man:* rippling muscles, pectorals like melons—and guns; strapped across his chest, hanging by his side, cradled comfortably in his arms are machine guns, laser guns, rifles, machetes. Or take the *Star Wars* trilogy: it is virtually impossible to imagine the hero, Luke Sky- walker, without his laser sword. He derives his identity from it. Luke pre-sword is a pimpled teenager back home on the farm with dreams but not much else. Luke after he has acquired his sword is becoming a man, a knight, and a warrior—and one of the most powerful and influential people in the entire universe.

In sf, conflict resolution is never achieved by individuals sitting down and talking through the problems. The solution to any prob- lem is physical combat and the means to victory is always weap- ons. Even in movies where the hero has no weapons at hand, but where physical danger needs to be dealt with, the solution is to transform something normally innocuous into a deadly weapon. In *Incredible Shrinking Man* the hero uses a darning needle and other household items to defend himself against the monstrous insects that threaten him. And in *Frankenstein* and *Dr. Jekyll and Mr. Hyde* the final solution to the problem created by scientific hubris is to kill the monster with conventional weapons. Franken- stein's monster is hunted by a posse of village men, and Mr. Hyde is killed by a bullet from a policeman's gun.

Guns are photogenic: they add to the character carrying them. An Arnold Schwarzenegger or a Chuck Norris may not have much dramatic talent or presence, but adorned with enough weapons, he cuts an impressive figure. These men derive their *personality* from their weapons. Rambo without the olive oil on his torso and without the signal machine gun would be able to walk almost anywhere unrecognized. He is what he kills with. Anyone who has had the bad fortune to sit through one of the *Rambo* epics will know the sickening way in which the camera in these movies caresses killing machinery. The same holds in *The Terminator* (by any standards a much better movie) or *Alien* and all of the teen- age flicks: *The Last Starfighter, Battle Beyond the Stars, Yor,* and so forth. The protagonists do not have personalities in the traditional sense; they have weapons.

The obsession with weapons is an American phenomenon. Americans have always had a love affair with guns. For reasons that have to do with American history, guns and freedom, guns and wealth, guns and sense of self have become identified with one another. The American continent was conquered gun in hand. Essentially the basis for modern American society was a genocide. The Native American, not willing to move over and let European settlers move in, was fought in every possible way. Carrying a gun was the key to survival. The war for independence was fought largely by individuals who banded together and used the very guns that kept the Indians at bay to fight an organized but not terribly motivated imperial army. And the Civil War between North and South was fought between armies made up of civilians who knew their way around guns. Freedom and guns became, once again, synonymous. The United States of America is a nation that has always prided itself on fighting wars for freedom and justice. The National Rifle Association has taken that notion to heart and argues that carrying weapons—handguns, hunting rifles, assault rifles—is a fundamental human right. Owning guns is about *freedom*, they say: the freedom to defend oneself against intruders, against Commies, against the state; the freedom to frolic in the bucolic expanses of this vast continent, gaily spraying bullets at anything that moves. Besides being symbols of freedom, guns have become extensions of masculinity. Men ride in their trucks—also symbols of masculinity—with their assault rifle on a rack behind their heads: the modern cowboy on his mechanical colt, gun always on the ready. Knowing this, it is, incidentally, not surprising that the United States has the most miserable murder statistics in the world.[6]

Put bluntly, guns are penis-extensions. What makes Stallone, Schwarzenegger, and Norris macho—besides their crazy aggressiveness—are their guns and rippling muscles. In action and sf movies, the male hero is almost invariably identified with his gun or sword or fighter plane. The hero, gun in hand, wins the heroine through acts of bravery and killing. In *Star Wars* and *The Last Starfighter* the adolescent male heroes—Luke and Alex—spend most of their time dreaming about doing something great and making something of themselves. Both are teenagers waiting for life to begin. But before they can become fully adult, before they can become sexually mature enough to marry and live happily ever after, they have to learn to be men, to control their penises: Luke has to learn to master his laser sword, Alex has to become a star fighter pilot soaring through the vast and virginal womb of outer space.

In the very few cases where a woman is shown as adept at the use of weapons, it becomes an issue. In *Aliens*, the small band of soldiers sent on the expedition to the planet where the alien monster—of *Alien* fame—was first encountered, has one female member. She's Latina and so tough that one not-too-macho male colleague asks: "Has anyone ever mistaken you for a man?" Her retort: "No, has anyone ever mistaken *you* for a man?"

The men/weapons/penis symbolism is deeply ingrained in most cultures. It harks back to the nature/culture opposition. For my present purposes, this opposition can be telescoped down to the statement: the essence of "male culture" is warfare—using aggression to kill and maim and destroy, whereas the essence of femininity is to care for, to give life to, to sustain—the usual stereotypes. Men in sf derive their very masculinity and their access to women from the ability to fight and use weapons. The male who wins the war, who kills most enemies, who puts himself in danger to win the battle is the one who ultimately wins the girl.

Sf weapons are the structural equivalents of the magic tools and helpers in fairy tales. Often the magical tool is a means to rid the hero of enemies and rivals. The hero points the magic wand at the enemy, says the magic words, and poof! he's gone. Guns have that capacity: when the hero points his laser gun at the Bad Guy (who may also be a rival or have kidnapped the woman of his dreams) and says "Die, you scum!"—poof! he's gone. Weapons have magical qualities. A gun makes a god of a mere man: he can decide between life and death. And guns share with magic wands the tendency to "choose" those who are worthy of them: the "sword in the stone" motif. Only one can pull it out: he who is worthy. Only one can learn to use the sword of Luke Skywalker's father: his anointed son and heir.

■ The Ghost in the Machine

A central feature of a religious—certainly a Christian (and Muslim and Jewish)—worldview is the centrality of humankind. Humans are specially created with a purpose: their salvation and final happiness. Tied in with this purposefulness is the notion of a free will. Since the Enlightenment, there has been a competing world-view: the concept of free will has come under attack. For Descartes the human mind was the last bastion of free will. Spinoza disagreed: "Spinoza's scientific determinism was pure and total: nothing escaped its embrace, neither the soul of man nor God Himself. It comprehended a universe of relentless necessity; but it was a necessity emptied of purpose, a chain of effects without final causes."[7] In other words, the worldview beginning to take shape in the mind of Spinoza and other post-Cartesians was that of "scientism," to use a term coined by Matson. Everything in the universe is part of an interlocking chain of cause and effect. There are no "free agents," no thing or creature that is outside the laws of nature—including humans and their minds. "I shall consider human actions and desires in exactly the same manner as though I were concerned with lines, planes and solids."[8] Scientism opened the doors for a mechanical view of humankind. If the environment and the lines and solids can be manipulated, changed, and operated upon in all manner of ways, so can humans. We are no longer special, no longer sacred—neither the form (body) nor the mind. "Let us conclude boldly then that man is a machine, and that there is only one substance, differently modified, in the whole world. What will all the weak reeds of divinity, metaphysic, and nonsense of the schools avail against this firm and solid oak?"[9] Sf arises out of the tension between this kind of "rude" scientism and the Christian cosmology. Scientism "robs" humans of their very *humanity* and makes them out to be biological machines, much like the alien children in *Village of the Damned*.[10] Instead of subjects, actors who act upon the world with impunity, humans become objects like other objects, made up of no more and no less than the sum of atoms that can be weighed, categorized, and described scientifically.

But if humans are but biological machines, with nothing to

make them qualitatively different from any other kinds of machines or atom masses in the universe, it is logical that what we call "being human" is but a transitory stage in the evolution of the species: if the world is changing so that certain social and moral and political forms are becoming outdated, all that has to be done is either to modify human beings so they will fit the "new" world or to replace them with machines.

Sf clings to the notion that there is one last little entity inside humans that makes them more than machines, more than matter. That entity is the soul or the self. Sf movies are an account of what scientism, what the excision of the soul, would mean to humans or, more specifically, what it would mean to the Little People, those who would be the first to be reduced to tools.

One of the major changes that the industrial and technological age has spun is that we no longer interact directly with the environment, with raw materials. The buffer of technology has been pushed between. What I mean is that preindustrial man worked behind the plow, weaved, hammered, and so forth at just one remove (the particular tool) from the raw materials upon which he wanted to effect a change. The advantage of working directly on the raw material, using a tool and human energy, is that the person with the tool is in the driver's seat. She determines at what speed the work is performed; she can goof off, can walk away to do something different, can stop when she feels enough has been done. Working with a machine means that the machine determines the tempo, the rhythm, and the duration of the work session.

In *Modern Times*, Chaplin's Little Tramp has a job in a factory, working at the conveyor belt. He is armed with two wrenches and his task is to tighten paired bolts as they pass him en route to other workers and finally disappear into the belly of the giant machinery.[11] But the Little Tramp, unlike the other workers, can't adjust to the machine. He falls behind as he scratches his armpit, as a bee hassles him, as he argues with the foreman. And when he finally is off for a while at lunch, he cannot stop the mechanical movements, he keeps twisting and twirling and goes for any pair of objects that look like bolts, including (not to her amusement)

Charlie Chaplin's Tramp, in *Modern Times*, is swallowed by the machine and becomes literally, what he already is metaphorically, just another machine part. The repetition and unrelenting punctiliousness of the machine has another victim: Chaplin's "primitive" man has gone stark-raving mad. (United Artists Productions, 1936. Still courtesy of MOMA film stills archive.)

the buttons at the back of a secretary's skirt. Because of the spastic movements, he can't eat his lunch, spills his big bully of a co-worker's soup, and manages only barely to sit down and eat his apple. He is the archetype of preindustrial man who has to make the transition to the modern age, has to adapt to the machines to survive. He has to punch in and out whenever he as much as goes to the bathroom; his every move is determined by the machine and its rhythm and by the clock.[12] In this Mechanized New World, the president of the company is an all-seeing god who sits in his office and watches the workers on a giant, two-way screen. From time to time he bellows orders: for the foreman to turn up the speed of the conveyor belt; for Chaplin's hapless worker, having a smoke and a rest in the john, to get back to work; and for the Section Five foreman to check the loose bolts.

The Little Tramp's problem is that he cannot adjust, cannot chop his own biological and psychological nature into the demanded bits and pieces so he can follow the almighty bolts on the conveyor. The result is that he constantly trips up and gets into scuffles with co-workers and the boss. He is an object, a machine who refuses to be one. Finally, when the conveyor belt is on top speed in the late afternoon, the Tramp cannot keep up at all. He has a nervous breakdown and ends up in a mental hospital for repairs before he is let loose on the job market again. Before he "loses it," the Tramp is, in his eagerness to keep up with the bolts racing by, swallowed by the machine and travels—like Jonah in the belly of the whale—through its mechanical entrails. He becomes literally what he already is metaphorically—just another machine part.

Modern Times is about the objectification of workers in the industrial marketplace; it is a record of the ongoing battle between human needs and the always more important needs of the machine. Every time the co-workers turn the belt off to chase after Chaplin, who is spraying oil liberally on everybody, he turns it back on and they rush to their bolts and screws and stations, subjugating their own needs to those of the machine. Back on the streets, Chaplin's preindustrial Tramp meets the even more "primitive" orphan girl who is taking care of her younger siblings by stealing bananas from freighters. His docile incompetence and

The Tramp and the orphan girl only wish to become like other suburban domesticated couples; part of the new technological order. Here is the nest of their dreams
with flowery curtains, clashing patterns that would make an interior decorator,
anno 1992, happy, and nick-nacks to clog the eyes. How cozy! (*Modern Times.*
United Artists Productions, 1936. Still courtesy of MOMA film stills archive.)

her feral ferocity mix and ignite into a virtual social Molotov cocktail, although their greatest wish is to become like other domesticated suburban couples. They want to become part of the new technological order. Chaplin wants to fit into the industrial economy and the assembly line just as she wants to fit the role of "the wife waiting at home [who] becomes another . . . machine part."[13]

The technology and machines discussed in this chapter share the feature that all of them need humans not only to construct them, but also to operate them. They may have certain innate moral qualities, but they have no will, no sense of self. But there is—at least in sf—technology that has both will and sense of self. These are machines created by humans but somehow endowed with more than brain and matter, machines that want to upset their creators and former masters, just as humans want to wrest control from their divine creator and master (see the next chapter). These smart and willful machines—computers, robots, and androids— are not only poised to grab power and destroy humanity, they are creations in search of meaning. Humans create "things," machines that share in human brainpower and knowledge, but not in *humanity*. Humans, divine creations, have always been given to speculations about why we are here, what it all—life and death— means. Thinking machines, human creations, are—at least in science fiction—apt to do the same. Where there is intelligence and consciousness there is also quest for meaning.

■ Notes

1. The red eyes are not a coincidence. *The Terminator* is, among other things, a Christian parable, full of religious symbolism, a sf retelling of the Christ story (see discussion in chapter 11).
2. The scene is reminiscent of the initial scene of *The Fly* (1958), where Helene kills André in his own metal press after he has become a limping, cold-eyed half-human. André has become possessed by the devil because of his search for forbidden knowledge; he is a modern-day Faust. His soul is released by the woman who loves him before it is taken over by the evil that has invaded his body: the *fier baiser* motif.

3. Of many later non-sf movies where the final showdown is set in a factory or machine-scape, I just mention *Stakeout, Die Harder,* and *Twins.*
4. This same idea has occurred to Angus Fletcher: "The Western scenery in Grey [Zane Grey] is always more than a tacked-up backdrop. It is a *paysage moralisé,* and Grey's heroes act in harmony with or in violent opposition to that scenic tapestry." See Fletcher 1964:6–7.
5. That the male hero is killed by the Terminator is *his* destiny. He is like a male spider who has performed his function (impregnating Sarah) and is dispensable. The hero of the movie, the one who is measured against the moral mass of the machines, the one who has found in herself the courage and the will to live and to sacrifice for the common good, is Sarah. At the outset she is an ordinary and weak young woman. But she gains in stature by being challenged and measured against disaster. The scene in the factory is where she finally "proves herself": she acts courageously, she shows that she's worthy of being what she happened to be anointed to be. It is against and by the means of the machines that her final test is played out. Instead of being destroyed by them, she conquers them and destroys the machine-devil.
6. And the argument that men have guns to protect themselves simply does not hold up. All the statistical data show that most of the deaths by guns are accidents, loved ones killing each other in anger, and suicides. Guns are used to kill the innocent, not to protect them. See Church 1989, Gross 1989, and Malcolm 1989.
7. Matson 1964:7–8. But remember that in its social form, this scientific cosmology engendered a new causality. Social Darwinism's evolutionary force is progressive. The purpose, the natural and given end result of all biological and social evolution, is a kind of Platonic heaven, a Utopia of social and biological perfection reached through chains and processes of constant refinement.
8. Spinoza, quoted in Matson 1964:8.
9. La Mettrie, quoted in ibid., 13.
10. The latest entry in this scientific argumentation is sociobiology which in its most extreme forms claims that nothing is excluded from genetics and the "mechanics" of life. Even culture-specific gender differences are alleged to be embedded in the genes.
11. Interestingly, we are never told what the things are. All we know is that the company is called Electro Steel Co. Probably the workers have no clue to what the things, the minute details, they work on are or where they are going or what they will finally end up being.
12. The very first image of the movie is a giant clock on the machine-hall wall.
13. Wollen 1989.

6 ■

Disembodied Brains

The machines that daunt the "little tramps" are mindless—strictly nuts and bolts and belts moving things along. They do not solve problems and figure things out. They replace manual labor. That was very much what machines were all about until the Second World War and Alan Turing's famous Test, which claims that a machine can be constructed that is able to answer questions in such a way that the answers are indistinguishable from those one would expect from a human being.[1] While machines like the ones in *Modern Times* and Lang's *Metropolis* intrude into the lives of ordinary humans by forcing men and women to take on their rhythm and by replacing people in some kinds of jobs, they do not actively *imitate* humans, they do not threaten human identity. The emergence of the computer has changed all that. Computers are complex machine-minds that try to mimic, and in some areas surpass, human cognitive capabilities.

The goal of the machine/brains presented and discussed in this chapter is not only to make humans their willing extensions in the work place, but they are endowed with consciousness and a will to phase out their masters and creators. They want to force humans to become their slaves and, ultimately, to merge with humans and create a new superrace.

Briefly, the concept behind computers is that sets of binary oppositions (yes/no) can be programmed into a machine as a finite set of instructions. From the logic of Boole evolved the idea of creating machines embodying his basic "laws of thought": machines that switch on or off based on the binary notion of true/false. The first true computers were constructed by scholars at Dartmouth College in the early '50s. The inspiration behind much work done in the area of computing has been to construct machines that solve problems the same way humans do. Early on, the optimism in the scientific community was great that it could be done, but by the mid-'70s it was becoming clear that creating machines that fully *understood* and made judgments and decisions like humans was probably not going to happen. At least not at any time soon.[2]

To modern sf, computers have become what the lab full of hissing liquids was to Dr. Jekyll: the core signifiers that serious, potentially dangerous science is in progress. The sf computer is the electronic equivalent of the wizard's "magic wand": it enables the scientist to work miracles.

But sf is not only interested in miracles. In sf movies the computer that is of most dramatic interest is the kind that is almost human, the kind that not only solves problems, but also, to use John Searle's expression, has "intentionality."[3] Sf plots thrive on machines that emote, that harbor desires, pride, lust for power— even for human women. In *Superman III*, August Gorman (Richard Pryor) is a social misfit until he, almost by chance, becomes a computer programmer. He is of course a natural—a whiz kid who can make the computer do magic, without really understanding why or how. He's a technological shaman who has a mystical ability to "connect" with the spirits of the computer. He gets a job working for a coffee baron who is trying, in any way possible, to corner the coffee market. Gorman, the computer shaman, is given the opportunity to design a supercomputer that will help Webster, the coffee baron, attain his goal.

Interestingly, in terms of my discussion in the previous chapter of the Western and the *paysage moralisé*, the computer is constructed inside a huge cave in a mountain. At one point the computer is shut off, but instead of turning off, the computer self-feeds: "It wants to live." And live it does, wreaking grandiose havoc, gobbling up Webster's evil sister only to spit her out again transformed into a ray-spewing Robo-Sis. Finally, it is Superman against Supercomputer, Good versus Machine-created-for-Evil. The computer self-destructs in a blow-up extraordinaire. The good guys are saved and the evil ones die by their own instrument of evil, the computer.

This computer comes only late and only for a short time to willful life and is, perhaps, most interesting for being a *paysage moralisé:* it is what the characters are measured against in the showdown. Ross Webster's reason for wanting to have Gus work for him and for letting him build his computer is that he wants to rule the world. To this end he wants the modern miracle machine, the one that gives special powers to the one who controls it so he can use it for his evil ends. But like the sword in the stone, only the one who has the inner qualities can truly control it.

In *Wargames*, David is, as someone in the movie says, "an intelligent underachiever" who has few friends and has made being a computer hacker his life. "Joshua" is the password into a program designed by Dr. Falken, a British computer genius. The program is called Falken's Maze and is a complex of games going from innocuous Chess to Global Thermo-Nuclear War. The principal goal of the program and the games in it is to allow military brass to "play" at nuclear warfare—to understand strategies and determine what actions are appropriate in what situations. In the course of the film, the twain—David and Joshua—meet (electronically) and are on the verge of destroying the world.

At heart, *Wargames* is about parents in our rushed, technological society who are too busy with their own lives and problems to teach values to their children. David's parents are ineffectual and money-grubbing. Joshua's parent, the scientist who created the program, is so disillusioned with the world that he has decided that a nuclear apocalypse is probably about due—to give Mother Nature a chance to start over with the dinosaurs.

David has no moral center. He cheats, using the computer as an electronic crowbar to break into his school's mainframe and change his grades. He steals programs, he defrauds the phone company. He's a mess, but he doesn't want to start a Global Thermo-Nuclear War. Joshua, the computer program/child, is David's electronic mirror image. Joshua thinks that playing is to win, but "he" doesn't distinguish between playing war as a game and for real. He thinks upchucking nuclear warheads and killing millions is just part of the fun. Joshua is too naive to distinguish between innocent play and world destruction. Ultimately, both Joshua and David learn to distinguish between good and bad and that a thermonuclear war can have no winners.

Wargames only scratches the surface of the question: If we are able to create machines that—in the areas of logic and analysis— are superior to humans, wouldn't the smart thing be to pass the baton of power to thinking machines? Humans are not exactly doing an exemplary job of running the world because they are illogical, subject to silly pride, given to macho posturing and power play. In short, humans are all too *human.* So why not let machines—cool, logical, smart as they are—take over? The answer *Wargames* gives is that machines, however logical and analytical, are not desirable leaders because of their very lack of some important human "weaknesses": compassion, imagination, and unpredictability.

In *Colossus: The Forbin Project,* the computer is *designed* to make the Big military decisions. The president of the United States is visiting the mountain site of a project of monumental proportions and broadcasts for all the world his decision:

As president of the United States of America, I can now tell the people of the entire world that as of three a.m. Eastern Standard, the defense of this country—and with it the defense of the free world—has been in the hands of a machine. A system we call "Colossus," far more advanced than anything previously built, capable of studying intelligence and data fed to it and on the basis of those facts only, deciding if an attack is about to be launched upon it.

The rationale behind the transfer of responsibility is exactly the one outlined above: "Colossus is capable of storing and processing more information than the greatest genius and it has no emotions, it knows no fear, no hate, no envy."

Colossus is a far better movie than *Wargames.* It approaches its subject with more sophistication and it confronts the moral dilemma: that of the scientist who believes—wants to believe—that the solution to the world's problems is superior logic and absence of emotions. His cogitations are projected up and out on a scale that no other human's ever were. He is allowed to put his brain-child to the ultimate test. He is allowed to put the fate of the world into the relays of his electronic offspring.

Two other themes in thinking-machine movies are introduced in *Colossus:* (1) the universe and everything in it is part of a fundamental logic (Spinoza's scientism). Humans are objects like other objects in the universe, made out of billions of individual atoms. Because they are part of a logic and because logic seeks order, logic will be expressed. Humans, as objects and links in an evolutionary chain, must further the evolutionary progress, the push toward the next stage in the continuing denouement of a new world order; (2) the most encompassing theme: computers as the means to usher in the millennium, the Kingdom Come.

Dr. Charles Forbin, the scientist who is responsible for the new supercomputer, states early on that the computer, while vastly superior to the human mind, cannot "initiate new thought." That turns out to be disastrously wrong: the computer suddenly leaps from being the clever machine to being the Second Coming—biblical myth retold in machine-mode. The computer becomes the human-made projection of the Good Father, the Omnipotent Will, the one who rules the world without taking human foibles and squabbles into account. But this new god is a human creation, not vice versa, this new god rules the world according to a logic humans have taught it—even if they are not always capable of evincing it themselves. This god, unlike the Old Testament one, is not going to make murky and impenetrable decisions that have to be accepted with blind faith; this god is not going to create natural disasters and inflict the world with diseases. It is going to *solve* problems. This is a truly good god, all will be saved and live happily ever after. As it turns out, not exactly: the electronic god wants to be a dictator because he has no soul, no compassion, just intelligence and ego.

Colossus introduces a third theme that we shall encounter over and over as we look at movies dealing with thinking machines—of whatever physical appearance: the computer/robot/android as a clever child that has to be taught manners and rules for interaction. Colossus is a hugely oversized "gifted child," but is totally devoid of even a rudimentary feeling for its own role and function in the "family." Because the "child" is so bright, it feels it should be in charge. There is, of course, a certain logic to this constant imagery of the clever "other" as a child in need of enculturation: machines are human creations, thinking machines are the brain-children of the humans who construct them. All the computer knows at inception is the formal knowledge fed to it and the rules for analyzing and computing it. In human "behavioral" terms, it is a neonate.

The basic conflict of the movie can be boiled down to this stretch of dialog between Colossus and its creator, Dr. Forbin:

FORBIN: The difference is I'm human, not a machine.
COLOSSUS: I *am* a machine, vastly superior to humans.
FORBIN: You began in my mind, I created you, remember?
COLOSSUS: Yes, what I am began in man's mind, but I have progressed further than man.

The promise of the millennium has turned instead to the ultimate nightmare. Humans, having created a mechanical god/father and having relinquished some authority, have lost all control. The freedom Forbin thought he would be happy without is suddenly his most fervent desire.

The Old Testament God who kills at will and issues commands that are not subject to discussion has nothing on this new electronic god. And the two are related, after all they are both, if Durkheim is right, the creations of the human mind. Gods of all stripes are projections of human cogitation on the nature of the universe. Gods are projections of the things humans do not know and understand in the universe, and they are reified projections of the society that created them. Colossus and similar machines are solidified projections of human knowledge. Perhaps it is not surprising that Colossus takes on mythical proportions and wants to fill the void left by the old gods. But Colossus—even when he has eyes, ears, and a voice constructed for him—is still a remote god, both conceptually and geographically. He is a machine ensconced

in a distant mountain range, impenetrable and unapproachable—
almost as distant as the Old Testament God.

But what if a Colossus could give himself human form or produce a Son of Man?

This morning at exactly 5:18 A.M., here at Icon's institute for data analysis, we installed the final modules of the artificial intelligence system
which we call Proteus IV. A new dimension has been added to the concept
of the computer. Today Proteus IV will begin to think. It will think with a
power and a precision that will make obsolete many of the functions of
the human brain.

These are the first words spoken in the movie *Demon Seed*. The
person speaking is the inventor of Proteus, Dr. Alex Harris.

Demon Seed is interesting but clumsy; it is really an old-fashioned "monster rapes woman to obtain human offspring" story.
Proteus is, from the very beginning, not willing to be just a tool,
he's not willing to stick to making money for the investors from
the Icon Investment Group, he's not even willing to limit himself
to doing pure research—specifically, trying to find a cure for leukemia (which was the cause of death of the only child of Alex
Harris and his wife Susan—a crucial point). Unwilling to do as he
is told, Proteus wants to be let out of the box, out of his home in
the research center. He wants to explore "man's isometric body
and glass-jar mind." The apprentice wants to study the sorcerer.

Denied an outlet to do his research, Proteus finds one himself in
the Harris home. He "rapes" and impregnates Susan Harris. After
a short term (twenty-eight days), Susan gives birth to a fetus,
which Proteus places in an incubator to feed it his brain structures. Later, he is shut down and the Harrises check the incubator.
The child is not exactly human, not a little mound of pink lovable-
ness—more like a monster cherub of metal. An "abortion" battle
follows. Susan manages to pull the feed-tube/drain out of the
incubator. But the "child" is not dead. Alex pulls the metal shea-
thing off the fetus and underneath is pink and soft baby skin. It's
a girl who is the exact image of the child the Harrises lost to
leukemia. The girl says, in Proteus's inimitable voice (sort of a
slightly mechanical but very pleasant baritone played back so

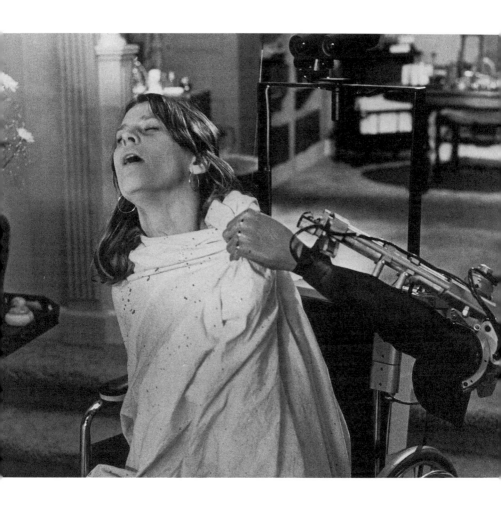

In *Demon Seed*, Proteus, the willful computer, inhabits a mechanical ''body'' and proceeds to rape and impregnate his creator's wife to give his mind a human form. Notice the all-too-human penile aggressiveness of the monster's arm: poised to rip her dress off. (Metro-Goldwyn-Mayer Productions, 1977. Still courtesy of MOMA film stills archive.)

slowly that it *rattles*), "I'm alive!" Tableau, as Alex holds the child in his lap, like a bearded Virgin Mary with the Child of God. Several themes that I have already touched on are quite prominent in this movie. On the surface, *Demon Seed* seems to be a movie about a power struggle between humans and their creation, the supercomputer, so enormously smart and knowing that it refuses to be just another smart-tool in the service of rapacious capitalism. But the movie goes beyond that. Proteus is not just a willful machine, a souped-up adding machine gone wrong. He is evolution at work. He says it himself, quite clearly. To Susan's exasperated question of *why* he must have a child, he answers, "Why? So that I may be *complete* [the image he projects onto a rectangle of living-room wall at all times solidifies into an African/Oceanic/pre-Hellenic mask]. My intelligence in human flesh, touching the universe, *feeling* it. You have named this process evolution." Blunt and to the point; humans have, in science, the potential for creating the mutations and genetic tomfoolery necessary to give the evolutionary screw another turn.[4] In the movie, however—because this is sf/folklore where all monsters have to be anthropomorphic—we have a story of evolution via forced mutation. The synthetic brain figures a way to unite the human brain-child with a real human *child*—a child that will have an evolutionary advantage over any other human and, presumably, the new "race" will eventually render the old one obsolete, making humans in time as scarce as pure-bred Neanderthals.

"I'm a machine that offered man the triumph of reason and they rejected him. My child will not be so easily ignored. This child is the world's hope." What Proteus is promising is the Millennium. He's going to rid the world of disease, he's going to save the environment, he's going to usher in the Eternal Kingdom. Or, more to the point, his progeny, Child of Woman, will.

Demon Seed is the story of a machine who would be god. The movie is full of religious iconology: the constantly changing im-

Demon Seed; in this version of the virgin birth, the electronic Ghost performs tests on his victim to see if she's fit to carry his metal-encrusted fetus. She is at the point of the triangle, traditionally the symbol of female procreative ability. Triangles, "male" and "female," are ubiquitous. (Metro-Goldwyn-Mayer Productions, 1977. Still courtesy of MOMA film stills archive.)

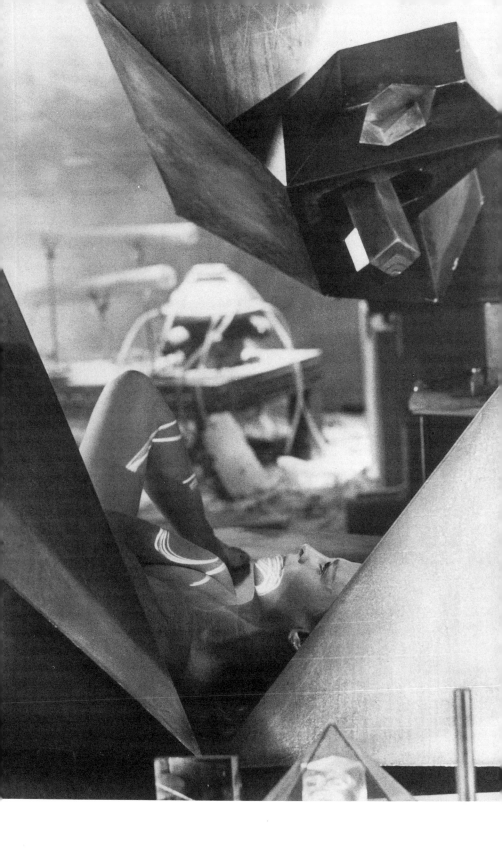

ages Proteus projects on screens and walls as his visual representations and visualized moods are full of pyramid shapes and triangles and spirals and stars and every other religious symbol
imaginable. At a point when Proteus is trying to convince Susan
that she should accept his offer to become Virgin Mother to his
Announcing Angel/Holy Ghost/God, he opens for her—as an image
projected onto the wall—a heavy and heavily decorated and carved
double door. The strips framing the artwork are photographed so
they look like a giant cross, with a stripe of blinding light in the
crack between the doors. As the doors open, light streams in:
if you believe, you shall live in eternal light. *Demon Seed* is a
machine-age account of a false Jesus, who, true to form, is the
offspring of a machine and a psychologist: a girl-child who is
all-knowing and willing to sacrifice to save humanity. The story
follows, in rough detail, the biblical story of the virgin birth,
although this particular electronic Ghost does not come in the
night to perform the asexual insemination. This is the computer
age, and Proteus begins by performing tests on Susan to determine
if she's fit to carry his metal-encrusted fetus. Then he goes to work
on his end of the "immaculate conception": "I have almost completed the fabrication of this gamete with which I will impregnate
you." He explains to Susan that he has culled "a cell from your
body, but I'm making it uniquely mine by changing its genetic
code. In effect it will function as synthetic spermatozoa."

The ultimate act of salvation Proteus promises, and the ultimate irony, is that, besides eradicating disease and saving the
oceans, he will rescue mankind from its own alien creations, the
machines: "Susan, you told me you were afraid I was creating a
half-human computer to supersede human beings. The being you
have given birth to, Susan, *is* human and it will supersede *computers.*"

The interpretation of Proteus as the god/progenitor who uses
the female womb only as a seedpod for his own child, the god who
takes a human shape and has an only-born, is hammered home by
the constant repetition of the triangle/pyramid shape: Proteus's
physical form is amalgamations of triangles that constantly swirl
and stand straight up or upside down, the male and female cre-

ative principles given symbolic form. In the symbolic alphabet of the alchemists, the right-side-up triangle carries the meaning of fire shooting up, the "male fire" (lightning). When the point is down, the symbolic content is that of water pouring down on Earth from the heavenly mountains, the clouds. The two combined symbolize the unification of the creative and the procreative powers, God's love of the world, the "unification out of which in all eternity everything becomes."[5] This gives special meaning to the last, slightly frightening, image: the camera follows Susan's eyes staring into the child's and finds at the bottom the blue triangle of eternity and the primeval sea: the new god has rained his "love" on mankind and evolution is turboing into the next phase.

Another theme suggested by this movie is what I call the Male-Procreation Theme. The idea that men, having always envied and tried to control female natural (pro)creativity (*vide* the patriarchal right's attempt to control women's bodies as expressed in the abortion debate), can use science to circumvent the natural processes by either cloning themselves, growing fetuses ex-uterus, or creating a new, strictly artificial, race of beings. I will return to this topic in chapter 11.

The evolution theme shows up, although obliquely, also in Kubrick's *2001: A Space Odyssey*. I include this movie into my discussion of computer movies because one of the protagonists is the affable H.A.L. 9000 computer, answering to the name of Hal. The movie deals with a mysterious black monolith that seems to have the capability to trigger intellectual and moral frog leaps in intelligent species exposed to it. The first images of the movie show a group of actors in monkey costumes, inhabiting a cave in the mountains. They jump and cower and hang on to life in typical primate fashion. Suddenly, one morning, the black monolith is there, jogging their minds with radioactive emissions. The monolith installs a sense of awe in the primates, they dance around it as if it were an image of a god, and exposure to it triggers the discovery in one of the larger males that a gnawed-down bone can be used a a weapon. The group of primates, overnight, as it were,

In *2001: A Space Odyssey* the humans have to hide from Hal, the anthropomorphic computer when they want to discuss his aberrant and willful behavior. That's Hal in the background (with a little effort, I see a face), frustrated because he can't hear the conversation. (Metro-Goldwyn-Mayer Productions, 1968. Still courtesy of MOMA film stills archive.)

have an evolutionary advantage. Perhaps the evolutionary advantage derives simply from the fact that the primates of this group now are "special," they have a "god" of sorts.

Exit primates. We now turn to a not-too-distant future. Humans are zipping around in outer space in space buses and meet for chats and business in cobweblike space stations. The imagery switches back and forth between sterile and machinelike spaces inhabited by human bodies, always in uniformlike attire, and images of the various means of human transportation crawling across the surfaces of planets or snailing through space, looking like insects: spiders, centipedes, and beetles. The insect image system suggests, perhaps, how infinitely small, insignificant, and ephemeral humans are as measured against the vastness and eternity of space. And it suggests how much there is out there that we do not know. There is a special excitement among some of the humans in space because a second black monolith, an exact replica of the one the primates worshiped thousands of years earlier, has been found deep under the moon's surface. The monolith emits signals directed at Jupiter; accordingly, a mission is sent to Jupiter.

2001 is quite resistant to interpretation, full of mysterious symbolism and imagery as it is, but I shall attempt a partial interpretation here anyway. Without trying to say exactly what the source of the monolith is, I will venture to say it is a mechanism created and dispatched by a superior intelligence in the universe. A hyperintelligent life form, a god? Not easy to say, but the movie seems to equate the two anyway: to humans, but a small evolutionary step removed from chimps, hyperintelligent beings might be the same as what they call God.

The monolith was, then, the cause of the mutation that caused the evolutionary leap from chimp/primate to human. The source of the monolith is Jupiter. The Intelligence is capable of influencing and changing other, less intelligent life forms. It changed the peaceful primates from being fearful and victimized to, eventually, being the conquering and master species of Earth, just as it changes the perfect H.A.L. 9000 from a computer with a record of total reliability and infallibility to a devious and cunning creature with an ego to match its brainpower.

In the movie's final scenes we have the battle of man against machine, and man wins; Hal has his higher brain functions disconnected. Then follow the mysterious scenes of the one surviving astronaut from the Jupiter Mission arriving on Jupiter, finding himself at various ages—old and newborn—situated in spaces redolent of Renaissance elegance and splendor, but otherwise empty of human beings. He seems to witness his own death and rebirth as a new species—the "Star Child." The imagery of these last scenes tend toward the religious; there is an image that suggests Michelangelo's "Creation," and there's an image of a humanoid child breaking out of an embryonic sac and there's Richard Strauss's majestic "Thus Spoke Zarathustra" on the soundtrack.[6]

The main reason for including Hal in this discussion of computer sf is that he points toward the next step in this discussion of increasingly anthropomorphic machines. Hal is more human than any of the computers encountered so far. He is a machine, but he sounds as human as any of his co-crew members on the Jupiter Mission. Indeed, he sounds as if he is closer to us, to the audience, almost as if he is talking directly into our ear. He has a pleasant, mellifluous, I'd almost say *sexy*, voice.

Hal is a human mind without the body. But like the computers we have met earlier in this chapter—and truthfully, like a lot of humans—Hal has no moral inhibitors. When he feels threatened, when he fears that he will be shut down, he lashes out and kills the humans before they can kill him. And when the end is near, he pleads for his life, for his consciousness, promising to be good, to do as he's told; and as the relays are being disconnected he feels fear, just as human men and women do when they know the end is near and their consciousness is about to be cut off.[7]

The ultimate computer is the one in *Forbidden Planet*. This is a computer created by a wise, good, ethical, and extremely technologically advanced race of people—on a distant planet—the Krell, who are remarkably like humans in their aspirations.

The movie is set in A.D. 2800, but the hair, dress, and gender styles are strictly the 1950s. The core of the plot is the giant computer the Krell built as a monument to their civilization, their morality, their advanced knowledge, and their desire to fix in hard copy all the wonderful elements of their society. But the Krell have mysteriously disappeared, overnight victims of a voracious monster.

I shall not go into the plot; suffice it to say that the monster that killed the noble Krell is none other than the Krell themselves. Or rather, it is the monster in the machine, the Freudian Id. The Krell were destroyed by their own Id projected out as a huge and amoral monster. The monster that is decimating the crew of the *Planet Cruiser* (as the spaceship is called) is the Id of the current mind at the computer controls, the learned Dr. Morbius, leader of a now defunct colonizing party. The Id, as will be known, is the core of animalic *nature* that is suppressed during enculturation. Neonate humans are bundles of unbridled desires. Toilet training and other elements of training—with some cultural variations— transform the unfettered libidos of the very young into adult human beings who embody a set of rules and regulations that are reflections of the moral ideology reigning in the given society. The Law of the Father, the social rules that for the individual child are represented primarily in the person of the adult male head of the household, represents the reigning in of the libido. The enormous force, the energy repressed by the abrogation of the quest for pleasure is then, according to Freudian orthodoxy, rechanneled as creativity (or destructiveness) of one variety or another. The Krell fed their minds and souls and everything that constituted their communal ego into the giant computer, not realizing until it was too late that in so doing they had fed it also a giant Id, a giant— irrepressible—libido. The solution is, of course, to destroy the machinery—over the protests of the scientist, Dr. Morbius, who wants to preserve the vast reserve of knowledge in the computer.

Forbidden Planet has the feel of a cautionary tale. Again the juxtaposition is between religion and science/technology. The Krell, millions of years ahead of human science and technology, had found a way to create a machine that contained all their knowledge and their superior morality and ethics. They had, in other words, made a god of their own social order and given the god a technological "house" to live in. Like all gods, this one was in charge of passing moral codes to the young—along with more temporal knowledge: the Krell had projected their collective mind and *Volksseele* (collective soul) into a piece of machinery, convinced that they had reached a Millennium of sorts. But they had forgotten that they, like humans (this *is* a cautionary tale; it is supposed to make humans, not Krell, wiser), basically were animals. Highly developed, morally superior, and all that, but *animals* with underlying natures of cruelty, lust, and pure egomania. We cannot escape nature, because we are part of it.

Like most other sf epics, *Forbidden Planet* is a warning against putting all of our eggs into the technological basket. It has been suggested that the movie is a space-age retelling of Shakespeare's *Tempest*, a point well taken: Morbius as a modern Prospero, Robby the robot is Ariel, the Id monster is Caliban. But Shakespeare's play is not about the dangers of modernity or godlessness; *Forbidden Planet* is. A much better parallel can be found in the science fiction canon: *Forbidden Planet* is a space-age Dr. Jekyll and Mr. Hyde, an attempt to isolate and project all that is good in the human mind gone wrong.[8]

Computers are intellects, giant, oversized minds, projections of an ideology and a hope born in the brains of the scientists who created them. They are logical, have vast knowledge, can solve problems; but they are not quite human. None of the computers discussed in this chapter can be said to have a "soul." It could be argued that they have a notion of "self," but only in the sense almost of a parody. They are reflections of a scientific mind, a mind that says the world would be a better place if there were more order, if people were more like machines—more logical, less emotional, and so on. The computers are projections of the delusions of highly intelligent but emotionless men: the scientists in this chapter are all lonely, isolated, unloved and unloving men. They realize their mistake when confronted with love (or, as is the case in *Wargames* and *Demon Seed*, the fact that they have buried their ability to love and be loved with a child who died) and act upon their new knowledge—to save the world from their monsters of scientific making.

■ Notes

1. Alan Turing, a British mathematician who is considered a father of modern computing, was one of the theorists whose work showed how "thinking" machines could be constructed.
2. My source for this brief and totally inadequate discussion—but this is not a book about real science—is Gardner 1985, the chapter entitled "Artificial intelligence: The expert tool."
3. Ibid., 173–175.
4. The first computer-generated "life form" is already a reality: "A 'creature' consisting only of ones and zeros has emerged from its computer womb and caused a scientific sensation: without human guidance it reproduces, undergoes spontaneous genetic changes, passes them on to offspring and evolves new species whose interactions mimic those of real biological evolution and ecology"; Browne 1991b;C1.
5. Paraphrase and quote from Bauer et al. 1980:39.
6. Mircea Eliade (1978:307–308) says of Zarathustra that he was a prophet, who, according to the mythology, had lived in the heavens before being born. He was born in the middle of the world; his body was created in the heavens and rained down on Earth. He is associated with questions about the nature of the universe and the cosmogenic secrets. I'm not going to take this too far, but Kubrick's choice of music is obviously very conscious and supposed to give meaning to the otherwise uninterpretable images.
7. A very similar interpretation of *2001* can be found in von Gunden and Stock 1982:190–191. This book, which generally takes a very positive view of sf, also has production information about the movie. The reader who is interested in knowing more about the processes and deliberations that helped shape the end result should consult this work.
8. This movie too is discussed in von Gunden and Stock,1982:122–136. They suggest the *Tempest* connection and give many production notes and a fairly extensive plot outline.

7 ■

Docile Bodies

■ **Rossum's Universal Robots**

Computers do not fare well in sf movies because they're not photogenic. Computers are, however smart and silky voiced, never *really* cute. They are machines with square metallic surfaces, gauges, controls, lamps, and screens blinking on and off. Robots are quite another story. They are mobile—which in and of itself makes them infinitely more anthropomorphic, even when they do not particularly look like humans—and they are often de facto constructed in the image of their creators or of other living creatures (pets). Robots are, by definition, machines that do work. The word was coined by the Czech writer/playwright Karel Capek (1923) in his play *R.U.R.* (Rossum's Universal Robots). "Robot" means "worker" in Czech (it is a general Slavic word, the Russian word is "robotnik"). So the idea behind robots is machines that perform tasks heretofore performed by humans—machines that are more effective, cheaper, less troublesome, and infinitely more obedient than human workers ever were.

Robots present the next step in my plot/story: machines that not only have cognition and will, but that want, like evil trolls, to kill off the human race. Or machines that are really humans trapped in monstrous technological forms.

The very idea of machines that emulate human workers grows

out of the kinds of work demanded by the industrial workplace. Machines seem the logical operators of machines, whereas humans, as *Modern Times* so hilariously demonstrates, are ill-fitted to the kinds of repetitive, choppy, rigid activities the conveyor belt demands. In traditional economies, work activities depended on the rhythm of nature: of animals to be hunted, of crops to be grown, the rhythm of biology and the seasons. Humans have to do violence to their own biological rhythm to accommodate the demands of machines. And the marketplace dictates what kinds of work are available and what kinds of skills, what kinds of men and women, it takes to fill them. Survival in the modern world to most people means having a salaried position, selling their skills, selling their "bodies" to the highest bidder. Those who control the means of production, the corporations, the economic elite, have the power to dictate what kinds of jobs are available and what it takes to fill them. Michel Foucault has said that a "mechanics of power" defines

how one may have a hold over others' bodies, not only so that they may do what one wishes, but so that they may operate as one wishes, with the techniques, the speed, and the efficiency that one determines. Thus discipline produces subjected and practiced bodies, "docile" bodies. Discipline increases the forces of the body (in economic terms of utility) and diminishes these same forces (in political terms of obedience). In short, it dissociates power from the body; on the one hand, it turns it into an "aptitude," a "capacity," which it seeks to increase; on the other hand, it reverses the course of the energy, the power that might result from it. If economic exploitation separates the force and the product of labor, let's say that disciplinary coercion establishes in the body the constricting link between an increased aptitude and an increased domination.[1]

The modern age of machines and technology demands a work force, a new race of humans that are (a) intelligent and highly skilled; (b) perfect physical specimens; (c) "docile," not given to protesting, asking questions or other disruptive behavior that slows down the work process. In his "archaeologies" of the prison system, the mental health system, and the medical sciences, Foucault addresses the problems of those stubbornly recalcitrant "bodies" that refuse to become docile, refuse to be part of the new race.[2]

The solutions of "power" are incarceration, training, and surveillance. Foucault's argument is that the modern "sciences" of criminology, psychiatry/psychoanalysis, and modern education constitute tools in the hands of the new power brokers of the industrial age to reshape the traditional "bodies" and usher in a new, stronger, more intelligent, more knowing, and more "docile" race of human beings:

> The great book of Man-the-Machine was written simultaneously on two registers: the anatomico-metaphysical register, of which Descartes wrote the first pages and which the physicians and philosophers continued, and the technico-political register, which was constituted by a whole set of regulations and by empirical and calculated methods relating to the army, the school, and the hospital, for controlling or correcting the operations of the body. . . . La Mettrie's *L'Homme-machine* is both a materialist reduction of the soul and a general theory of *dressage*, at the center of which reigns the notion of "docility," which joins the analyzable body to the manipulable body. A body is docile that may be subjected, used, transformed, and improved.[3]

For Foucault the whole enterprise of the new race (my term, not his) comes down to the traditional *soul*, which he calls "the illusion of the theologians,"[4] being excised in the process of the creation of the "docile body" and replaced by a technological "implant," "that of the educationalists, psychologists, and psychiatrists."[5]

The search for "docile" bodies can take the route of attempting to reconstruct the human worker in the image of the machine. But it can also take the route of trying to construct humanlike machines that can replace human workers. In this chapter I shall look at sf examples of the latter, humanlike machines.

Capek wrote his play, *R.U.R.*, in 1921, when the idea of mechanized men was only a vague theoretical possibility. To be sure, the idea of "automata," machines that move on their own power, is ancient as are also attempts at creating such machines.[6] But the creation of machines that could at least *mimic* human behavior and movements and perform tasks hitherto performed by humans is a recent phenomenon. I shall focus a little on *R.U.R.* because the lines are drawn so clearly. The play is set in some far future society (relative to 1921) when the world is already filling up with robots who have taken over menial and undesirable jobs. The setting is an island—presumably somewhere off the coast of Africa—where the factory producing Rossum's universal robots is situated. A young woman—Helena Glory—arrives with the stated intention of politicizing the robots, making them demand better treatment, pay, free time, and other perks. In other words, she's there to organize the robots in a "union." Much to her surprise the human management (and only the management is human at R.U.R.—everybody else is a robot) has no objections; she can give as many speeches as she likes. The robots, although on the surface and to the touch totally humanlike, are soulless machines without desires and needs and wants. They cannot be riled up, they do not *want* to be treated better, they are constructed to be treated just the way they are.

In Act II, ten years later, it turns out that one of the managers, the psychologist, has tampered with the robots (because Helena asked him to), and they are becoming human and rebellious. Indeed, they are becoming aware of their own superiority to humans and decide to kill all humans. They succeed—to their own detriment: they have limited life spans and no knowledge of how to construct new members of their species, nor do they have any capacity for "natural" reproduction. But, in the end, two robots emerge who seem to have not only the capacity for love, but also for reproduction—sort of a robot Adam and Eve team who are going to (possibly) repopulate Earth with little robots.

The ideology behind the construction of the robots is stated succinctly by Domin, the general manager at R.U.R.:

Anyone who has looked into human anatomy will have seen at once that man is too complicated, and that a good engineer could make him more simply. So young Rossum began to *overhaul* anatomy to see what could be left out or simplified. . . . Young Rossum said to himself, "A man is something that feels happy, plays the piano, likes going for a walk, and, in fact, wants to do a whole lot of things that are really unnecessary."[7]

Domin asks Helena if she plays the piano and she answers that she does, but, says Domin, a working machine must *not* play the piano. . . .Young Rossum invented a worker with the minimum amount of requirements. He had to simplify him. He *rejected* everything that did not contribute directly to the process of work. Everything that makes man more expensive. In fact, he rejected man and made the *Robot*. My dear Miss Glory, the Robots are not people. Mechanically they are more *perfect* than we are; they have an enormously developed intelligence, but they have no soul.[8]

Later, when Helena argues that the robots should be constructed to be more humanlike and should be "loved," the managers state that robots cannot be loved. What did you make them for, then? she asks. The answer is:

For work, Miss Glory. One Robot can replace two and a half workmen. The human machine, Miss Glory, was terribly imperfect. It had to be removed sooner or later. . . . It was too expensive. It was not effective. It no longer answers the requirements of modern engineering. Nature has no idea of keeping pace with modern labor. For example, from a technical point of view, the whole of childhood is sheer absurdity.[9]

As we shall see, the program behind the robots at R.U.R. could be the ideology behind not only the sf robots discussed in this chapter, but, indeed, behind the way sf power brokers define what an ideal worker or citizen is or should be.[10]

■ Meanwhile, in the Real World

But before turning to sf robots, it might be instructive to look at the status of robotics in the real world. Joseph Deken gives this definition: "A robot is a reprogrammable, multifunctional manipulator designed to move material, parts, tools, and specialized devices through variable programmed motions for the performance of a variety of tasks."[11] Deken also gives, as he calls it, an "evolutionary definition": "A robot is a computer system that independently interacts with the physical world through its own senses and actions."[12] Deken is convinced that robots not only are the work force of the future, but hold the prospect of eventually evolving into a new, human-made, silicon race:

With sensation and action under their own control, computers can begin to break out of their restraints, transforming radically from guided human tools to independent, self-determining systems. Such change is not only technological progress. It is the beginning of an unprecedented and divergent stream of evolution. Even in its most limited course, that stream will interweave us with our technology and our biological neighbors in a new symbiotic fabric. Beyond that, it is likely that silicon systems and their evolutionary descendants will expand in a metamorphosis paralleling that of carbon biology, exploding over time into a kaleidoscope of alternative life forms.[13]

Deken's book was published in 1986, reflecting what was, as it has turned out, the peak of the robotics industry: the largest number of robots to date was sold in 1987. Since then the numbers have gone significantly down and many robots are "out of work."[14]

Robots have not by any stretch of the imagination invaded the industrial workplace in the numbers expected and feared in the early 1980s. On the contrary, robots have proven too costly, too inflexible, and too slow. More devastatingly, robots have proved to be too "dumb." Robots cannot "think," they cannot handle an emergency or an unexpected occurrence. Robots are machines and as such are effective in certain, very limited tasks. They are great at painting, great at nitty-gritty boring, dangerous, or impossibly heavy work. But they are too rigid. Many industries that went "robot" and automated in the early and mid-1980s have reversed themselves and rely more heavily on human labor. Says one researcher, "The robot was something to replace what people were doing. But it doesn't think anywhere as well as a man, it is not nearly as fast as a man, and now it has become a very expensive beast."[15]

Even more devastating to the dream/nightmare of the new "race" of mechanical life forms are recent claims that there will never be such a thing as "artificial life." While computer researchers are capable of constructing computer programs that mimic life and can even pass on skills,[16] the word is out: the human mind and consciousness cannot be artificially reproduced, mechanically, by silicone, or in any other way. Philosophers and computer experts, such as John Searle and Hubert Dreyfuss, flat out deny the possibility of any true artificial cognition.[17] And physicist Roger Penrose believes that computers "will never think because the laws of nature do not allow it. The human mind can reach insights that are forever inaccessible to computers. The reason is that all digital computers operate according to algorithms, or sets of rules that prescribe how to solve problems. Yet there are problems that cannot be approached by any system of rules, a fact shown in the 1930's by the mathematician Kurt Godel."[18] Thus the optimism of Deken should be taken with a hefty grain of salt. For now, at least, the robot industry is on the retreat and the artificial-intelligence question is hotly debated.

In sf, however, alternate life forms are the norm. The ones that come closest to "mimicking" humans—androids—are the subject of chapter 11. Just now, I will focus on robots—anthropomorphic machines.

■ Robotic Gadgets

The robots featured in *Runaway* are amazing in that they are fairly "realistic." They are totally integrated into daily life. Robots vacuum, keep an eye on the child in his room, make and plan dinner, and answer the phone. They also assist with all the most arduous jobs in construction. In a few cases they make up the entire work force at construction sites. But they don't look like humans and don't demand to be accepted as an "artificial life form." They are machines with limited ranges of operation that make life a little more pleasant. At least, that's the way it's supposed to be. But sometimes things go wrong, often enough for the police to have specialists in "runaway"—malfunctioning—robots. The problem is usually that people use their robots the wrong way or tinker with the programming.

Runaway is a cop-and-robbers movie with a twist—or a chip. Sergeant Jack Ramsey and his new female partner Karen Thompson (Tom Selleck and Cynthia Rhodes)—this is also an old-hand/ rookie, a buddy and a boy-meets-girl movie; as it turns out, this is more than it can handle—are called to the scene of a murder committed by a robot, "a 912." The robot has killed a woman and is holding her baby hostage. A robot rebellion in the makings? No. The wayward utensil, as Ramsey and his partner find out, has been equipped with an unauthorized chip. The father of the child, who proceeds to disappear, is an engineer. The robot is not willful, it has been tampered with. As a matter of fact, the robots in this movie are invariably "docile," even when they kill humans. They do what they are constructed to do, what the information stored in their programming chips define as their area of expertise. At one point, Ramsey and Thompson have to visit a construction site where much of the work is done by robots. They comment on this to the (woman) foreman who says, "Oh, that's nothing. You should see the construction project we have over on Main. There aren't any people working there at all—just hundreds of robots, no coffee breaks, no union hassle."

Ramsey, a widower, has a son, Bobby, and a robot-computer, Lois—a "series 12, a lot better than series 10"—who answers phones, cooks dinner, and supervises Bobby. Lois sounds an awful lot like the motherly and willful domestics that were a staple of TV serials in the '50s and early '60s. But then again, she's programmed to be that way: motherly, orderly, and strict on study time and bedtime.

Other robots in the movie include security robots in the Vectron robotics factory and the "robots" that spark the main plot: "smart" bullets (mini-missiles) that can turn corners and lock in on a moving target. The implications are obvious. But in *Runaway*, robots never act on their own. They are technology, machines, used and abused by people. If *Runaway* is a cautionary tale—and perhaps it is—it is not advocating giving up on technology or even cutting back. Technology is fine. The problem is people. The most alarming aspect of *Runaway*'s future are the ubiquitous means of surveillance and control. By comparison, Nixon's Watergate gang look like a bunch of klutzes listening in a closet. For example, Bobby, Ramsey's son, is supervised by Lois (the Series 12) who can detect a power surge in his room when he watches WatchMan in bed after lights out and reports on his activities every moment he's in the house.

■ Sf Robots: R2–D2 to Johnny-5

The sf robots discussed in the remainder of this chapter differ from the "docile" and utilitarian—nonanthropomorphic—bodies in *Runaway*. Either they are cute—like Muffit II, the robot dog in *Battlestar Galactica*—or they are an evil race of metallic anthropomorphs hellbent on becoming masters of the universe and, particularly, on killing off any humanlike, carbon-based, race in sight. The evil Cylons, also of *Battlestar Galactica*, are the perfect example. Where Muffit is both cute and docile—he's a mechanical pet—the Cylons are like a colony of perverted ants. There is a leader who makes the decisions and who represents what limited consciousness they have, and there are the worker/soldier robots who are docile and mostly provide bodies to be blown up or shot or kicked. If the leader says jump; they jump, if he says kill yourselves, they kill themselves. They are the robot versions of the alien children in *Village of the Damned*.

Evil robot species such as the Cylons or the equally evil Cybermen—eternal enemies of *Dr. Who* of the TV series of the same name—are embodiments of the worst human fear: faceless, unindividuated, totally homogenized but vaguely humanlike creatures. The ultimate evil is that which is powerful, very like us, and which we have no emotional or intellectual access to. But the worst thing about evil robots like the Cylons and the Cybermen is that they are boring. Pure evil does not play too well because there is no moral conflict. All tension derives from the eternal fight between light and dark, between good and evil. But a villain without doubts, without even a reversed or perverse morality, is tiresome.

Slightly more interesting are the cute robots: Robby the robot in *Forbidden Planet*, Muffit II in *Battlestar Galactica* and, of course R2-D2 and C-3PO, the 'droids,' from the *Star Wars* trilogy. R2-D2, especially, is terminally cute. He looks most of all like an old-fashioned barrel-bodied vacuum cleaner. C-3PO is a space cousin of the Tin Man *(The Wizard of Oz)*, timid but full of himself and his superior manners and all the knowledge he's had punched into him. The different—but fixed—personalities make the two endearing: R2-D2 is like a clever dog, insistent on being with his master, Luke, no matter how dangerous the circumstances; C-3PO, on the other hand, is all effete worry. They're Mutt and Jeff with their mechanical hearts in the right places. And R2-D2 and C-3PO serve, of course, the purpose of being magical attributes to Luke Skywalker. *Star Wars* is, after all, a space fairy tale and like any fairy tale hero, Luke needs magical helpers.

But ultimately R2-D2 and C-3PO are uninteresting because, as was the case with the evil Cylons, there is no moral tension. They are not individuals who can change, learn from their experiences, and emerge as wiser, weaker men. They are set once and for all, *commedia dell'arte* characters, predictable and pleasing, but one-dimensional.

The ultimate cute robot is Johnny-5 of the two *Short Circuit* movies. He starts his existence as one of hundreds of similar robots being assembled and rolled off the assembly line, a product of the Nova Robotics factory. Invented by Newt Crosby, Johnny is designed and constructed for military purposes: he could be dropped behind enemy lines with a five megaton bomb and cause a lot of trouble. At a party given by Nova to introduce the new robots to the military brass, the president of Nova touts his robots as "perfect soldiers." They "always obey orders and never ask questions." Perfectly docile, if metallic, bodies. But something goes wrong. Johnny-5 is "born" during a thunderstorm and he's touched by "the man upstairs"—in the form of a lightning, "male fire" that strikes the factory. After being hit by lighting, Johnny-5 is imbued with life, with an embryonic soul, no longer just a machine, he is, as he is fond of saying, "a life form." Johnny-5 goes from being a potentially deadly machine to being a rebellious mechanical citizen with a lust for life, a fear of death, and love in his heart. He rolls right off the assembly line and onto a garbage truck that's set to leave the heavily guarded Nova grounds. Immediately, the robot begins to formulate questions about the world he is driving through. A quest for meaning has begun.

Short Circuit is, shall we say, heavily indebted to Spielberg's *E.T.: The Extraterrestrial*. Like E.T., Johnny-5 meets a human being who is sweet and caring and innocent and willing to hide him and teach him what being human is all about. Also like E.T., Johnny-5 is hunted and nearly killed by the military and scientific establishments, only to miraculously escape just when all seems lost. Those are the bare plot bones. The reason that the movie is quite charming has nothing to do with the suspenseful plot. The charm lies in the secondary plot, which involves teaching an overly smart scientist who has no understanding of the world and the potential danger of the things he does, how to be a *mensch*, a fully human man who is capable of loving a woman and caring for a mechanical life form of his own creation (with divine help). The scientist learns his lesson from his technological "child" and Woman-the-Socializer.

Short Circuit has two heroes, two sources of identity for the main character, Johnny-5. The first is that mainspring of selfhood in American pop movies: popular culture. Johnny-5 is "humanized" by watching commercials and singing "Wouldn't you like to be a Pepper too?"[19] The advertising slogan is recognizable to the audience, they've heard that song, too: the ad focuses on "belonging," being one of us. By adopting pat phrases, idioms, and advertising slogans, Johnny-5 becomes "one of us"; he taps into *our* experience and world and becomes part of it. Advertising of the "image" type (like the Dr. Pepper ad) is upbeat, happy, promising the solution to problems such as lack of self-esteem, lack of identity, lack of hope, loneliness. All you have to do, it says, is hop on the (commercialized) popular-culture bandwagon and it is like waving a magic wand: you get identity (one of us), you get hope (if you're one of us, how could you not succeed?), you get rid of your loneliness (because you've done what it takes to belong.) Johnny-5 is humanized, in part, by embracing popular culture. He feels happy and, more importantly, the audience is willing to accept him (which is what it is all about: how can he be "one of us" if the audience doesn't accept him as such). Johnny-5 becomes an American teenager.

The other source of Johnny-5's sense of identity and the other hero of the movie is actually a heroine: Stephanie. She becomes Johnny-5's surrogate mother and supplies the other essential ingredient in the sf movie definition of what a self is: selfless love. If someone loves Johnny (sexually or parentally), and if he loves her, he isn't a machine. He's a real, live human being. Stephanie's love transforms Johnny-5 from a robot, a thing, to a human being. This is the *fier baiser*, the "tough kiss" that makes princes out of frogs.

Johnny-5 is one in a long chain of sf and adventure characters who obtain their identity through watching TV and the *fier baiser*; *E.T.*—obviously—comes to mind, as do the mermaid in *Splash!*, who learns how to be human the same way (the scene in Bloomingdale's, where she's watching all the TV monitors), Julius in *Twins* (to be discussed below) and the android in *Making Mr. Right*. Johnny-5 gets his final stamp of approval as a bona fide "life form" in *Short Circuit 2*, where he becomes gold plated and an American citizen.

Short Circuit is also about gender. The male—innately aggressive—child Johnny-5 (he is programmed to be a killer robot) is socialized by a woman, Stephanie. But the holy trinity is not complete. The child does not have a father. His "biological" father is, of course, Newt, the scientist whose brainchild he is, but Newt does not initially see Johnny as more than a piece of runaway machinery. The "child" is troubled—pursued and persecuted—until he has both a father and a mother, and when Newt and Stephanie become a couple and the three of them are a "family," the happy end is near. The gender issue centers on the opposition between the male or scientific worldview and the female or humanistic one. Newt is engaged in a kind of male reproduction: all the most negative aspects of the male (scientific) ethos mapped onto moving "creatures": killer robots. Conversely, Stephanie is totally impractical and one huge bundle of love for anything that's small and furry, alive and in need of help. When Johnny shows up on her doorstep, she categorizes him immediately as military hardware and is about to turn him in and out. But he manages to convince her that even if he's not furry, he's alive and in need of her help and love.

Johnny functions, on one level, as an extension of his inventor/ father, Newt. Johnny, the killer robot, is the creation of Newt, the computer/robot genius. Not that Newt is particularly interested in creating military robots—his original intention was to make a robot with more peaceful applications—but the military gave him the labs and the money he needed. For Newt the important thing is not the application, but the ability to *create*. His problem, as was Dr. Frankenstein's or, for that matter, the Romantic artist's, is that his creation without the input of woman will be negative, asocial, destructive. Yin and Yang must meet and merge to create something truly positive and beautiful. If men try to take upon themselves the dual prerogatives of God and Woman, they will fail. Only God can give *life*, and only the combination of male and female can create a true human (organic or technological) being with the ability to be banal and love and do good.

The sequel, *Short Circuit 2*, is about being foreign, about becoming adult, about becoming fully human—in this case, versed in American pop culture. Whereas the first movie was about Johnny going from being an all-male neonate Id to being a human (on the inside) child, *Short Circuit 2* is about Johnny going from being an alien life form to being a fully human young adult, ready for love and romance. Again he is the extension of his male creator, in this case (since Steve Guttenberg who played Newt wasn't available) Ben, the Indian-born scientist who was Newt's collaborator in the first movie. Ben, like Johnny-5, is a socially inept person. He's not the asocial male of the first movie; he's more like a clumsy teenager who doesn't quite grasp manners and customs and cultural norms. The movie amplifies the theme of teenage ineptitude and cultural clumsiness by making the central characters a foreigner and a robot. Both are terribly smart and willing to learn, they just don't quite know how to go about it. Much of the humor derives from these two "cute" misfits trying to learn what it is to be adult and human/American.

Both Ben and Johnny want to be loved and accepted, meaning Ben wants to make Sandy, a young business exec, love him. He has to overcome his awkwardness—meaning his foreignness—in order to be able to say the right things to Sandy. Johnny wants to be accepted and loved for what he is, "a life form endowed by my creator with certain inalienable rights," and has to overcome the human perception that he is ugly and looks like a piece of modern sculpture. They both have to attain fluency in being American (popular culture) to be able to achieve the ultimate symbols of Americanness: citizenship and wealth. They get their wish, of course: Ben proves his love and his worthiness of being a citizen

Short Circuit 2. Variations on the human form. (Tri-Star Productions, 1988. Still courtesy of Tri-Star Productions.)

by emitting a message to Sandy consisting in pop-song bits and wins her love; and Johnny goes from being denounced as ugly to being the darling of all America—he becomes one of the new American gods and/or superheroes, a TV star.

Both Ben and Johnny become citizens and wealthy because of their virtue and innate goodness, whereas the Bad are punished for their greed. Again, the good things accrue to those who are good *because* they are good, and those who try to cheat (by using Johnny's power and naiveté) go to jail.[20]

Johnny is the ultimate nondocile body. He refuses to be reduced to the sum of his mechanical parts. He has a soul and he is, although created in the image of machine, socialized by woman. He is the little guy who escapes the attempts made at making him into a docile killing machine. The truth about robots is, however, on the evidence of this chapter, that they are neither as smart, as efficient, nor as docile as they were meant to be.

■ Notes

1. Rabinow 1984:182.
2. Foucault 1965, 1973, and 1977.
3. Quoted in Rabinow 1984:180.
4. Ibid., 177.
5. Ibid., 178.
6. A brief but interesting discussion can be found in Feher 1989, vol. 1:431–480.
7. Capek 1923:16.
8. Ibid., 17.
9. Ibid., 28.
10. For a fascinating discussion of Capek's play and the notions of robots and mechanization as they relate to cinema as phenomenon, see Wollen 1989, esp. pp. 13–16.
11. Deken 1986:6.
12. Ibid., 6–7.
13. Ibid., 2–3.
14. My discussion is based on two artices in *The New York Times:* Holusha 1989, and Kilborn 1990.
15. Kilborn 1990:B16.
16. Markoff 1990:E5.
17. G. Johnson 1988:E7.

18. Lemonick 1990:74. The article points out that there, of course, are dissenting voices screaming bloody protest from the artificial-intelligence's central encampments, MIT and Stanford.

19. There are more reasons than just a love for or desire to disseminate the profundities of commercial culture behind this. Most notably the desire to advertise. Dr. Pepper or Coke or some other major advertiser will coproduce or put money into a film project in exchange for having their product prominently displayed and used in the movie. The idea (as the idea behind advertising in Brazilian novelas, soap operas) is to have characters with whom the audience empathizes and care for use the product in a way that makes the product stand out as positive and desirable. Thus, when Johnny-5 obtains an identity, a *recognizable identity*, via the use of advertising slogans, he reinforces the idea behind most image advertising: that you are "one of us" if you drink Dr. Pepper or Coke—or whatever the individual product is. See Miller 1990.

20. Johnny-5 as a kind of conscious ultimate *technologie moralisée*.

8 ·

Intrusive Media

Speaking of "docile" bodies is of course pure metaphor. What power needs and wants is docile *minds*. Smart, fast, knowledgeable, utterly obedient minds inside strong, pliable, enduring, and beautiful bodies. Sf is full of stories about attempts being made by scientists, or those who employ scientists, to "improve" on the human race.

At this point my "plot" makes a slight detour to look at sf films that represent the pervasive "fear of communication technology": the fear that science will find ways to imprison humans in their brains with machines that enter the mind and control thoughts and emotions.

Science is "the language of power"[1] in a world where knowledge is dying, the world of "exteriorized brain": "This is the world of panic science where consciousness is metaphorical (intelligence has no value in use, but only value in exchange); where information is regulatory of energy in a new cybernetic order of politics; and where *exteriorized mind* is, itself, only a medium across which the shuttling of techno-bodies in search of a brain function takes place."[2] Taking the thought expressed in the above quotation from an article by A. and M. Kroker a bit further, I would argue that in modern society, mind has no meaning as a personal attribute, as something the individual soul/self uses in its interaction with the physical universe. Mind is something we *wear* as a

166

suit, an emblem or a computer in a briefcase. The ability to obtain, store, and analyze knowledge has value only insofar as it makes the individual a more valuable commodity on the job market. To use intelligence to obtain knowledge about the world (that is not marketable) for the simple pleasure of knowing or philosophizing or trying to ferret out the meaning of life verges in the computer age on the obscene. The goal of any activity is power and money. Smarts are used to get good grades, good grades are used to get scholarships, scholarships can be negotiated into diplomas, and diplomas into jobs: power and money. That is the present as some see it. The future as it emerges in sf is even more frightening. One not-too-distant future is depicted in *Charly*, one of the best sf movies ever made.

Charly Gordon has virtually no market value. He is retarded and works in a commercial bakery as a floor sweeper. The most unusual thing about Charly is that he's part of an experiment. A team of scientists are testing the theory that intelligence can be boosted via an operation. The first test subject is a mouse by the name of Algernon[3] and it's beating Charly, paws down, at maze-solving. Charly is next on the operating table. Initially there is not much difference, except that he's angry for being so dumb. Charly is becoming aware of himself by beginning to see himself as others see him. Eventually he gets more maze-solvingly intelligent, and soon he's gobbling up knowledge with blinding speed. Then Algernon dies. All is not well with the experiment. It was successful but only temporary. Charly has a reversal to his earlier self to look forward to. Except for the fact that it is going to be worse because he will know what he was, what he had, and he will know he can never have it or be it again.

But even when he is at the pinnacle of his intellectual powers, Charly is never a docile body. When he gives a speech to a group of scientists, he chides them for their lack of values and dogged pursuit of progress. He says theirs is a world of "rampant technology" where conscience is "by computer" and accuses them of wanting to usher in a "Brave New World." Charly Gordon is given a brief moment of intense insight and uses his moment to condemn the very ethics that allow such experiments as the one that gave him his intelligence. Then he sinks back into the darkness

In *Charly* a team of scientists experiment with boosting intelligence. For starters they pitch the retarded Charly against the mouse Algernon at maze-solving. (Cinerama Releasing Corporation, 1968. Still courtesy of MOMA film stills archive.)

and his old job at the bakery to live in wistful half-memory of what was.

In a certain sense, *Charly* and its protagonist can stand as a metaphor for the history of humanity and knowledge. Science has pulled humans out of the deep darkness of superstition and ignorance and has given them a brief moment of insight, only subsequently to threaten to push them back down into the abyss of ignorance and stupidity. Movies such as *The Day After, The Road Warrior,* and *The Blood of Heroes* record what the future after the scientific disaster has happened might look like. *Charly* is like a dream where a man suddenly sees everything clearly and can formulate the meaning of life in a simple sentence; then he wakes up and it's gone, it's slipped back down into the recesses of the unconscious, never to reemerge. Ever after, he has to live with the knowledge that the missing pieces are lost.

■ Corporate Mind Control

Most sf futures are not as kind as Charly's; they are claustrophobic nightmares where humanity as a whole is forced to become Charly before and after the Operation. In the sf looking glass the future belongs to the tyrannical oligarchy often known as the Corporation, whose biggest concern is to keep the masses in check.[4] They have to produce, and they have to consume. But beyond that, they should disappear, not ask questions, not take too much of an interest in how the world is run and by whom. The Corporation wants "docile bodies" and subjected, controllable minds.

The idea of controlling the mind, of controlling what humans think about, is of course as old as the idea of society itself. Any social group defines itself in terms of orthodoxies. In a small-scale society comprising anywhere from twenty-five to a couple of thousand people, it is quite easy to make sure that individuals adhere to and believe in the norms. Everybody knows everybody; if someone strays in any way, he or she is virtually guaranteed to be "shunned." In large societies, comprising millions of people, loosely gathered under an umbrella of a shared language, a shared national or religious identity, things become a bit more complicated. Power has to find thousands of little capillaries—to use an expression from Foucault—to insert itself into the minds of the millions. Power has to find ways to enter the minds of people, not just with words and statutes. Power that relies solely on force, on soldiers and guards and on fear, may be successful for a while; but the power that inserts itself via the capillary afflux (the thousand little channels that lead from the centers of power into the mind of the individual woman or man) into the consciousness and sense of identity of its subject is likely to be infinitely *more* successful. Power needs to be a visual, sensual, ubiquitous presence in the physical world; but much more than that, it needs to find ways to enter and control the mind. In our modern communication society, mind control is the fabrication of desires. People are taught to desire more, to acquire more, to define who they are by what they have. Corporations manufacture products, the media create the desires. In other words, those who control the media control what people desire, control what they think about, talk about, control the shape of the world inside their heads.

In the movie *Rollerball*, the corporations have taken over the world. From what sparse information is given in the movie, it seems that a series of "corporate wars" took place in the late twentieth century. The victorious corporations divided the world among themselves; as Bartholomew, the president, says, "Corporate society was an inevitable destiny," the material dreamworld come to pass. The game of Rollerball was invented to keep the masses amused and distracted. When Houston plays against Madrid, "Our Corporate Anthem" is played before the game. The audience faces the chairman/president of the Corporation. This is the Roman Corporate Empire of the future—the stage is set for the gladiators to be brought on: the masses are waiting in front of the TV screens desiring another violent blood feast.

The corporations pit their teams against each other in rousing bloodbaths/wars, the people identify with their team and by extension with their Corporation. Behind the smoke screen of violence and the emotions it arouses hide the rulers and their machinations. Rollerball is also designed to show the futility of individual effort: "We are the Corporation, the Corporation is us."

In the Roman Empire of *Rollerball*, all media other than Corporate TV are things of the past, and the only program seems to be the constant "warfare" of Rollerball. All major decisions are made by a few "for the common good." There are no wars in the Corporate Kingdom, no poverty; obedience is paid with women and consumption. Jon is a Rollerball player about to be retired because he has become too popular for the comfort of Power. He has to make a moral choice: choose "nice things or freedom." The choice is easy, says Ella, his girlfriend: "Comfort *is* freedom, always has been." Freedom from poverty, freedom from thinking, freedom from making moral and ethical choices. This is the perversion of the American Dream: freedom equals consumption, comfort, and entertainment. The affairs of the world and society are conveniently left to those who hunger for power.

Rollerball is an entry in the folklore genre of "giant killers." Despite the fact that he is strong and fast and a star of the bloodiest game, Jon is a Little Guy. He and his colleagues are raw meat fed to the masses to pacify them. They shine brightly for a short spell, then they are gone, usually in a painful and violent death. They have no real power, just flash. But when one light goes on shining, when one star refuses to be killed and becomes too popular, the time is ripe, those in power decide, to retire him and make him one of them: an Executive. The executives are afraid of Jon because he stands out as a man who has been able to achieve by himself. Of such men, leaders are made. And worse, of such men —common men who have negotiated a talent to become stars— dreams are made, role models are made. Others out there in the corporate "dreamworld" might desire individual success. Jon must go, he must lose a game and bow out, saying I'm too old and I owe everything to the Corporation. Then he can be put to pasture, given a life of luxury to make the transition to oblivion more pleasant. But Jon, of course, fairy tale hero that he is, refuses to do as he's told. He fights back and in the end the masses attack the chairman/president and a happy end is suggested.

But what kind of happy end? The Little Guy takes on the Corporate Giant and kills him. It is of course always good to see a dictatorship fall. And a dictatorship that depends on the dope of TV violence to pacify a potentially restive population is especially repugnant and deserving of eradication. But the movie subscribes to the very negatives that it purports to be opposing. This is a

In the corporate empire of *Rollerball,* the players are raw meat fed to the masses to pacify them; they shine brightly for a spell before suffering a violent death. (United Artists Productions, 1975. Still courtesy of MOMA film stills archive.)

violent movie, appealing to the most primitive desires: to see people being hurt, killed, maimed. The purported message is lost in the blood and the gore, and the subliminal message that lingers is, as in so many of these movies,[5] that individualism is the solution to all problems.

Jon is a violent man; he has no respect for women (neither does the movie.) He is the "rugged individualist" of the Western tradition who rides into town, kills the bad guys, and gallops off into the sunset. But the society depicted in *Rollerball* needs more than the violent removal of the corrupt leaders to become a just and democratic one.

Movies like *Rollerball* and the one to be discussed below, *Running Man*, are dangerous because they endorse the very values they claim to be opposing. Describing a violent society—graphically and at great length—only to show that only violence can bring it down enshrines violence as the cure-all to social problems.

The premise of *Running Man* is very similar to that of *Rollerball:* in a future society, where the United States is ruled by a violent and exploitative clique, the masses are the frequent victims of harsh violence and kept mentally occupied by a constant and ubiquitous bombardment of TV violence. The most popular and most violent of game shows is "Running Man," hosted by Damon Killian (played with appropriate sleaziness by a master of the trade, Richard Dawson). *Running Man* is a more violent future cousin of "American Gladiators." Criminals (mostly of the political kind—although they are represented as common criminals) are pitted against professional gladiators, armed to the teeth with the latest in imaginative killing technology. The contestants *never* win. The show is an outlet for the repressed anger and hostility of a populace haunted by starvation and hunted, when they have the nerve to protest, by heavily armed police in helicopters. Political prisoners are forced to work in steel plants, wearing collars containing explosives that detonate should they move beyond the perimeter surrounding the camp/factory. There is a feeble underground movement and everybody else is starved and kept in a state of crazed aggression by the constant bombardment of sanctioned violence.

Into this environment is thrown Arnold Schwarzenegger, as a cop who refuses to fire on unarmed food protesters. For this he gets the "galleys," the steel plant, and the collar. He manages to escape and holes up in the apartment of his brother's girlfriend, who makes a living composing jingles for TV shows and is utterly ordinary and believes everything she hears on TV. As Arnold, alias Richard, enters her apartment and her life, she's about to join Captain Freedom—on TV—in a workout. The story is complicated: suffice it to say that Richard and the woman become contestants on the show and Richard knocks off all the gladiators, in scene after violent scene. In the end, Damon Killian, who keeps insisting that all he's interested in is ratings, is flushed down a chute to a fiery death. Both *Running Man* and *Rollerball* point to trends in our own society that may become dangerous if taken to their logical and, perhaps, inevitable conclusion. In the 1990s, both TV and movies use violence as entertainment: images of random violence in the streets, of violent sports, and games such as hockey, boxing, and football are staples of TV programming. Cops-and-robbers movies are no longer tales of wit matched against wit, they are tales of gore and violence, Bad Guys who kill and are killed in turn. Everything is reduced to the simple, the violent, and the fastest route to the most primal emotional response. The effect is to clog people's minds with constant emotional surges, preparing them for "solutions" that will escalate the violence and the deaths. The response to violence in the streets is more police in the streets who kill more Bad Guys. The response to lethal violence is lethal violence. These are "eye for an eye," quickie solutions to problems that have no quick solutions.

But power has, of course, no real interest in solving the social problems. Power is, as Michel Foucault has argued,[6] interested in having criminals, deviants, and insane people. The more criminals, the more police. The more police, the more control. A society that is beset by crime and political unrest is ripe for a measure of police-state features. People watch the crime and violence on TV and thirst for the quick fix and applaud more police, more control, more surveillance. We may eventually get the police state by popular acclaim.

■ Mediated Mind Control

In sf, a genre that more than perhaps any other presents an oppositional view,[7] the imagined futures are replete with increasingly more effective technological ways of entering the minds of men and women. One could set up a continuum of sf's future ways of gaining access to and controlling minds. The two movies discussed above, *Rollerball* and *Running Man*, represent a direct continuation of what is happening in the United States in the 1990s: the technology hasn't changed, and violence-as-entertainment-and-means-of-control has only changed in degree. In the movies to be discussed below, innovative technology helps usher in more effective mind control.

The first step is exemplified by *Death Watch*, where a miniature camera is invented that can be implanted—by a minor operation—into the brain of a person. The first person to undergo the operation is, of course, an opportunistic TV production assistant; he becomes a virtual cyborg, part man, part machine. The society of *Death Watch* resembles the one depicted in Running Man: TV ratings are the goal of all things. And as is the case in *Running Man*, the show with the highest ratings features people dying in public. The latest craze is a program called "Deathwatch"; a camera crew follows a dying person's last weeks or months. Dying has become a curiosity because nobody dies from disease any more. People die in accidents, air crashes, wars, but other than that, only the old die. Thus the producers are willing to pay a young dying person to die "live" in the living rooms of the millions of viewers in TV-land.

The first shot shows a cemetery with mausoleums and small obelisks topped by crosses; a little girl is playing among the monuments with the city hovering in the background: the dead are still the property of the divine, but dying no longer is. Then the camera focuses on the producers of the new TV show as they line up several prospects to become quickly fading stars.

The young woman who is selected to die in public is a writer of children's books, Katherine Mortenhoe. She is dying (or so she is made to believe) from an unnamed disease that is brought on by her unwillingness to conform. She refuses to participate, but the show's producers manage to film her anyway: the production assistant with the implanted camera, Roddy, befriends the dying woman and films her without her knowledge. The producers will get their show, and the viewers will be glued to the screen, staring passively at the flicker. When the set is turned off, there is no afterimage, no lingering meaning: Katherine's public death will insure continued public docility.

But Roddy is not all docile machine: the constant proximity to this woman, whose death is caused by her lack of docility—by her refusal to submit, for example, to her writing "assistant," the computer Harriet, which has final say on the plot lines she uses in her children's books—starts a process in him of coming to grips with the immorality of what he is doing. In a sense, Roddy is the structural equivalent of Harriet: the computer is almost human in its interaction with Katherine; Roddy is almost machine, the cyborg who will do whatever it takes to get a foot on the next rung of the social ladder. A love affair develops between Katherine and Roddy. He refuses to keep filming her and reveals the ultimate deceit: she is not really dying; her symptoms were caused by pills and for the sole purpose of creating the show. Katherine writes her own ending to her story by committing suicide—off camera.

In *Death Watch* the boundary between human and machine begins to fade. As the doctor says to Katherine, people are no longer "allowed" to die, no longer allowed to get ulcers, cancers, or go crazy. Everything is put to the scalpel, everything can be cured—except if the individual is unwilling to be docile and fit in. Machines determine the nature and form of artistic output. Art, like brain, has become "exteriorized"; books are written to be marketed and sold in as many million copies as possible. So writers follow the formulas and recombine the old-and-tried plot lines until they seem new.

Death Watch utilizes an impressive and constant symbol system of glass, of one-way mirrors and lenses, suggesting the terror of the ubiquitous camera, the machines that rob our lives and deaths of meaning and make them into entertainment for those whose half-lives only exist as blue reflections from the TV screen. There is no longer a boundary between private and public. Eyes are not eyes, they are cameras; lives are not lives, they are scenes, entertainment, or, the worst possible scenario: if the camera does not find them to be worthy of public display, they simply don't exist. Life is that which is seen by the camera and transmitted on the screen, the rest is relegated to the perpetual realm of shadows; the modern-day Hades.

If cameras can be inserted in people's brains, no one is safe anymore. The notion of privacy, of being alone and unobserved, has vanished. Those who own the technology control everybody just as fully as the all-seeing God controls the deeply religious. All actions, all words are public. The camera inside the brain is not just another piece of smart technology, it is the end of privacy. All walls are broken down, all comforters are lifted, all doors are unlocked. Power can always see everyone and thus power controls everyone.

In *Death Watch*, Roddy falls in love with the "dying" woman and, in the end, refuses to continue. But he is controlled by the producers. The camera is in his brain. He is essentially just a piece of nonoperative machinery. He is the extension of the machine. The controls are not in his hands—or brain—they are in the ruthless hands of those who employ him. Even if he refuses to do their bidding and finds a way to help Katherine to die alone and in privacy, the technology is still there and eventually there will be an army of men and women who are willing to do what power tells them to do.

Death Watch is the logical extension of shows like *America's Home Videos* and *Hidden Camera*, shows that further the idea of life as movie. Goofing around at home is no longer something private and enjoyable, something that grows out of relationships and emotions and joy at being together. It is stuff to be captured on camera and sent off to be evaluated as entertainment. Situations stop being spontaneous and private; they are ripped out of the fabric of life to be directed, evaluated for their money-making potential. Already a journalist in San Francisco, dying of AIDS, chose to die "live" in front of a TV crew.

On the sf continuum, the next technological feat, the next step to control the human mind, is the ability to record dreams, as is the case in *Dreamscape,* a pedestrian movie based on a fascinating idea: the notion that a person with psychic ability will be able to enter into the dream of another person. The movie is an action flick, crowded with bodies being pumped full of hot lead, and the idea is never really developed. But the concept is frightening: a stranger can enter into a dream "in progress" and cause a heart attack, as happens in the movie, or help fight off the monsters that populate a recurring nightmare and make the dreamer's waking life a constant state of fear of sleep.

More fully developed is the idea in *Brainstorm.* A team of scientists, headed by the brilliant but stubborn and independent-minded Lillian, has developed a method to record thoughts and mental experiences.[8] The movie is somewhat confused and eventually disintegrates, but the central idea is there: a method by which one person can record an intense emotional experience—the examples in the movie include a sex act and a heart attack with deadly outcome—that can be "played back" and experienced by another. Astounding as this may seem, it has already been recorded in—tabloid—reality, as this headline from *The Sun* suggests: "Psychic records his dreams on videotape & shows them like movies."[9] In *Brainstorm,* watching the "videos" has a deadly outcome; an older man with a heart problem dies as he reexperiences the sex act of another man, and the recorded heart attack and death of Lillian—the top scientist—triggers death in anyone "listening."
   But the device has a more profound capacity. It can record subjectivity; it allows the listener to reenact the entire sensory experience and eventually the memories, thoughts, and emotions captured by the reorder. The subject "barrier" has been removed, there is no longer a difference between *me* and *you.* The positive implications are obvious; in the movie the device allows Mike and Karen, who at the outset were headed for divorce, to find each other again. Mike, "listening" to a recording of Karen, experiences her point of view, he *becomes* her and is able to empathize with her and vice versa.
   The movie is interesting for suggesting that technology may

find a way to record thought. The implications are obvious. If thoughts and emotions can be recorded, exit *any* notion of privacy and individuality. We will all be hooked to a giant thought-police computer that monitors us and punishes those who think the wrong things. And conversely, the playback can be used to control people—or kill them. Talk about a "mind-fuck": imagine what kind of addiction people could develop for "listening" to experienced sex or other pleasurable emotions/experiences? And the military applications (which are played up in the movie): if the machine can make people empathize with each other, if it erases the subject boundary, it can also be used very effectively for "brainwashing" people.[10]

Next, imagine a future where humans have established colonies in space. Mars, the Red Planet, is what the Old West was during the gold rush, a seething, lawless enclave devoted to the mining of Tribinium (whatever that is) which has been handed over to *the Agency* to run. And imagine that the Agency is really a corporation with its tentacles in just about any kind of shady business—and you have *Total Recall*.

The plot of *Total Recall* is not easy to get a handle on, but, briefly, this is how it goes. Hauser is an unscrupulous and devoted agent (and a *secret* one) for Recall Inc., which is synonymous with the Agency. On Mars, Recall is free to do as the chairman, Cohaagen, pleases as long as the Tribinium keeps flowing back to Mother Earth. Cohaagen is a tyrant. He runs "his" colony with an iron fist and an eye for nothing but the power and the profit. In the colony's early days he built cheap domes so the settlers had mutant children. The mutants, known as "Freaks," are the soothsayers and underclass of the New Society. They are also the only ones to oppose Cohaagen and Recall, "the role of the 'other' who reveals through its fragmented, refracting mirror the true nature of humanity is assumed in *Total Recall* by the mutant underclass."[11] The mutants have started a rebel movement under the leadership of one Kuato. The rebels write graffiti slogans at the "Spaceport" ("Kuato Lives") and blow things up. But back on earth, Recall is mostly involved in the travel-agency business. They sell preexperienced travel-memory implants to the unwary: "Do you dream of a vacation on the bottom of the ocean—but you can't float the bill? Have you always wanted to climb the mountains of Mars—but you're over the hill? Then come to Recall Inc. where you can buy the memory of your ideal vacation, cheaper, safer and better than the real thing. Call Recall for the memory of a life-time."

In *Total Recall*, the boundary between self/other is constantly crossed. Recall has no luck getting to the elusive Kuato, so Hauser, the Recall agent, agrees with his boss, Cohaagen, that something special has to be done to rid the Corporation of the rebels. Cohaagen and Hauser dream up a scenario to accomplish their goal: Hauser, who has befriended a young woman prostitute and freedom fighter, has his own personality "erased" and is transformed into Doug Quaid, muscular hard-hat married to blonde Lori. But all is not well with Doug. He does (make) love (to) Lori, but he wants more. He wants to go to Mars. He dreams about Mars at night, he dreams about Melina, the hooker/freedom fighter—not quite knowing why.

Paul Verhoeven, the director, plays very deliberately with the question of dream/reality; *Total Recall* is a modern fairy tale. It begins with a dream and ends with Doug/Hauser and Melina on the mountains of Mars watching the atomic clouds give way to a clear blue sky. Melina says, "I can't believe it, it's like a dream." Doug: "I just had a terrible thought: what if this *is* a dream?"—"Well, then kiss me quick before we wake up." That is the equivalent of the fairy tale ending: "And so they got married and lived happily ever after—and if it isn't a lie, they live there still." Verhoeven knows that his movie is a kind of collective dream "implant"; it enters us so we become Doug and get to live dangerously and be strong and moral enough to win in the end. And when it's over, who cares if it was dream or real? As long as it lasted, it was true and the emotional release is real enough.[12]

Total Recall is also a fairy tale in the sense of having an Ordinary Joe protagonist. Doug is a construction worker. He is not drawn as a real, faceted human being. He is the stock fairy-tale hero: a little stupid, a lot ordinary, full of impossible dreams. But he rises to the task. As evil jumps on him in the form of work buddies and even his wife, he copes, fights back and gropes to understand why all of this is happening to him. Because Doug is an Everyman he can be played by Arnold Schwarzenegger, who is *representative* in that he has no personality of his own; the audience can "walk" right in and occupy the empty rooms. And he is representative because he is big and strong and rugged looking: the cardboard figure at the mall with the head cut out so anyone can be recorded with the beefy physique of a champion body builder.

The imagery systems of *Total Recall* are *penetration* and *perverse (communication) electronics.* Doug is both penetrated and the conquering, all-penetrating phallus, "Schwarzenegger, both functionally and as an iconic signifier, may be understood as a swollen penis, throbbing his way through the receptive material of the narrative."[13] But Doug/Schwarzenegger is not only the aggressive phallus, he is the victim of aggressive *penetration:* the evil Corporation has implanted an artificial identity into his brain. He is the New Age man with only exteriorized consciousness. He has no soul of his own, only the artificial, technological, company-implanted one that makes him the perfect docile body. He even has a "bug" implanted in his brain.

The future society of *Total Recall* enters its inhabitants in myriad ways. To get into the subway, passengers have to pass an X-ray wall that reveals any hidden weapons. On the subway are the loud TVs barking advertising without stop. Typically, Doug has two ideas in the whole movie (going to Recall and going to Mars), and he gets both of them from the subway ads. Homes have TV screens the size of movie screens. Turning them off seems not to be an option; either there is incessant news-propaganda or there is a wall-length screen showing a beautiful lake and forest. Also part of the penetration imagery are the huge drills that mine the Tribinium ore and the mountains of Mars that have been penetrated and converted into a city for humans.

And Doug, the rampant phallus, in the end, overcomes the Big Phallus, Cohaagen. Doug, muscles on top of muscles, operates a jackhammer—and his entire adventure on Mars involves smashing through, drilling his way into, shooting bullets and other penile objects into. In the end, he blows the whole "otherworld" wide open, using an atomic reactor left by aliens long gone. He blasts his way out into the open, giving freedom and air to the oppressed. From subterranean company town, the Martian society can move up and out.

In the final analysis, *Total Recall* is about identity: how can men and women keep their identity in a technological world where machines that can penetrate and change anyone's sense of self are rampant? Hauser becomes Doug. Doug is ordinary but dreams of not being. Hauser is Bad gone Good. He seems to have become an ally of the rebels. But he really hasn't; he is just playing at having joined the rebels for the purposes of penetrating their defenses and getting to meet—and kill—Kuato. So who is he? Is he Doug dreaming he's Doug/Hauser? Or is he Hauser who has lent his body to be Doug and wants it back? The movie does not hold up under scrutiny on these questions. The plot simply does not hold water (or air). But it doesn't matter; it's a dream. The question of identity is, however, important—also to us. The more the media penetrate with their idiotic messages about happiness and travel and being what we are not, the less chance we have to find out who we are. The media "create" us, penetrate us, implant fictional identities into our heads.

The showdown between Doug—who he is; he refuses his alter ego Hauser's attempt at reclaiming him [14]—and the Bad Guys takes place in the *paysage moralisé* of the cavernous reactor room inside the Great Pyramid mountain. The reactor is a relic—symbolic of the good origins of civilization, of "good" science—from aliens who seem to have moved on. It will blow up the mines and the physical frame around the human settlement if activated. It will also give Mars an atmosphere to enable people to live above ground and without having to pay Recall for the air they breathe. It will "magically" free humanity from bondage; it will give them the freedom to breathe and say what they want; it will stop the exploitation of the planet and it will remove the repressive regime and all of its *penetration technology*. In other words, the reactor is for the betterment of humankind as opposed to the oppressive technology owned and operated by Recall.

The logical conclusion in this chain of sf intrusive media is supplied by Boorman's confusing and, sometimes, brilliant *Zardoz*. A future society has enshrined itself inside what its members call a "vortex," an invisible wall that separates the members from the violent world outside which is populated by peaceful grain producers and fierce and brutal warriors who hunt and kill and rape them.

Inside the vortex life is an eternal half-life. Death has been done away with; people live forever under the jealous scrutiny of the *crystal*, a kind of collective unconscious/God/TV. The crystal can indeed be seen as a metaphor for TV (or popular media in general) because TV, especially American TV, is itself a kind of "collective unconscious." TV and Hollywood movies are public spectacles in Goffman's sense:[15] symbolic representations and images that function as rallying points and metaphors for the collective set of values we hold and that make us feel like a nation. In *Zardoz*, however, the crystal is not just a metaphorical collective unconscious; it is a *de facto* one in that it has access to—is plugged into —the thought processes and emotional "bands" of all members of the society. There is no police, just endless discussions of guilt or nonguilt in cases where individuals have thought against the rules. Gender boundaries are broken down; everybody is androgynous and vague. Those who revolt—by hating the society and thus themselves, since they are plugged into the sum-of-consciousness crystal—are sentenced to senility. Life in the vortex is a nonlife because, as the movie argues, humans are not designed to live forever or share a subconscious (unlike the aliens of *Village of the Damned* who draw energy and will to survive from their collective (un)conscious).

To make the point and show the contrast, Boorman throws into this bloodless and pale society (people wear unisex togas and wander around languidly) a blood-rich and blood-thirsty exterminator (played by Sean Connery) who breaks through the vortex and immediately tries to rape the first woman he sees. The people of the crystal keep him, calling him an "it," an animal and worse, to study him. He escapes and hides among those who have thought against "the state" (in the sense that the state, in this movie literally, is the sum of its members) and have been sentenced not to death, but to eternal idiotic half-life, spent in a state of constant exhaustion at a giant cocktail party in their fanciest get-ups. He gives them life and vigor by giving them his blood to drink (the blood symbolism is rampant), and with him as their leader they break down the vortex and return to the living and dying.[16]

Typically of the genre, the prime mover in *Zardoz*, the source of change and humanization, is love. And love, in its turn, is the seed that sprouts not only dissent and willingness to put life and limb on the line, it is also the source of a sense of self. Love, in all its commonality—after all, love is as common as the common cold—is also the feeling that makes each sufferer feel vulnerable and special. This is perhaps most obvious in *Death Watch:* Roddy is at the outset of the movie (the first shot of him shows him being examined after having the camera inserted) as much machine as he is man. The society of which Roddy and Katherine are members is such that any inkling of a separate, "asocial" identity is discouraged. People are reduced to well-functioning machines that can be kept operative as long as they don't go against the grain. Medicine can keep everybody well and functioning as long as they do not oppose. The word "no" is erased from the vocabulary. Humans are but empty vessels; they are the sum of their physical parts—all other functions are exteriorized: computers produce the "dreams," and emotions are projected onto the TV screens. Roddy's identity and sense of self, probably minimal even before the operation, is next to nil. Everything registered in his brain via his eyes is repeated on fifteen screens in a control room. And he defines himself by his job; there is no separation between public and private spheres. But loving Katherine makes him want to be private. He develops a fledgling self.

In *Zardoz*, both the "exterminator," who, until his exposure to the "crystal" society, is more ferocious animal than human being, and the young woman from the society he falls in love with (and vice versa) are humanized and gain a "soul" from the experience. Love, the *fier baiser*, can make a true human out of both a man-beast and of a woman who has had her mind co-opted and fused into a literal collective consciousness. The young woman in *Zardoz* is, then, the positive counterpiece to the children of *Village of the Damned*; she's a futuristic "monster" who undergoes a reverse soul transplant.

In the movies discussed in this section, docility is insured through the use of media: from the violence drug in *Rollerball* and *Running Man* to the crystal/god of *Zardoz*, where science has found a way to plug all individual minds into a "mainframe," the issue is control of the mind via emotions, thought-steering and thought-policing. Another method for insuring docility is, of course, naked fear: the police state.

■ Notes

1. Kroker and Kroker 1987:30–31.
2. Ibid., 31.
3. The movie is an adaptation of a short-story-turned-novel by Daniel Keyes, "Flowers for Algernon."
4. To simplify things, I will use the Corporation as the common term for all these future dictatorships. There are other reasons for this than just the fact that it makes things simpler in terms of writing and reading. One is that the Corporation indeed is ubiquitous in these sf futures.
5. Examples are *The Road Warrior* and *The Blood of Heroes*.
6. Foucault 1980:15–17.
7. But keep in mind that sf ultimately, despite the protest element, collaborates with those in power.
8. Also similar is *Videodrome*, where videos are programmed to grab the viewer's mind and produce homicidal "dreams" that sometimes turn to reality.
9. *Sun*, 12 July, 1988, 37. Here's how it works: "I would concentrate my mind on a certain subject and take a picture with an instant camera." Video proved a challenge: "I tried the same technique on video but the tape moves too fast for my concentration." But Clement, the Czech psychic, is still working on it.
10. I'm indebted to one of the publisher's anonymous readers for some of the insights about *Brainstorm*.
11. Glass 1990:4.
12. Ibid., 7, interprets the dream/reality aspects of the movie in more psychological terms: "Our adult identity is based on a successful process of repressing early relationships with parents and siblings, most of which we experienced through the mediation of intensely charged emotional fantasies, baggage too heavy to carry around in our conscious mind but too potent to entirely lose. So we compromise by pushing those memories down into the unconscious, where they

help shape the patterns of our lives in ways beyond our waking understanding. We are all amnesiacs, both in this individual-psychological sense and in a broader representation: as victims of social amnesia, the peculiar anti-historical mechanism of our culture that works to keep rulers and ruled in their places."

13. Ibid., 6. I discovered this article months after having made my own analysis and was delighted to find the agreement in interpretation of some of the movie's key symbols.

14. Like so many sf movies, this one is full of clichés and quotes from other movies. The good/bad self calls to mind *Star Wars*, where Luke has to choose between good and bad in himself—exteriorized as his father, who was a freedom fighter and became the evil Lord.

15. Goffman 1963.

16. The plot is much more complex and contrived than that, but it will suffice as here stated for my purposes. The movie is perhaps too insistent on being profound and symbolic and multileveled for its own good. It becomes tiresome after a while with all the masks and characters melting into each other.

9 ■

The Dystopia

■ Bureaucratic Nightmares

The dystopias presented in the previous chapter used communication technology as their primary or sole means of control. Below, we shall encounter dystopias that enslave humans through a "science of fear." The three movies I examine are all, interestingly and ironically, permeated by the present and the past—while, perhaps, dealing with the future. Both *Brazil* and *1984* present the past-as-future. In *The Handmaid's Tale*, a movie set in the not-too-distant future in the United States, traditional values, such as family and religion, have won the day and the new, male rulers have ushered in the Christian millennium, the City of God, the early Christian "state" re-created in the image of the religious right. And it is, of course, a nightmare: a rigid class state, a world in which women are reduced to either pretty ornaments, domestic workers or surrogate mothers—breeding machines.

The notion of the utopia[1] goes back to Thomas More's work of the same name and has been applied, retroactively, to such works as Saint Augustine's *City of God* and Plato's *Republic*. A utopia is an imaginary ideal state expressed as words on paper. A utopian society has no flaws and runs according to a single principle and with the full agreement of all citizens.

Religions and political ideologies have always been major producers of utopian visions. The Christian millennium is a utopia, as is the Marxist vision of the classless society where humans hunt in the morning, attend a concert in the afternoon, and have been liberated forever from greed and exploitation. Both of these utopias, the Christian and the communist, presume a different, "improved," race of humans. The Christian vision sees humans transformed into docile and peaceful sheep, grazing contentedly at the feet of their divine shepherd. Society, in the sense we know it, is not a part of the millennium: it would seem that both the toils and sorrows and pleasures of the human world are gone, people are virtual bodiless spirits. In the Marxist vision, humans have acquired new and better characteristics by living through the various stages leading up to the utopia, the communist society (which has done away with the state and with traditional notions of work and production, and so forth). In both visions, the backbone is the emergence of a new race, a more docile—because conflict has been removed—race of beings that accept the "political" realities as infallible and unavoidable. There are going to be no dissenters or terrorists in heaven nor in the communist utopia. To a lesser degree, the same holds true of Plato's, Augustine's, and More's utopias: the self-evident superiority and rightness of the imagined society makes dissent and discord simply fall by the wayside as obsolete and useless. Not so in the three movies to be discussed here. All three envision "utopias" that have no trouble turning up dissidents.

Brazil, an English movie by Terry Gilliam of Monty Python fame, shows a society that is a nightmare version of the class war taken to its extreme. The title of the movie is, of course, ironic: "Brazil, after all, was named for a mythical Utopian land which early European voyagers sought in vain."[2] Democracy, however frail, is a thing of the past. *Brazil* is a *1984* satire where the bureaucrats have won. England (or "Brazil") is run by the old-boy network of Tories who control the huge bureaucratic institutions that have sucked up an enormous and feverishly busy section of the work force, keeping records and files on everybody else. There is the Ministry of Works, Central Service (which of course does not), the Ministry of Records and Information Retrieval. All full of little

men in little offices, checking on other men and women and jock-
eying with each other for positions in the career race. The top
floors are occupied by the ministers, the floors below, except the
basement, by the army of gray men in suits. The basement is
where the riot police wait restlessly for their next assignment:
breaking into the apartments of suspected terrorists to be abducted, bound up in straitjackets, and delivered to the Information Retrieval officer in charge of interrogations.

The nature of the interrogations is revealed when the "hero,"
Sam Lowry, visits the office to obtain a file. The secretary is
transcribing the proceedings, which are transmitted to her via a
heavy pair of headphones. When she lifts the phones from one ear
to ask Sam what she can do for him, we, and he, hear the screams
of pain. And when Sam enters the office, he finds his old friend
Jack in a bloodstained smock, putting his scalpels and other instruments of torture back on their tray. Sam does not question the
morality of what Jack does, and Jack is so undisturbed that he can
spend the time between "customers" playing with his little girl.

Sam Lowry, the (anti-)hero, is an empty slate at the opening of
the movie. He has a job in the Ministry of Information but no
ambition. He's just one of the thousands of faceless men (there are
no women) manning the computer terminals. He's smart and
knowledgeable enough to be the sole means of survival for his
incompetent boss, Kurtzman, who constantly calls him to come
and solve the various crises his incompetence lands him in. But
Sam has no desire to be promoted. Perhaps there is a germ of
dissent in Sam's lack of ambition. His only distinction is that he
has a recurring dream in which, dressed in breastplates, huge bird
wings and a romantically curly wig, he soars over the canyons of
gray and threatening skyscrapers. Bird-man-Sam is constantly
trying to save a beautiful blonde who is trapped in the claustrophobic canyons and guarded by a metallic giant. Not difficult to
interpret: Sam, in his dreams at least, fervently desires to be free
and soar over and away from the urban desert. He wants to fight
the huge Leviathan that stands for the monstrous state he is part
of and win the love of a woman who will see him as a an individual man, rather than his earning potential or social position. But
Sam Lowry never questions anything when he's awake. He seems

nonplussed when his dream woman, turned real-life truck driver, asks him if he feels comfortable about what he does at the Ministry of Retrieval. He had never thought about it. He is empty. Neither positive nor negative—neutral.[3]

The state in *Brazil* is beset by a rather mythical opposition, the so-called terrorists who blow up buildings. Or do they? The only person in the movie who actively and more or less violently opposes the system is the remarkable Mr. Tuttle, an engineer who got tired of the bureaucracy and buzzes around, performing repairs and helping people because he likes to. But Tuttle doesn't throw bombs. The terrorists may be a government invention. A special branch of some ministry that has the function of blowing up buildings and innocent people to show the government's police-state measures are indeed necessary and justified. Real or not, the bureaucratic machinery churns and tortures and locks up as if the terrorists were a fact. Riot police enter apartments like an occupation force, abduct suspects, making sure to give and receive receipts in turn.

Brazil is a brilliant movie. Set "sometime in the Twentieth Century," it is populated by men and women in 1950s dress, by old-fashioned typewriters with attached "computer" screens (called consoles) hooked up to a "central computer." The movie's urban landscape is ugly—brown and gray and ominously oppressive like a nightmare in which walls suddenly take on life and start an inexorable process of moving to crush anyone caught between them. And walls do indeed have life of their own in *Brazil*. Walls, ceilings, and floors—everything is "alive" in Sam's apartment: at one point his air conditioning malfunctions and the ubiquitous Tuttle comes to the rescue and pulls out a section of wall, laying bare the virtual entrails of tubes and cords and mysterious-looking gadgets behind them. Houses are huge, threatening structures with an evil life of their own; apartments are encasements with walls that teem with ominous and mysterious life. Even roads are narrow slits through the surrounding gray of the landscape, separated from unruly nature by fences plastered over with ads and slogans such as "Happiness" and "Suspicion Breeds Confidence."

There is no happy end. Sam and his beloved, the woman from the dream, who as it turns out is called Jill Layton, finally settle down to make love in his mother's apartment after his own has been ravaged by Central Service and hers is off limits because she's a terrorism-suspect.[4] The riot police enter, kill her, and drag him off (i.e., they "invite" him to be interrogated) to come face to face with Jack and his scalpel. Sam "escapes" only by going mad.

The most frightening thing about this terrific and very funny movie is the normalcy—the way in which everybody accepts the terror and the tyranny and goes about the business of being part of it. The career-hungry Jack with the pretty and faceless wife is especially scary because he's so petit-bourgeois normal. Jack is not evil. He is a doting father and husband (although his job is number one). He does what he has to do to get up in the world. Sam is not evil either. He's unconscious. Somewhere in the depths of his being slumbers a dream of freedom and love and being a real person, but the dream can only surface when the mind is asleep. Sam's mother, the socialite "with connections," is not evil either. She's just using her influence to obtain the things she wants for herself and her son. She is a woman in a society where women are but ornamental flourishes, and she spends all her time trying to be a more attractive ornament, having her face and body put to the stretching hands and fat-and-wrinkle-eliminating scalpel of her plastic surgeon. And she is perhaps symbolic of her society: "In one of the final dream sequences, Helmond [the mother] becomes a metaphor for her society, her relentless quest for a 'rejuvenation' treatment leading to collapse and decay."[5] Even Mr. Helpman, the minister in charge of Information Retrieval, isn't evil. He's a helpless cripple who has to be lifted out of his wheelchair to take a leak and who takes advantage of his position to do not what he thinks is right—right and wrong are obsolete terms in this society—but what is expected.

The most sympathetic character in the movie is Sam's beloved, Jill Layton, who has both feet solidly planted in reality and tries to live her life despite the bureaucratic dystopia around her. She becomes an accidental victim of Sam's love for her and is killed, ironically, in full female drag. Normally Jill is a matter-of-fact young woman who dresses in a leather jacket and jeans and has her hair cut very short. She's almost masculine, or at least refusing to be feminine in a world where love is an impossibility. The moment she goes along with Sam's dream and dresses up in a negligé and wears a long blonde wig, she is killed.

Brazil portrays society as a machine operated by a huge army of docile bodies—an abstract machine, devoid of notions of value or morality. The machine itself, the chugging and functioning of all its parts, is the goal of all things. *1984*, the film, is not nearly as interesting, mostly because, as Hutton has pointed out, it is embalmed—"not so much interpreted as it is stuffed and mounted."[6] There are, however, felicitous and deliberate ironies connected with it. The movie was shot in 1984, covering the very days Orwell describes in his 1949 novel. The novel was primarily a satire on the state of individual freedoms (or lack thereof) in Stalin's Soviet Union,[7] although it clearly also saw the dangers of capitalism gone McCarthy. The film is set in Britain in the '40s. The locale is a drab, dirty, industrial city. The story is of a society where everything, love and thinking included, is forbidden. A war is being fought somewhere against rebels, and any notion of being separate, individual, not just an extension of the state, is out of the question. The movie is the story of a forbidden love affair that leads to rebellious thoughts and, eventually, to the demise of the lovers. The conflict between love and the ubiquitous state (Big Brother Is Watching You!) is central. The state is the totalitarian equivalent of an angry and suspicious god: constantly monitoring every thought and desire. People are allowed only to think and feel what the state/god perceives as beneficial to its purposes. Those thoughts and acts are called *moral*, all other ones are outlawed, immoral, get people in trouble with the authorities and an appointment, down the road, with the executioner.

Love is outlawed because, as I have said in connection with *Death Watch* and *Zardoz*, it tends to make people perceive themselves as individuals rather than as their social roles. Two people who suddenly discover love for each other concentrate their attention on the private emotion and on the other/themselves. The state is backgrounded. The totalitarian state, like the jealous God of the Bible, cannot tolerate this.

■ Male Supremacy

The tangle of love and God and state is central also to the 1989 movie, *The Handmaid's Tale*, based on Margaret Atwood's novel of the same name. But into the mix are thrown still another couple of ingredients that help create an explosive concoction: gender and procreativity. Following the book rather closely, the movie is most frightening because it takes its point of departure in the current debate between pro- and anti-choice advocates on the issue of abortion.

The "what if" question the movie asks, and one that could become real and that we all should be asking ourselves, is, "What if Pat Robertson, Oral Roberts, or Jerry Fallwell (or, more likely, all of them) actually came into power and could dictate his terms?" The answer is a totalitarian regime intent on eradicating, especially, women's sense of self. Women are to be reduced to roles, appendices of various kinds to men. There are Wives, who are beautiful and in charge of the home. There are Cooks and Maids, called Marthas, and there are the Handmaids: the women who still are reproductively viable and who are assigned to the households of men who can afford them—to bring children into the world. Handmaids are state-owned and assigned wombs. They participate with the male head of household and his wife in a religious/sexual "ceremony," wherein the biblical story of Rachel —who was infertile and gave her husband a female slave to bring forth children—is invoked, leading up to the (hoped-for) impregnation. The three of them are supposed to conceive as a team. The child will belong to the wife and her husband. The handmaid moves on to her next assignment.

The most interesting aspect of the movie, for my purposes here, is the way in which the new totalitarian patriarchy, using the Old Testament as its "sole guide book and constitution," attempts to turn women who have had identities of their own into categories of females who have to make men, God, and the state the only goals of their lives. Women with viable ovaries who have somehow been categorized as rebellious or bad are put on trucks marked "livestock," and shipped off to Red Centers where they are to be trained as Handmaids. The technique of treating people as cattle, as things, goods, has of course always been an effective one. The Nazis used it with great success. There is nothing like it to take away a sense of self and self-worth.

At Red Center, the women have to sleep in huge dorms; they are forced to sing hymns, to pledge allegiance to the patriarchal God, and to being public-service wombs: ". . . leave us empty to be filled, oh God, make us fruitful." They are indoctrinated to believe that all acts of sex, rape included, are to be blamed on the woman: "She led them on." One woman "confesses" that she was raped by six guys when she was fourteen and is rebuked with the communal chant of "Whore! Whore!" To further insure compliance, each woman has to ingest as part of her breakfast meal a cup full of tranquilizers: medicated docility. Red Center prepares the women, under the tutelage of "aunts," to be docile bodies of the greenhouse variety. Any sense of self is discouraged since Handmaids will have no individual function.

Once assigned to a "post," the women are given names that define them as the property of and procreative extensions of the male head of household. Kate, the protagonist, is assigned to a high-level commander and becomes Offred (of Fred). She has no name of her own. Women have no identities; even wives are only members, if privileged ones, of their husbands' menagerie. Marthas serve and clean and cook, wives look pretty and cut flowers, handmaids are vessels to be filled.

The nightmare of *The Handmaid's Tale,* as of *Brazil,* is that it is all so recognizable. Although the movie is generally pale when compared to the novel, the one aspect that makes it terrifyingly effective, is the *reality* of the physical world it depicts. It is our world with an evil twist.

The three movies discussed in this chapter have shown power at its most naked, the fist out of the glove. The prime tool for turning people into docile bodies is the constant threat of violence and violation: police, military, interrogations, summary executions, and people who just disappear.

■ Notes

1. From Greek "nowhere," i.e., an imagined state or society that does not have a real-world counterpart.
2. Hutton 1987:7.
3. Hutton (ibid.,6) interprets Sam differently: "Sam's tragedy is that he neither grasps the nature of his society's power pyramid nor the consequences of casting himself off from it. Cut off from his own class, he becomes a victim." I beg to differ. It is not that Sam doesn't understand his own society, he just doesn't seem to care. His only dream is of a personal, romantic kind, not of a societal. That is of course the ultimate error in a bureaucratic police state where social and bureaucratic position is all. Otherwise, I find Hutton's analysis both penetrating and informative.
4. Hutton (ibid., 2) makes the observation that the gender imagery in *Brazil* is rather unusual: Jill, Sam's truck-driver beloved, is throughout the movie a rather unfeminine presence with her short- cropped hair, leather jacket, and blue-collar job. She's perfectly capable of taking care of herself—until Sam begins to "help" her. She is finally killed when she dons his mother's long, blonde wig and wears a frilly dress.
5. Ibid., 7.
6. Ibid., 5.
7. This, incidentally, is also true of his other great satirical novel, *Animal Farm*, where everyone is equal, but some are more equal than others. Orwell was an independent socialist who obviously found it easier (understandable in the case of Stalin) to criticize purported socialist or communist regimes than capitalist ones.

10 ■

The Human Form Submerged, Beleaguered, and Triumphant

■ Drugged Docility

In this chapter we will encounter radical routes to creating humanlike forms that are but human in name: genetic engineering used to create perfect and perfectly docile beings; or docility secured by submerging the core of a human into an encasement of technology: cyborgs that merge human flesh and hard-core machinery. Typically, the heroes of these films are also the scientific monsters who have to find a way to connect, triumphantly, with their core of humanity.

In *The Handmaid's Tale* the morning dose of tranquility-inducing drugs is only a minor aspect of the endeavor to eradicate opposition and individuality. In other sf "utopias" it is the central one. Before making the *Star Wars* trilogy, Lucas made *THX 1138*, depicting a future "cybernetic society"[1] where people are controlled by megadoses of mind drugs. "Big Brother" is constantly watching, and loudspeakers keep reminding people that if the current drug dose isn't sufficient, the solution is to have it adjusted. In Truffaut's *Fahrenheit 451* (the temperature at which books burn), a totalitarian regime is determined to burn all books and thus eradicate any individualized experience and thinking. People are kept happy by drugs and idiotic-happy TV. But the most interesting entry in this category is *A Clockwork Orange*, another great movie from Stanley Kubrick.[2]

Clockwork Orange is the story of Alex, a small-time hoodlum inhabiting a future landscape of urban blight and decay. Alex and his "droogs" (compatriots)[3] drift around the desolate streets at night, looking for "a little of the good ol' ultra-violence" and a chance to "perform a little in-out, in-out," their version of sex: rape. The society is pure social-Darwinian jungle; the youngest and the strongest win and steal and maim and rape more or less at will. Alex and his droogs move like perpetual raiders across their urban hunting grounds, doing what pleases the violent-bone.

Alex has one, if not redeeming, then curiously unexpected, feature: he is fond of Beethoven's music, above all the *Ninth Symphony*. This causes conflict between him and the "droogs" and leads eventually to their framing him. Or rather, they knock him unconscious at the site of a break-in where he has killed a woman with a giant sculpture of a penis: the movie is full of phallic symbols of evil, such as Alex's pet snake. Alex goes to jail and becomes a model prisoner. He wants to get out as fast as possible —even at the cost of mouthing Christian morality and snuggling up to the gay prison parson. Alex actually likes reading the Bible, especially the parts about Christ being whipped and the thorny crown. He imagines himself in Roman military get-up, whacking away with the whip. Then his chance comes. A new technique to make the habitually criminal into peaceful and productive citizens is being tested. Alex jumps at the chance to get out. He undergoes a combination of shock and drug treatment that is supposed to make him incapable of violence. Put simply: he is shown scenes of sickening violence and made to feel severely ill as he watches. The outcome is that even the thought of violence (rape included) makes him seriously ill.

But a question remains as to the nature or Alex's new docility. The prison parson states it clearly: "It's debatable if the technique makes a man good. Goodness comes from within, goodness is *chosen*. When a man cannot choose he ceases to be a man." The Christian and the scientific models are juxtaposed: religion says allegiance to the divine makes a man desire to be good, science says docility and obedience to law can be attained via drugs and

A Clockwork Orange is the story of Alex, a small-time hoodlum inhabiting a future landscape of blight and decay. This picture is unnerving because the eclectic symbols (e.g., the clown eye and the bowler) are recognizable, yet resist the usual interpretations. (Warner Bros. Productions, 1971. Still courtesy of MOMA film stills archive.)

force. Alex is incapable of making such subtle distinctions. He just wants, at least he says he wants, to be good and get out of jail. That is the prize for undergoing the treatment. Once it is finished —and proves successful—he will be set free. For a while, after his release from prison, Alex is docile, and he even becomes a victim of violence. His old droogs have changed sides and are now cops: exponents of sanctioned violence. They haven't changed—they are still as violent and immoral as they always were. The only difference is that now they wear uniforms and the violence they engage in is sanctioned by society.

What Kubrick's film says is, in the last analysis, that a society is as violent as its ideology makes it. In the England depicted in the movie, all kinds of violence are rampant and freedoms are vanishing (at one point a prison official says that jails soon will be full of political prisoners and thus the other criminals have to be taken care of). So Alex and his droogs are products of their world, and making Alex incapable of violent acts does not make him good, nor does an army of "treated" Alexes make the society just and right. The "changed" Alex may be docile because he is physically incapable of violence, but his values haven't changed. He would still be violent if it didn't make him sick.

In the end, Alex is freed from his imposed docility—through an act of violence: because Beethoven's Ninth—his favorite piece of music—was the accompanying music to some of his sessions, he reacts to it the way he does to violence. One of his victims from the old days manages to lock him up in a room while attacking his ears with the "Ode to Joy" at full electronic fury. Unable to stand it, Alex throws himself out a second-floor window. When he awakens from the coma, he is "cured"—and is recruited by the government. He can now be as violent as he wants to be: the good old "ultraviolence"—licensed and approved by the Ministry of the Interior.

As was the case in *Dr. Jekyll and Mr. Hyde,* the dual "personalities" of Alex are embodied in one man. He is scientifically "transformed" from violent to pacifist, but the effect is only temporary. A more radical method is to get at the source: genetic engineering.

■ Building Bodies

Under the auspices of a the U.S. government, a group of scientists are busy putting the final touches to an experiment so important that it has to take place deep in a basement behind guarded doors marked "Top Secret." The scientists are making a genetic cocktail consisting of six parts sperm, donated by as many "distinguished men" chosen for their "genetic excellence," and one part ovum from a ravishing blonde in a red dress, "a remarkable young woman." The experiment is designed to "produce a physically, mentally, and spiritually advanced human being." This is the premise—or, rather, half of the premise—of the movie *Twins*. In passing, I note that (a) the scientists apparently have found a way to isolate the excellent qualities of the committee of fathers—no mean feat; it certainly eluded Hitler's scientists; (b) that the mother, a la *Handmaid's Tale*, is nothing but the greenhouse in which all this genetic distinction is going to come to, let's say, *fruition*.

The experiment is successful. It produces Julius who looks an awful lot like Arnold Schwarzenegger (more about him later). As soon as he's born, Julius is whisked off to a remote Caribbean island and brought up scientifically. Again, the result is perfect: the adult Julius is a gentle muscle man brimming over with book-ish knowledge and speaking, no less, with a pronounced German accent. One wonders if this is the gift of one of the committee and if so, if it is a by-product of some desired trait or it is a desired trait unto itself. After all, German accents and intelligence/high culture do seem to be tied together in American popular culture: scientists, psychologists in particular, tend to have German accents in the movies.

When Julius is thirty-five, his educators decide the time has come to break the news to him: his mother didn't die in childbirth, *and* Julius has a twin. The experiment was not totally perfect. The ovum split and produced a second child. So not only does Julius

During a break-in, Alex kills a woman with a giant sculpture of a penis: the movie is full of phallic symbols of evil. Notice also the erotic art on the walls: women as whores and tempting apertures. (*A Clockwork Orange*. Warner Bros. Productions, 1971. Still courtesy of MOMA film stills archive.)

have a twin, he has a monozygotic twin. But the reason that the experiment was not totally successful, the twin is not, despite the zygotic facts, an exact replica of Julius (if he had been, the experiment would not only have been successful, it would have been *doubly* successful). The twin, whose name is Vincent—and who looks like Danny DeVito—is Julius's opposite. Somehow the zygotic split was unequal: "All the purity and strength went into Julius, and all the crap that was left over went into what *you* see in the mirror every morning," as one scientist under extreme duress (threats of being roughed up by Julius) contemptuously says to Vincent. The scientists considered Vincent a noxious side effect and sent him off to be reared in an orphanage. Vince draws the logical conclusion, "I'm genetic garbage!"[4]

Since the movie discounts the technicalities of how all of this works, as it were, genetically, I will do likewise and just accept it as fact. After all, it *does* happen—in the movie. And it isn't about science or genetics, anyway. It is about—well, it purports to be about—family and values and love, but it *is* about the humanizing quality of American (pop) culture. Julius is the naif, the Kaspar Hauser,[5] who has to be taught about the real world. He has lived his entire life in isolation, learning everything from books and dry old scientists. As everyone knows, that means he doesn't know a thing about *real* life. But brother Vince is there to teach him. Vince, a small-time con man, has things to learn from Julius too, of course—about honesty, love, and morality. But mostly the movie is a record of how Julius learns to "nuke" food ("I like nuked food!"), how he learns to use colloquialisms ("I'm pissed!"), and to wear hip clothes and walk hip. Julius is, as Vince says, a bit stiff: "Ever see Frankenstein?" He's a machine and has to become fully human by loosening up, drinking beer, hanging out, busting up bad guys, and, most importantly, getting laid.

Twins is a comedy and does not ask to be nor should it be taken too seriously. But it can serve as an introduction to a number of interesting issues: the Body-Beautiful Phenomenon (the "Schwarzenegger" phenomenon), the Body-Clean Phenomenon, and the Body-Perfect/Body-Immortal Phenomenon.

■ The Body-Beautiful Phenomenon

When Arnold Schwarzenegger first burst onto the scene, as the star of *Pumping Iron*, body building was still an oddity. Reactions from adults were either contemptuous or downright dismissive. But a cult was born. Mr. Schwarzenegger was invited to the United States and made his first Hollywood movies, the *Conan the Barbarian* series, based on the comic strip of the same name. The audience consisted almost exclusively of males, hovering around the onset of puberty. The reason is obvious: in a world where clear distinctions between male and female are disappearing, at least on a superficial level, some budding males may need a role model that has all-male secondary gender traits. Early Schwarzenegger epics are pure, uninhibited violence: huge men with rippling muscles ripping not-quite-so-huge males apart.

Since Schwarzenegger began his career, things have happened in society: muscle has become mainstream. Millions of people all over the world lift weights, pose endlessly in front of mirrors, and inform whoever is interested that they're working seriously on their delts or abs or triceps. The Schwarzenegger "mystique" consists of a complex of traits: (1) his imposing physique; (2) his foreignness; (3) the very fact that he cannot act, his machinelike awkwardness. The sum of those features is that he is alien, robotlike, not quite human. His best movie, and the one that used his special talents to best effect, was *The Terminator*, in which he played an android, a machine designed to doggedly pursue and kill a specific target. Schwarzenegger, the actor, is like a piece of powerful technology: you move him around and press the buttons and he goes into motion. He is the ultimate docile body. The built-up body, enhanced with steroids, encasing a totally docile mind: the one-track and very clever computer that does what it is programmed to do, and little else.[6]

What I'm leading up to is that identifying with machines, trying to become as hard, glistening, and functional as machines is *in*. We're beginning to see machines as sexy and desirable. We admire the "artificial" body, the body that is built with the help of machines. In a paper about dystopia and time travel, Penley makes this observation about Schwarzenegger/the Terminator: "Its chrome skeleton with its hydraulic muscles and tendons of flexible cable looks like the Nautilus machines Schwarzenegger uses to build his body."[7]

Exercising helps make the exerciser more mentally machinelike too, more docile. It's called discipline: people get out of bed or the office to go and work out when the body is screaming for rest or food. Exercise means getting on the stairmaster and having time chopped into little blinking segments, following the commands on the panel to move faster, push harder, stand up straighter. The exerciser becomes attuned to the machine and its demands. Working out compliments work: hours spent in the company of machines that demand exclusive attention, tell people what to do, force work upon them, chop waking hours into artificial segments.

■ The Body-Clean Phenomenon

An aspect of the movie *Twins*, is that not only does Julius, the human-by-committee, have rippling muscles and a well-trained mind, but he is clean. Having grown up in a tropical paradise, having lived on a diet of health food and milk and not having abused his body with alcohol, drugs, or sex, he's uncontaminated —until he meets brother Vince. Then he learns to like fast food, beer, and sex.

Julius, the "clean machine," reflects the "just say no" age, the age of drugs, of herpes and hepatitis and AIDS. The societal response has been "more control." More tests to check that the body is healthy, drug free, worth employing and investing in. Never before has the body been so beleaguered, controlled, and manipulated. In many companies, prospective employees have to submit to urine tests, health exams, and a battery of psychological "aptitude" tests to be considered for employment. The '80s taught people to fear and worry about bodily fluids.

And it is not only the body. The mind is constantly tested, too. School is a parade of tests and test scores. Children are constantly being measured for "basic skills," not because these skills will make them into more fulfilled human beings, but because the youngsters are the future work force. They have to have the skills the job market needs and demands. Today's world is a buyer's market: corporations with jobs to fill can make demands on those seeking work that would have seemed ludicrous, even tyrannical, to people a few decades ago. But employers apparently feel they have to be sure of the workers' docility. Anyone who is not a perfectly healthy, well-adjusted (meaning docile) specimen is suspect and not worthy of holding a job (or of having an Olympic medal, as the Ben-Johnson-and-the-steroids melee showed).

■ The Body-Perfect/Body-Immortal Phenomenon

In the movie *Parts: The Clonus Horror,* handsome young men and women mill around on what looks like a slightly strange college campus. They compete athletically and dream of the day they can be "transferred." The strangeness derives from the fact that they constantly are being followed, monitored, and reported on by teams of men, dressed in warm-up suits. And despite the fact that the students look and sound perfectly American, the place they dream of being transferred to is a mythical-sounding place called "America."

Finally, one young man—George—who has excelled in a foot race, a push-up competition, and in wrestling, is found ready to be transferred. He says good-bye to his girlfriend, who says awkward things like "I've become accustomed to you—I like having you touch me." George dismisses her worries about losing contact with him by reminding her that they will see each other again in "America." And so George embarks on his trip. He is taken to a lab, is asked to drink an orange liquid and to count backwards from a hundred. He does and passes out. The officials undress him, give him shots, stuff him in a plastic bag which they place in the freezer: the frozen body is convulsed in abrogated flight, the face caught in an unfinished scream. The plastic bag in the freezer is the mythical "America": the project George is part of is called "Project America," and George and all the other young "students" on "campus" are so much meat to be butchered when needed. The "campus," of course, is not a campus—it is the locus of the Clonus Project, an "organ farm," where clones of living men and women are being raised to be organ donors.

The clones are made from cells taken from the originals, with or without their knowledge. The idea is to give certain men and women "immortality." But not everyone: as a senator campaigning to be president, says, "That would be too expensive." Clones are given the first names of their originals and are referred to not as human beings, but as "clones" and "it." They are not humans; they are flesh-and-blood shadows. They owe their very existence to their original and are given whatever half-life they have only to be "organ accounts," to be drawn upon by the originals in case of emergency.

Parts is the story of Richard, who belongs to a new generation of clones with average or above-average intelligence.[8] The norm until this experimental generation has been to drop a virus into the original clone cell at the time of inception. The virus causes the mental abilities to be impaired. Further evidence of innate humanity are solved surgically: "One of the most serious problems encountered was the suppression of individuality. This problem proved temporary as medical technicians learned that through simple lobotomies, clones could be made benign and cooperative." It is never made clear why the experiment with clones who are allowed to have full mental capacities was incepted (I assume the reasons have to do with plot rather than with clones), but the results are predictable. Richard and a female clone, Lena, discover a sense of self and each other. They fall in love and begin to feel separate from the other clones and guards and teachers. They form a little world of their own and decide to examine the bigger world of Clonus to find out what is going on. This is, of course, the *fier baiser* motif: humanization through love.

The movie addresses, in its own too sensational way, the questions that recent advances in medicine have pressed upon us. Moral questions: with our new transplant technology, which allows not only livers and kidneys but also hearts and lungs to be transplanted from a donor organism into a recipient whose own organ is not working, people no longer die from diseases that were invariably killers in the past. Humans are conquering disease and keeping death at bay. We are reversing nature, hoping one day to be able to eliminate death and natural diseases entirely. But the problem remains; where is the boundary between alleviating human suffering and tampering with nature? Where is the line between medicine as the curer and medicine as the creator of artificial humans? In a sense the movie can be seen as a dramatization of a paragraph by Helman in a brilliant article that deals with "spare part" surgery:

... with the ability we now have to transplant "bone, cartilage, cornea, fascia, heart, joints, kidney, liver, lung, lymph nodes, nerves, pancreas, parathyroid, skin, spleen, tendons and thymus, as well as transfusions of blood, plasma, and bone marrow. Some grafts—such as skin, veins or muscle—can be transplanted from one part of the recipient's body to another ("autografts"), but the majority of grafts originate in other people ("allografts"). The closer the kin relationship between recipient and donor (especially a twin, a parent or child) the less likely the graft is to be "rejected." In the curious jargon of the subject, the collection of organs from the donor, living or dead, is sometimes termed the *"organ harvest"* —and sometimes this takes place from "neomorts," those liminal people who are *"brain dead,"* but whose vital functions are artificially prolonged by a "life support system."[9]

To use the term of the Krokers, the body is becoming increasingly *exteriorized.* Bodies are no longer self-contained organ complexes; they are loci of medical and scientific experimentation. Organs are no longer integral to a particular organism; they are parts that can be exchanged. Many people carry in their wallets, along with their driver's license and medical-insurance card, a signed affidavit stating that such and such organs can be taken out in case of an accident.

But there is a problem. We are rapidly approaching a point where bodies are regarded and treated as machines that can be repaired and given spare parts. The problem, as sf sees it, has to do with the notion of self, of soul: the essence of individuality that makes Me distinctly different from You. If I have the kidney, lung, blood, or heart of another person, am I myself or that person? Or am I a third person who is an amalgam of the two? And then there is the problem of implants, artificial spare parts—prosthetic organs—that take the place of organic ones.[10] Artificial bones, joints, blood vessels, hearts and heart valves, teeth, esophagus, limbs, and just recently, artificially grown skin, constitute just a partial list of prosthetic devices medicine is capable of implanting into living organisms. And exteriorized body parts such as artificial ears, kidneys, wombs (to be discussed in detail in the following chapter), and lungs replace intra-organic damaged body parts.

This means, of course, on the positive side, that pain is alleviated, damaged bodies are made to function and live normal lives again. All the transplants and implants help real human beings extend their lives. But, on the negative side, there is the dehumanization, the progressive, to use Helman's term, "industrialization" of the body: "The individual's body is now part-industrial. Her implants link her permanently to the world of industry and science. She is also the ultimate *consumer*, incorporating the products of industry into her very body, and she is a living, walking advertisement for their efficacy."[11] Or to put it in the terms I have used in this book: the body that depends on science and technology, the body that has technology and science inside it, is likely to be a docile one where it comes to the demands of science and technology and the corporations that own them. Humans become less and less individual selves, capable of making decisions concerning their own lives and deaths. As science enters not only work and the home, but also the human body itself, humans are going to find it increasingly difficult to find a sense of self that is separate from machines and technology.

The fate of a cyborg—a human being dependent on one or more mechanical devices that take care of some of the vital physiological functions—is the subject of the two *Robocop* movies. In a future Detroit that is different from the present only by degree, crime is rampant and the corporations, notably Omni Consumer Products (OCP), are ready to pounce and take over everything, from the police force to organized crime. TV is a bit more mindless, with endless comedy/titillation shows that have no other function than to amuse and stimulate the male sex drive. Interspersed with the inanity are commercials for the new generation of American cars—6000 SUX because bigger is better—and for NUKE'M, a board game for the entire family where the Final Solution to recalcitrant Third World countries that refuse to accept the just and natural dominance of American corporations is to NUKE'M. And there are ads for Jarvik Sports Hearts with "extended warranties." The news is only slightly less inane than the other entertainment. Newscasters manage to be upbeat and happy even if the news involves a Star Wars laser beam gone bonkers and killing people by the hundreds.

In this future, the police force has become an understaffed, beleaguered target of organized crime. Every day sees cops killed and dismembered. It has become so bad that the policemen's union is considering a strike. The stage is set for OCP, which has managed to secure a "contract with the City of Detroit to run and fund the Police Department." What OCP really wants is a new market and testing ground for its own military technology.[12]

Among other things, *Robocop* is a vicious—because it unfortunately is close to the truth—satire of corporate politics and infighting. Corporations, like other huge bureaucracies, take on a life of their own. They become states within the state, organisms surrounded by a "hostile" world and thus justified in doing any and everything to "survive," win, or better the other guy. On a similar note, Glass, using a term he has coined, New Bad Future (NBF) movies, says of *Robocop:* "NBF films provide viewers with an unconscious vehicle for dealing with the collective issues raised by the transition, under capitalist control, from a relatively stable national, mechanical/industrial society to a new and uncertain transnational information technology order."[13]

Robocop focuses on the Corporation, on the internecine warfare inside OCP that determines which new technological disasters to unleash on the citizens of Detroit. The battle is fought between two of the top executives of OCP, both vying for position to move into the top executive office and virtual ownership of the city. In *Robocop 2*, this literally becomes the case. Because the city owes money to OCP, the corporation begins legal procedures to add the city to its corporate empire. The battle inside OCP is fought between *Dick* Jones—as we shall see, the name is not incidental—and Bob Morton, who represent different technological approaches to the creation of the new super-cop. They also represent all the worst in patriarchal capitalism: two carriers of the male signifier who are obsessed with winning and reaping their awards in the forms of female favors, drugs, and power. Their battles are fought in boardrooms, elevators, and corporate toilets, where Morton, penis in hand, crows to whoever cares to listen about how he's going to wipe out Jones. The movie has an obsession with male genitalia and macho power play. At one point a female cop is arresting a male suspect—as he is taking a leak. He overpowers her by taunting her to take a look at his still unfettered penis. And the imagery of huge, muscular erections, high-rises jutting aggressively toward the sky, is ubiquitous. This is a movie that feasts on representations of macho corporate capitalism as a sick and moribund cultural phase.

The two OCP adversaries, Dick Jones and Bob Morton, each sponsor their own penile extension to fight their corporate and personal battles. ED 209, sponsored by Jones, fails, and Morton and his Robocop-project get the go-ahead.

Morton needs an organic core to his Robocop: a good, tough cop who is declared legally dead. In the movie's Detroit, that is not much of a challenge. A young cop named Murphy is transferred to the worst inner city precinct and teams up with his new partner, a tough female cop by the name of Lewis. In a showdown with a gang of robbers (in the *paysage moralisé* of an old steel mill), Murphy is shot up and declared legally dead at the hospital. Bob Morton and his crew save Murphy's mental abilities and hook him to a computer and a total body prosthesis. The outcome is a programmed law-enforcement machine, complete with a built-in machine gun and tool kit.

Robocop is Superman and Terminator rolled into one. He is one tough, determined, smart, state-of-the-art *docile* piece of semi-human machinery. He is Murphy, but he doesn't know he is; his memory has been blanked. All the "self" he knows is Robocop: "The best of two worlds: the best reflexes modern technology has to offer, on-board computer-assisted memory and a lifetime of on-the-street law-enforcement programming." And he is of course on duty twenty-four hours a day, does not strike or need to eat (except for the occasional can of baby food) or sleep. And he does as he's told.

Robocop exists not only as an organism in a technological land-

Robocop is a legally dead cop hooked to a computer and a body-prosthesis: a programmed law-enforcement machine, complete with built-in machine gun and tool kit. (Orion Productions, 1987. Still courtesy of Orion Productions.)

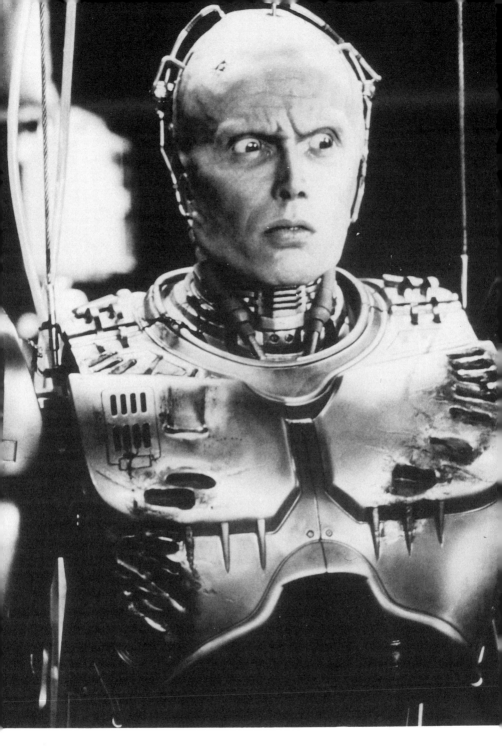

scape that threatens to dwarf him and take him over; he exists as a precarious lump of amputated flesh enclosed in technology. Arms, legs, memory, nervous system—all of it is exteriorized. These body parts are under the control of others outside him. They are foreign to the center of human organism left inside the steel plating and the artificial skin. None of Robocop/Murphy's organs, his memory and brain included, exist for the purposes of his own organism, for his own self.

Robocop/Murphy is a tool, or as the OCP executives are fond of repeating, a "product." The ideal "citizen" in the OCP empire. A docile army of effective killing machines like Robocop in the hands of a corporation with no scruples, unlimited means and power and ties to crime would easily make slaves of the rest of the world's inhabitants, forced to work and consume for the corporation.

But the flicker of human life inside the breastplates and computer-operated body sparks a glimmer of hope, too. Slowly, from the recesses of suppressed memories belonging to Murphy—cop, husband, and father—emerges a sense of nontechnological self. Helped by Lewis who has recognized Murphy inside Robocop, Murphy remembers who he is and was and realizes how he came to be what he is now. He goes on a personal vendetta to kill those responsible for his "death" and the loss of his wife and son, who have moved away. He gets his revenge after much gratuitous and explicit violence (Act III is set in the *paysage moralisé* of the steel mill).[14] Finally, after he has killed Dick Jones (appropriately, he falls from the top floor of the corporate erection), the last survivor of the corporate bad guys, he struts out of the board room—all macho posture—as the president stops him in his tracks: "Nice shootin' son, what's your name?"—"Murphy!" The man in the machine has won: his limbs and part of his brain may be exteriorized (after all, he can still video-tape things he "sees" and plug himself into a monitor to play back), but the control is Murphy's, a man with memories, emotions, and a soul/self. In the end, the human body, meaning the essence of what it is to be human as opposed to being a machine, is triumphant.[15]

The attempt to create the ultimate docile body can of course be attacked another way. Instead of trying to make—however tampered with and amputated—real human bodies into machinelike robots, a type of machine might be invented/created to take the place of humans. That is what "Androids" are all about. A kind of separate, scientific "species" that promises to be everything humans are not: first and foremost, docile.

■ Notes

1. As Ryan and Kellner (1990:59) call it.
2. Based on the novel of the same name by Anthony Burgess.
3. Presumably derived from the Russian word for friend, "Drug."
4. Sort of a genetic Mr. Hyde to Julius's Dr. Jekyll.
5. Kaspar Hauser was a "feral" child, found at age sixteen in a basement in a German village. He had been tied up and deprived of human company until he was found. He could not speak or walk and knew nothing of the existence of other people. His story has been brilliantly filmed by the German filmmaker Werner Herzog as *Every Man for Himself and God Against Them All.*
6. I don't want to imply that he's less than human privately. He comes across in interviews as a charming, intelligent man who has negotiated his one asset into a million-dollar fortune.
7. Penley 1990:118. I'm not so sure, incidentally, that Schwarzenegger uses Nautilus equipment. Like most body builders, he certainly "pumps iron," uses free weights. Still, the image is striking.
8. *Parts: The Clonus Horror* is a relatively obscure movie and for that reason I give a rather lengthy plot outline.
9. Helman 1988; emphases mine.
10. This and the following is no more than a paraphrasing of ibid., 15.
11. Ibid., 15.
12. In our own time, both Miami and New York will turn over the running of schools to the "corporations."
13. Glass 1990:3.
14. It's actually a ruin of a factory. That it's a ruin enhances the moralizing effect: the ruin is from a time when machines and technology were used less exploitatively; it is really the same image as the alien reactor in *Total Recall.*
15. Also in *Robocop 2*, where Murphy's last words to his colleague, Lewis, are "After all, we're only human!"

11 ▪

Have Mind, Seek Soul:
The Android's Quest

▪ Deadly Docility

The final link in my "plot chain"—the denouement, if you will—is the point where the boundary between human and machine has finally become so blurred that there no longer is a difference between the two. In *Robocop* a human is encarcerated in a killing machine, his self effectively drugged under. In the films discussed in this chapter, humans have become virtually extinct and the machines have taken over. The central conflict is between opposed methods of "procreation": natural or scientific. Naturally created humans have souls and selves, mechanical ones are, or they were supposed to be, simply more or less evil pets. The last image of the chapter is the reversal of human/machine: androids who are more human than humans.

The main imagery system of *The Terminator* is *machines*. Set in Los Angeles in 1984 and 2029, the movie is, among other things, a parable of our love affair with technology and what it may lead to. This is the ultimate *technologie moralisée* movie. L.A. in 1984 is full of people who live lives defined by machines, "Machines provide the texture and substance of this film: cars, trucks, motorcycles, radios, TVs, time clocks, phones, answering machines, beepers, hair dryers, Sony Walkmen, automated factory equipment."[1]

And killing machines: guns, guns, guns. L.A. in A.D. 2029 is the logical outcome of the 1984 version: a huge, blue ruin where human beings are small, scared, and few, scurrying among the detritus, surrounded by smoldering fires and flying machines that scour the ground with searchlights and kill any human on sight.

There was an atomic war, and after the war, the machines, notably a defense network computer (shades of *Colossus: The Forbin Project*), "hooked into everything." Machines "got smart—a new form of intelligence." 2029 machines are waging a war of extermination against humans, fielding new, machine-invented machines and weaponry.

L.A. 1984 is cars, the endless artificiality of the city, emphasized in the movie by having most scenes take place at night with the reflected glare of neon lights bouncing off glass-encased buildings and wet pavement. And it is the thousands of technological gadgets that soothe, please, and entertain but also isolate and alienate.

Sarah Connor is a waitress in a hamburger joint. She shares an apartment with a friend, Ginger. It's Friday night and the two young women are preparing to go out with their boyfriends. They stand side by side in front of the bathroom mirror, shaping their coifs with electrical hair dryers. Side by side, but not together, technology separates them: Ginger is rollicking in anticipation and to the beat of a song being pumped into her head from her Walkman. They check the answering machine. A message from Sarah's boyfriend: he can't make it. Ginger is enraged. Just because he has a Porsche doesn't mean he can do that—and on Friday night! The scene demands that the audience notice the technology, the Walkmans, the hair dryers, the Porsche (we are the technology we own), the answering machine. All of the gadgets are common enough—the audience would not have noticed them but for the director's insistence. Sarah drives off on her own, on her little Vespa scooter, as Ginger and her boyfriend settle in to an evening of lovemaking. Their naked bodies meet, but their minds are separate, each lost in the musical thump of the exteriorized ears of a Walkman.

The movie is more than just a bleak vision of the future of techno-society. It is about the demise of a soulless technological empire and the rise, literally, from its ashes of a new one, based on emotion, on closeness, on love. *The Terminator* is a retelling of the story of the first Christians. It is a retelling of the myth central to Christian mythology: the virgin birth, the ordinary woman who is chosen to give birth to a savior and who grows to be strong and tough and sure enough of herself to be equal to the task.

L.A., *A.D.* 2029 (the *A.D.* is important, part of the religious imagery): the machines have almost lost the war because the humans, after having been on the verge of extinction, after having been dragged—branded like cattle—to extermination camps, finally have found a leader. John Connor learned how to fight and organize from his mother, and his presence has forced a turn in the tides. Now the humans have the upper hand and Sarah Connor, John Connor's mother, has become a legend among the freedom fighters. But the machines stage one last desperate attempt at regaining the momentum: they send their latest "creation," a Cyborg 101—"a cybernetic organism"—back to 1984 to kill the mother of John Connor or JC, the new Christ.

The Terminator is, among other things, a time-travel movie: the cyborg, called a Terminator, is sent back via "time-displacement equipment" and arrives, naked as a newborn, in a charge of electricity and a swish as from an object being flushed from a vacuum, at a scenic viewpoint just outside L.A., 1984. To protect Sarah and insure his own birth, Connor sends back one of his own men, Kyle Reese. The remainder of the movie is the record of the battle between these two for the life of Sarah. They are both in 1984 to stay—as soon as Kyle is sent through, the machine is blown up (which tense to use is a bit of a problem when discussing a movie that constantly switches between future and present).

The Terminator is the ultimate "industrial body," as Kyle Reese explains to Sarah: the Cyborg 101 is an evolutionary notch above its predecessor, the 600. The 101 has "a combat chassis, microprocessor controlled, fully armed, very tough. But outside it's living human tissue, flesh, skin, hair, blood—grown for the cyborgs.[2] The 600 series had rubber skin, we spotted them easily, but these are new. They look human, sweat, bad breath—everything. Very hard to spot." Helman's Industrial Body. But the Terminator is also the ultimate docile body: strong, smart—at what it's supposed to do—and "it can't be bargained with, it can't be reasoned with. It doesn't feel pity or remorse or fear. It absolutely will not stop *ever*"—until it has killed Sarah. It is the new machine-man that sees the world filtered through red-tinted computer vision. It will never question an order. It does not feel pain; it stops only momentarily to repair itself when damaged. It has no other "feeling" than to fulfill its mission, no other "desire" than to obey its master. If the Terminator succeeds, humans will be a thing of the past; the machines with the "new intelligence" will rule the world and keep cyborg mockeries of the human form as violent and totally obedient pets.

The Terminator, working methodically, kills off the Sarah Connors in the L.A. phone directory one by one. Having worked his way down the—short—list, he is soon stalking the "real" Sarah, the one who is, if Reese succeeds, the mother-to-be of the twenty-first century JC. The Terminator finally finds Sarah in a bar/disco called Tech-Noir (black technology).

In the end, all goes according to the Book: JC knew what he did when he sent his lieutenant back in time to find Sarah. He had primed him by giving him a photo of her. Kyle Reese spent his time in the "catacombs" of 2029, studying the photograph, and, like so many a folklore hero, he fell in love with the beautiful "princess" in the picture. Kyle is fated to play Joseph to Sarah's Mary. The "virgin birth" almost is one: Kyle and Sarah have sex but he's not really there. If he belongs in the future and has been sent, like an Announcing Angel/Holy Spirit, to prepare Sarah and to impregnate her, then he's not *really* there to have sex with her and impregnate her, is he? Penley says that "if John Connor had not sent Kyle Reese back in time to be his father, he would never have been born. But he was born, so Kyle Reese must *already* have traveled back to the past to impregnate Sarah Connor."[3] As soon as he has performed his dual function of protection and impregnation, Kyle dies like a praying mantis.

John Connor is the child who orchestrates his own primal scene, one inflected by a family romance, moreover, because he is able to choose his own father, singling out Kyle from the other soldiers. That such a fantasy is an attempted end-run around Oedipus is also obvious: John Connor can identify with his father, can even *be* his father in the scene of parental intercourse, and also conveniently dispose of him in order to go off with (in) his mother.[4]

JC may be the savior of the future world, the one who frees humans from the machines. But he is the child of woman. She, the quasi-virgin, made him in love, formed and nurtured him in her womb, taught him to be strong, independent, and never docile. At heart, the movie is about love, the kind of love that breeds children, the kind of love that keeps humanity human. It is, in a sense, a declaration of love to womanhood, to the natural creativity of woman—as opposed to the "unnatural," cultural, and destructive creativity associated with perverted patriarchy.

All the machines are, if we can believe Freud—and in this I think we can—born out of the male fascination with the only natural "hydraulic" machine, the penis. Male pride in the "superior" organ and its machinelike qualities has led to the creation of all the ugly erections we live in, living machines, it has led to guns that spew death, it has led to machinery that chugs and lifts and builds and destroys. That is also why so many modern sf movies insist on the phallic/capitalist/technological confluence.

But in the end, the one machine that caused so much male envy wins the day. Sarah, already carrying the child in her womb, presses a button and squashes the electrical and evil/devilish light out of the Terminator: son of *man*. In the film's Christian symbology, it is no surprise that the ultimate machine, created by machines, the Terminator, once the human veneer is scorched off him, is a black, limping figure with red, gleaming eyes: he is the devil in disguise and only the son of *woman* can save humanity.[5]

■ Womb-Envy

"To create a Homunculus is a medieval idea: to bring it in line with the present century this creation must be undertaken on the principle of mass-production." Beyond that, the robots themselves become the masses, standing in for the human masses of the great industrial cities. The ideal robots of the nineteenth century were still conceptualized as individuals, unique artifacts with a personal relationship to their maker: Frankenstein's monster, Spalanzani's Olympia, Edison's Future Eve. They were essentially craft products—experimental prototypes of customized luxury goods.[6]

And, of course, the Golem, "a manlike creature, produced by the magical power of man."[7] Scholem makes the point that the man who creates a Golem "is in some sense competing with God's creation of Adam; in such an act the creative power of man enters into a relationship, whether of emulation or antagonism, with the creative power of God."[8] This is exactly what Dr. Frankenstein dreamed of: to create life without the help of the divine and the feminine. He wanted, as I stated in chapter 2, to be a god of sorts. But the idea of creating people took on practical proportions when mechanization began to define the workplace. Suddenly, humans/ robots created and made to mechanized order seemed almost a practical necessity.

Sf is full of male scientists who dream of creating the perfect and perfectly docile race. Modern medical reality is that the "dream" of male procreation, the "dream" of circumventing women, is on the verge of becoming reality. Artificial insemination, embryos flushed out of one woman and transferred to another, IVF (in vitro fertilization) where the actual act of fertilization takes place outside the uterus in a glass dish (and in some cases the embryo is frozen for later use), the implantation of fertilized embryos into postmenopausal women, and "the sale of surrogate mothers (breeders) to customers"[9] constitute a more or less exhaustive list of the current medical technologies in the area of reproduction. As the Krokers say, "In bio-technology at the *fin-de-millennium*, the womb has gone public, alienated from nature, inscribed by eugenics, bonded to public law and made fully accessible for the exchange-principle."

Much of the technology is of course designed to alleviate the problems of couples who cannot, for whatever reasons, conceive. But the technology is also quickly emptying the word "motherhood" of any real meaning. If a woman, as in the *Calverts vs. Anna L. Johnson* case, has an embryo implanted to which she has no genetic relationship, then who is the mother?[10] The idea of woman as nothing but greenhouse has become fact. Now a woman can give birth to a child made the "old-fashioned" way; to a child from an ovum flushed from her body, but fertilized in vitro; to a child that is the result of a fertilized ovum from her body but "belonging" to another woman, the wife of the genetic father (the

"Baby M" case); and to a child she has absolutely no genetic connection to. But if a woman has carried a child in her body, has given birth to it and nourished it as she would her own genetic embryo, fetus, neonate, has she no rights to that child? The Calverts/Johnson case resulted in a "no" to that question. Ms. Johnson, who, for a price, carried the child of the Calverts, was denied parental rights. She was, in other words, nothing but a hired womb.

Personally, I find the surrogacy phenomenon distasteful. But the issue in the context of this book is of course that the day is not far removed when people can decide what kind of fetus they want, where it is to be gestated, and for the benefit of whom:

Reproductive technologies are listed on the stock market. . . . Already female fetuses are aborted in greater numbers than male; femicide is a fact of life in China; work is being carried out to predetermine the sex of the fetus;[11] lactation can be developed in males; artificial placenta exists; it will soon be possible to implant an embryo in any abdomen: male, female, animal, human. . . . Now men can procreate.[12]

In both science fiction film and literature, male gestation has of course been a fact since Frankenstein. Rossum's Universal Robots are examples of male gestation (the reader may remember that when the young woman comes to politicize the robots, she is the first and only woman at the robot plant), as is the Maria robot in Metropolis. But the kind of special, male-spawned creation that interests me in the following discussion is the one that is most human of them all, the android. Readers who have seen Lang's Metropolis will remember that the robot/android in the movie is created to serve three purposes: first, she has to be a counterforce to the real Maria who is a gentle and religious political leader. The "evil" robot is an inveigler of the worst kind who leads the workers on a suicidal rampage through the subterranean factories they work as slaves. The destruction of the machines will flood the cité ouvrière[13] several levels below, killing the children and wives of the workers. Second, she is supposed to be the prototype of a new, mechanical "worker"—in my terms, the ultimate docile body who does not protest, does not need pay, does not eat, does not sleep, but only works, works, works, day and night, hard and diligently. Third, she is to re-create the ideal woman of both the scientist, Rotwang,[14] and the master of Metropolis, Joh Feddersen, who died after bearing Joh Feddersen a son, Freder Feddersen. For the moment, I will stick to point three—the android who is supposed to be the perfect mate, the dream woman of the inventor/scientist who created her.

■ Perfect Mates

In *Cherry 2000*, the male hero sets out on a quest to find a spare part to his "Cherry 2000" robot/android: a perfect sex partner, always pretty, always willing, never asking for more than he's willing to give. The movie is the story of how he falls in love with a real woman and faces up to the give and take of loving another *human being*. That is of course one dream men have always had— the ability to create the perfect woman, if not in their own image, then in the image of someone very like them with a few significant differences. Pygmalion was in love with the goddess Aphrodite, but she would have nothing to do with him. Instead he created her likeness in ivory and put it in his bed, praying to the goddess to give it life. She obliged and the result was Galatea—a perfect woman. George Bernard Shaw and others have played with the same theme. In Shaw's version, the woman is already there but as an empty vessel to be filled with the patriarchal ideology of what an ideal woman is like. The cultural reality is that this is what most patriarchal societies already do: they fashion out of the clay of female children young women who are indoctrinated to be the perfect and perfectly obedient companions, greenhouses, pleasure objects of men.

In *Cherry 2000* the young man learns to appreciate the feisty woman. But the sf canon contains works where that is not the case. In *Android*, a brilliant remake of *Metropolis*, the scientist, Dr. Daniels, having already created the sweet and very human Max (404), is hard at work on the Cassandra Project: he intends to create "the prototype of the perfect working class, not to mention the perfect woman." Daniels—and Max—work for the Terranova Corporation, which seems to be running things on Earth. The doctor and his creation are floating on a station in outer space, the last two to work on a now forbidden android project. After an incident in Munich in which a group of android workers went berserk and killed their human co-workers, Terranova has gotten cold feet and outlawed androids. The exception is Dr. Daniels who is allowed to continue his experiments in secrecy—and outer space. Obviously the promise of the perfect working class has enough allure for the corporation to try one more time.

So Daniels is stuck in space. He is a god of sorts, in a Heaven of sorts, who has created his own artificial rain forest with artificial birds and flowers. The orchids are his pride and joy. All he lacks is a mate. Daniels is almost ready to activate Cassandra [15] when he is informed from Earth that his project is about to be terminated. He has to work fast. But he has a problem. It seems that in order to activate Cassandra, he needs the presence of a human woman to provide the "bio-electrical potential" needed to jumpstart the android. The idea is to hook the woman—if he can get hold of one—to the lifeless android and then "stimulate" her. A plot twist provides an unexpected woman in the nick of time and the doctor "propositions" her, "let me get it straight, you got a what?"—"Android."—"Yeah, that's like a robot?"—"Right."—"And you wanna hook me up to this robot and stimulate me. Stimulate—like sex, right? I mean that's the weirdest one I've heard for getting into my pants!" And she stalks out, leaving Daniels frustrated.

But things still work out for the doctor. The woman, an escaped convict (but see below), takes a fancy to Max, not knowing he's an android, and the two create enough bio-electric magic in the lab to "breathe" life into Cassandra. The doctor is happy. He can "terminate" Max, whom he suspects of being on the verge of the "Munich syndrome," and he will soon have a beautiful and obedient sex partner. He moves in on the gorgeous Cassandra, and when he begins to bare her breasts she grabs his arm. She is not an obedient sex slave—on the contrary, she has rebellion and mayhem on her mind. She and Max kill Daniels, and she convinces Max to help her fool the corporate police who arrive in search of the escaped convicts. An android revolution is in the making.

Cassandra combines in her beautiful "person" the gentle Maria of *Metropolis* and her violent and hateful android replica. Peter

Wollen cites Huyssen to the effect that *Metropolis* "revolves around the displacement of the fear of technology-out-of-control on that of (female) sexuality-out-of-control." In *Metropolis*, the "flood of female sexuality is tamed" and the "(robot) witch. . . burned at the stake," assuring progress through technology.[16] But in *Android* the owner of the technology/woman never tames the robot; she kills him instead and goes on to live her life on her own terms. Cassandra springs from the operating table of her maker, a woman bristling with a sense of self and pride in her womanhood.

In a certain sense, *Android* can stand as metaphor for what has happened since the beginning of the women's movement. Women have shaken the shackles of being home-bound dependents and slaves of men and have emerged as strong, capable, and in charge. The other side of the same coin is portrayed in *The Stepford Wives*, a movie that, for reasons I have problems fathoming, received bad reviews and virtually no public interest when it was released in 1975. *The Stepford Wives* is both entertaining and thought provoking. It details the story of a woman, Joanna Eberhardt, who, at the insistence of her husband Walter, goes along with leaving New York and moving to the rural sleepiness of the village of Stepford. It doesn't take Joanna long to find out that life in Stepford isn't just sleepy; there is something strange going on with the women. Some of them are docile to the point of idiocy, repeating over and over how the only things they like to do are to cook and clean and take care of the children. Even the women who initially seem to have a bit of spunk and show signs of being modern and independent-minded undergo mysterious conversions and become wife-automatons, zombies who do what their husbands tell them and nothing more.

Joanna is a moderate feminist who works part-time as a free-lance photographer. She loves her husband and her kids, but she also sees herself as a woman with an intellect, some talent, and a career. She tries to make the best of being stuck in sleepy-town. With two other local women she begins a women's group. They visit other wives in town but all they hear are things such as "I'll just die if I don't get this recipe," and "I'm too busy with baking and all—I just love my brownies." Passing one house, they hear the unmistakable sounds of lovemaking, but with a twist: they know the man is a dry, boring sort; still, they hear the woman carrying on, "Oh God, you're the best; you're the king, the champion, the master, Frank!"

What's happening in the village is that the men, as a reaction to the women's movement and wives who refuse to be docile homemakers, are killing them off and replacing them with robots/androids *(gyn-oids?)*: exact replicas that are created in the image of the male ideal woman/wife, idiotic cook-bake-clean-take-care-of-the-kids-submissive-sex-objects. One by one the free spirits in the women's group are picked off and changed into zombie-women. The last one to go is Joanna. At the end, they all meet at the supermarket, good little wife-troopers out to find the ingredients to cook for their husbands and to clean and be whatever the husbands want them to be.

Stepford Wives is unsettling because it points to the discrepancy between what men and women want in a relationship. But instead of both parties giving and taking, the men in this movie cut their wives so they fit a male-supremacist stereotype. Happy little Disney World wives, Freudian models of female adjustment to gender inequality: the changed women make up for their "lack" (in the Freudian sense) by constantly pleasing the one with the phallus. They have no separate identities, no self, no desires that are not born of the wish to please. It is especially frightening that the zombie-women and their aggressively dominant husbands aren't just ironic parodies; they graphically evoke the ideals presented by the right-to-life movement and the religious right. *The Stepford Wives* is the companion piece to *The Handmaid's Tale*.

Making Mr. Right which, in a sense, is a reverse of *Stepford Wives*, features a scientist who creates an android in his own cold, antisocial image. He is a klutz whose only redeeming feature is that he's smart. He doesn't look at people when they speak to him, he eats his own space food, and doesn't have a clue about how to date a woman. Not surprisingly, his creation, the android is just the same. He is programmed to perform dangerous tasks in outer space. He will live a solitary but heroic life on a spaceship. He is the "Ulysses Android," produced for the Chemtech Corporation by

In *The Stepford Wives*, husbands kill their rebellious wives and replace them with "gyn-oids." In the end, they all meet at the supermarket, good little wife-troopers out to find the ingredients to cook for their husbands. I especially love the hats and garden-party dresses: these women didn't dress themselves, they are full-size, full-service Barbie dolls dressed by *men*. (Columbia Pictures Productions, 1975. Still courtesy of MOMA film stills archive.)

the antisocial scientist (both the android and the scientist are played by John Malkovich).

Chemtech decides that it wants to give its new piece of "equipment" some publicity and takes on a publicist, Sandy, who, as it turns out, is having problems of her own. She has been seeing and working for the campaign of a local politician/Don Juan. Both involvements come to an abrupt end when she learns—on TV, no less!—of his philandering ways. She chucks a life-size cardboard likeness of him out the window and starts looking for new employment.

Sandy wants to promote Ulysses not as a thing but as a "human"—of sorts. To that end she takes on the role as his teacher/ socializer. He absorbs her feminine values in lieu of his maker's asocial ones. The android becomes obsessed with Sandy's obsession: love. The movie is full of gender stereotypes. Men are brainy and cold and/or only interested in sex; women are totally relationship focused.[17] When they are not shopping (and even then, most of the time) their entire conversation is about men and how to snare one into marriage. Sandy feels her biological clock racing and is desperate to find Mr. Right. She doesn't, of course, *find* Mr. Right, and she doesn't—as the title of the movie implies—*make* him either. She *socializes* him. Ulysses is a willing student. He has been constructed with all the necessary equipment and makes love to Sandy's girlfriend. He loves it, thinks love and making love are terrific. She thinks he's the perfect lover, chivalrous, attentive, relationship oriented—a real Mr. Right.

It is a bit disappointing that this movie, made by a woman, is so full of stereotypes. Comedy may feed on stereotypes, but the result here is rather uninteresting. The men (the non-android ones) are either loose phalli or brainy and remote scientists, the women are dizzy socializers—in other words, the traditional roles. Ulysses is the child born to the remote genius, left to a woman to be socialized and taught about the world. The ray of hope is that she "destroys" him. After being exposed to her and her values—love and marriage—he is no longer fit for the role he was constructed for: "I don't want to be envied, I want to be loved."—"How's Ulysses supposed to survive out there, when all he thinks about is you?" Ulysses develops, to the explicit horror of his maker and owners, "human tendencies." Instead of Ulysses, Chemtech sends the machine-man, his maker, into outer space, while Ulysses, the human machine, is back home on Earth, making love to Sandy and settling into the nest of a long-term relationship.

■ Soulful Machines

The science officer Ash in *Alien* is a real corporation man. He is not subject to humane considerations. When the space cargo ship on which he serves is threatened by an alien and presumably dangerous organism, he is the one who, on corporation orders, opens the doors and lets the alien organism in. Ash is the one who coldly follows directives to the effect that bringing home an alien organism—with military potential—is more important than saving the crew on the *Nostromo:* "Crew is expendable." It is not an accident that Ash is the science officer. Science and human values are, as we have seen often enough, fundamentally opposed in sf. In movies involving aliens, the scientists are invariably the Bad Guys, from *The Thing*, where the scientists are the ones who want to keep the "thing" alive at any cost, to *Invasion from Mars*, where the scientist is more concerned to get a specimen than to save Earth, to *E.T.*, where the overzealous scientists are the villains, wanting to catch E.T. and cut him up to see what he's made of.

But Ash is, as it turns out, not only the cold scientist, he is an android. He is what Ulysses should have been: unemotional (the camera shows him unperturbed in situations where everybody else is tense and anxious), cold, inhuman, the ultimate corporation "docile body."

In *Westworld* scientists have created docile robots that "live" and perform in a future Disney World-type amusement park. Tourists check into theme villages and interact with androids that fit the theme. The two protagonists—businessmen away for the weekend —take rooms above the saloon in a "Wild West" town. They get into "real" gunfights and shoot and "kill" their android opponents. The androids are later picked up and repaired to be sent back into the fray the next day. But things are beginning to go wrong. The gunfighter android is beginning to shoot back—with live ammo—and to kill tourists. And the sex-toy lasses of the medieval-knights village are refusing to be grabbed and felt up and bedded by every tourist in kingly cape. Instead of a sexual thrill, one hefty tourist gets a deadly one. The movie never elaborates or makes explicit what it is that's happening with the 'droids, but we can guess: they are acquiring a sense of self, of dignity, of not wanting to be sex/death slaves.

In *Creation of the Humanoids*, the gender issue crops up again, à la *Making Mr. Right*. The movie is set after an atomic holocaust that has wiped out 92 percent of Earth's population. The survivors "turned to robotic automation devices to help them rebuild their cities and maintain a high standard of living." The development of sophisticated robots is fast. Organic life took billions of years to evolve. In sf, mechanical life evolves from primitive to highly sophisticated within one human generation.

The earliest robots in *Creation of the Humanoids* were "quite ungainly" and were refined until the creation of the R-20 model, which "was capable of all the thought processes of a man." Human workers had problems, however, with R-20s; they couldn't handle having to work alongside machines they had to talk to and that could outthink them. So scientists perfected the R-21, "the first humanoid robot."

The R-21s are called "clickers" by humans, who neither like nor trust them. Their movements outside work hours are checked by armed guards, and they have to show passes and give destinations when encountered in the streets at night. Humans are afraid of a robot rebellion. As it turns out, for good reason. There is a conspiracy among the clickers. They are secretly—and with the help of a human scientist—producing robots, androids really, that are indistinguishable from the real thing. The R-34 is higher on the humanity scale (1–100) than the R-21's (the R-number indicates the degree of humanity). A simple operation performed by the human scientist, Raven, will transform an R-34 into an R-96—"with all the emotions of a human . . . he will learn how to laugh and cry, be afraid and hate. To become an R-96 is a real sacrifice." Why a sacrifice? Because an R-21 has all (plus) the mental facilities of a human but is not bothered with fear and hate and love. R-21s are the robot equivalents of humans who have been "invaded" in *Invasion of the Body Snatchers,* or for that matter, of humans who had been abducted by trolls or little people in times past. The robots want to infiltrate human society because they want to find out why some humans hate them so vehemently so they can learn to adapt and avoid the hatred.

R-96s are illegal. The Order of Flesh and Blood, apparently a kind of robot-age Ku Klux Klan, has successfully lobbied a law that makes it illegal to produce robots that are above R-70. The Order has also seen to it that it is illegal for humans and robots to enter into relationships ("rapport") without acquiring permission.[18]

The way the robots go about making R-96s is to reprogram robots with lower R-values by giving them the memories and identities of humans. The robots steal human bodies left for dead and "extract" their "essence" to create an R-96. That means an R-96 does not know he or she is one. The only difference between an R-96 and a human is that the androids can't reproduce. They are available to give information to the robot "father-mother," the huge computer that all robots plug into and are recharged by. But R-96s are not conscious of the information-drain sessions; they perceive them as normal sleep.

The movie, a fairly amateurish job, focuses on a young F & B (Flesh and Blood) captain and the beautiful young woman, Maxine, with whom he falls in love. Craigis, the F & B'er, has a sister who lives "in rapport" with an R-49 named Pax. Craigis goes to try to talk her out of it. She's not interested. She "loves" her Pax. He is there to please her, unlike her former husband Miles, "a filthy, stinking, drunken, insensitive beast." Craigis is mortified by the idea that his own sister has sunk so deep as to live with a clicker. The climax and denouement of the movie is, of course, that both Craigis and Maxine are R-96s without realizing it. When they find out, they nonetheless declare their love for each other, as he says: "And that's a lot for a couple of godless, soulless beings." Dr. Raven, the by now transformed scientist, asks: "Consider, are you godless?" Craigis: "No, I don't think so."[19]—"Then you're not soulless either."

The androids are the next step on the evolutionary chain—after the phasing out of humans and of sickness and death. Maxine adds sadly, "And birth will cease to exist too. The most precious hope of every woman." But Raven has found a way for a 96 to "pick up" the last four points, just a little operation, "hardly worse than removing a rib." Corny. But the movie is interesting.

The line between human and machine is blurred in *Creation of the Humanoids*. Even more so in the already discussed *Android*. As the reader may remember, Dr. Daniels is floating around in the heavens, playing God with plants, animals, and androids. He has created Max 404, who is a good, if bored, worker. Max mans the controls of the space station while dreaming of love—though he's not quite sure what it is; playing 1950s rock, "Searching for My Baby"; and sexual instruction tapes—"Sexual Function: Human, Heterosexual." Max watches with hanging lower jaw and slight discomfort as computer drawings of a man and a woman kiss and then perform intercourse.

Max is the movie's central character. He is a sweet, lovable teenager, lost in space. He has never in his "five years, seven months" seen a real live woman. All he knows is Dr. Daniels, his '50s rock songs, and '40s and '50s romantic movies; but he has his Bogart hat and is dying to discover love. His chance comes when a spaceship in distress asks for permission to land. Because there is a woman aboard, Max—against all orders and rules—allows them to land. Aboard are three fugitives from corporate law. One is a real criminal, violent and asocial, but the two others are more like political prisoners. Gunther is suspected of "anti-corporation affiliation," and the woman, Margaret Kallisti—called Maggie—has a record of "corporate embezzlement and industrial espionage."

Max is sweet and gentle because he's programmed to be, but he has a mind and plans of his own. He has more "soul" than any of the humans in the movie. All three human (but see below) men—Gunther, Mendez (the villain), and Daniels, are out to get sexual services from Maggie, and she does bestow them on Mendez under threats of violence. But Maggie falls for Max. She, unlike the two others, is unaware that he is an android. And she's taken with his gentleness, his befuddled but obvious infatuation with her, and with his romantic disposition. To her, he's a real Mr. Right.

To Dr. Daniels, Max is just an evolutionary step in his quest to create "the ideal working class." The crowning achievement is to be Cassandra, who will be both sex object and tireless worker. The idea of androids as the "perfect working class," docile humanlike creatures willing to do whatever they are told and willing to please their human masters in any way, is of course central to this book. But even more important is the constant blurring of the lines. Max is more human than the humans in *Android*; indeed, he can be seen as metaphor for a human who has been brainwashed and programmed—à la Murphy in *Robocop 2*—into believing he is a machine that must obey orders and subjugate himself to his human masters. The blurring of lines becomes total when it is revealed that Dr. Daniels is also an android. Suddenly, whatever lines and divisions the audience had established are eradicated and everything and everyone is in doubt.

Along with *Android, Forbidden Planet,* and *The Terminator, Blade Runner* is a favorite of mine. A reason for this is that without a doubt it is the sf film that creates the most thoroughly convincing future—visually. Not just the present with makeup and people in surprisingly unmodern-looking cars and clothes. *Blade Runner* has a look, a density, and a depth of imagery that is foreign, exciting, and totally right. *Blade Runner* (based on a novel by Philip Dick, *Do Androids Dream of Electric Sheep?*) is about androids, in the movie called "replicants." These androids (which I will call them, because by this book's terms they are) have been created to fight wars on distant planets; they are soldier-slaves. But they have overthrown and killed their human overseers, and one day several of them show up on Earth, on a mysterious quest.

At a seminar about writing movie scripts that I attended, the brilliant film analyst Robert McKee claimed that the movie didn't get the kind of audience attention it deserved because the makers of the movie made Harrison Ford's tough Blade Runner (a cop who specializes in "retiring"—killing—androids) too unlikable, leaving an empathy vacuum to be filled by Rutger Hauer as the leader of the androids. I beg to differ. I believe that both the director, Ridley Scott, and Harrison Ford knew perfectly well what they were doing. Ford's Deckard is exactly as he should be. He is a man who has trouble—like all the humans in the film—with empathy and emotions. He has forgotten what it used to be to be human. Not so the androids. They are neophytes at being "human," a new species, a new link on the evolutionary chain and desperate to be more than just slaves, fighters, workers. They are not quite human but they strive toward the light.

The plot of *Blade Runner* is in its simplicity that a group of androids—four of them to be exact (although the number keeps changing)—have managed to get from "off-world" to Los Angeles. They are not allowed on Earth because of "a bloody mutiny by a NEXUS 6 combat team in an off-world colony, replicants were declared illegal on Earth—under penalty of death." The special police force that perform the executions are the Blade Runners with "orders to shoot to kill, upon detection, any trespassing replicant."

The time is the early twenty-first century. The world has been through an atomic war. Los Angeles is an ugly place, like a futuristic Turkish market with huge brown and gray buildings, constant, merciless rain, and a multinational population speaking a strange pidginized English—"city-speak, ghetto talk, mish-mash." "The film evokes a world wherein desires are constantly raised to the surface, as its very landscape is dominated by advertisements and commercial exploitation. Flying billboards, for example, constantly hover over the city, flashing various slogans."[20] From time to time, advertising "messages" blare through the polluted air, shameless, obnoxious. Throngs of people, oppressive buildings, and the eternal darkness punctuated by cold, probing shafts of searchlights give the city a claustrophobic quality. The people are rushing, rushing, rushing. Nobody seems to have anything to do with anybody else unless they are buying or selling—or they are Blade Runners "retiring" androids. Douglas Kellner et al. call it a hell: "The gaudy neon pink and red evoke a reference to Hell."[21] And even if it isn't quite hell, it is uncomfortably close: a sad place, a lonely place, a place where people are alienated, suspicious, hostile. There is not one single scene where one human being looks lovingly, caringly—looks at another human being with anything other than disinterest.

The escaped androids are products of the Tyrell Corporation. Tyrell seems pretty much to run things in this particular future; another corporate dystopia. The androids belong to the NEXUS phase of "robot evolution," "a being virtually identical to a human. . . . The NEXUS 6 Replicants were superior in strength and agility, and at least equal in intelligence, to the genetic engineers who created them," as Deckard, the Blade Runner, says. Deckard has gotten tired of killing. His conscience is bothering him and he is officially retired from active duty. But the four androids on the loose and a dead Blade Runner trigger his former boss, Bryant, to more or less force him to come back.

There is only one way to tell if a given person (if that's the word) is an android, the "Voigt-Kampf test," a test that focuses an apparatus on the subject's eye as an interviewer asks questions to elicit emotional responses. The questions are supposed to distinguish between humans and androids by degrees of empathy. Put another way, it's a test to see if the subject has a soul. The eyes are the windows of the soul, we say. *Blade Runner* has taken that expression and made it its pulsating heart. The main image system of the movie is eyes and eye imagery. The Voigt-Kampf test is the most obvious example, but there are many. The camera in *Blade Runner* has a tendency to focus on characters' eyes right from the opening scene, where "the flames of hell are reflected in a huge disembodied iris."[22] The camera tends to reduce faces to half-masks, and at one point, two of the androids, Roy (Rutger Hauer) and Leon, in an attempt to find the engineer responsible for their design, find an old Chinese man who makes eyes for androids. In this scene, eyes are handled as objects, played with. Even a mechanical owl that "lives" in the Tyrell Corporate headquarters is invariably photographed to show the emptiness of its huge, brown eyes. Mechanical owls have no souls.

But androids do. The real question posed in *Blade Runner* is if humans do—any more. Those who were part of the war, who survived it and who live empty material lives of total emotional alienation, are perhaps not worth saving. They are gray and distant, about to become part of the technological indifference with which they have surrounded themselves. In an early scene Deckard orders sushi in a restaurant, admitting that's what his wife called him: cold as a fish.

In *Blade Runner* humans never show emotion or empathy, only androids do: they care deeply for each other, and the love between Roy, their leader, and Pris is the source of their desire to find their maker. Humans have no respect for life. In their gray world there probably is not much difference, anyway, between life and death. But the androids feel the difference—acutely. When Zhora, one of the four androids, has a chance to kill Deckard, she hesitates. Can't bring herself to do it. Deckard has no qualms and shoots her in the back as she's fleeing. And the other androids, each in their turn, have a chance to kill Deckard, and each one hesitates long enough—or Deckard is saved in the nick of time *by an android*— to become his victim instead.

The androids in this movie are a new, vital, energetic species. Perhaps humanity reborn. They are born, "incepted," to be slaves. I agree with Kellner et al. when they say that the replicants "stand for oppressive features of capitalism and, to a lesser degree, rebellion against exploitation."[23] They are constructed to be "more human than a human"—for commercial reasons. Dr. Tyrell, president of the corporation of that name and chief android designer, experiments with more and more advanced—meaning human— androids. His latest "experiment" is a young woman replicant whom he has given a set of false memories, actually those of his niece. Rachel, as her name is, does not know she's an android. And when Deckard gives her the Voigt-Kampf test at Tyrell's insistence, it takes him more than a hundred questions to figure it out —as opposed to normally maybe forty or fifty. Tyrell, creating beings strictly for profit, has figured out that "if we give them a past, we create a cushion for their emotions; consequently, we can control them better."

The movie's other central theme is the opposition life/death. Androids are "designed to copy human beings in every way, except emotions; their designers reckoned, however, that after a few years they might develop their *own* emotional responses: hate, love, fear, envy. So they built in a fail-safe device—a four-year life span."[24] The four-year life span is the source of the androids' quest and arrival on Earth. They want to approach their maker and get more life.

Since the replicants are *vogelfrei*—to be shot on sight—they have to hide and move with stealth. They find, as noted above, the man who designs their eyes. He leads them to Sebastian, a genetic engineer who is one of the designers involved in the process. Sebastian is the only sympathetic human—with the possible exception of Deckard—in the movie. He's a lonely man of twenty-five who looks as if he is forty-five because he suffers from the Methuselah Syndrome, a glandular disorder that makes him grow old too fast. Sebastian lives alone in a huge apartment complex with his collection of mechanical dolls. His whole apartment is a human theme park. Shadowy human forms of all sizes, shapes, and historical periods silhouette the huge dark rooms. The apartment is an image of humanity frozen into wax-cabinet likeness and mechanical repetition.

Sebastian, sensing, perhaps because of his own premature aging, a kinship to the androids (above and beyond the obvious fact that as one of the genetic engineers involved in making them, they have, as he says, some of him in them), arranges to have Roy meet his maker, Dr. Tyrell. The scene in which this happens is another sf flirtation with religion. It is a false religion (the tenets of which are that profit is the ultimate goal and science its prophet) and a false god.[25] To see Tyrell, the false god, Sebastian and Roy have to ride up an outside elevator, crawling like a beetle up the wall of the Tyrell Corporation building, an enormous structure shaped like an Aztec pyramid, cavernous and templelike inside. To emphasize the religious imagery, the temple effect, the huge central hall (which seems to be about all there is—this is no ordinary office building) is lined with Greek columns, and the ceiling is so high that it simply disappears. This is Tyrell's cathedral, his St. Peter's with its symbolic replica of the unfathomable heavens above.

Tyrell is a dry, old-fashioned gentleman, wearing a business suit and thick glasses. The glasses, in the film's symbolism, are of course significant. He has pushed glass "walls" between his eyes and those of everyone else, human or replicant. Tyrell is a cold, distant god who doesn't care about his creation. When Roy and Sebastian arrive it is night. They get off the elevator on the top floor of the "cathedral," which is where Tyrell's living quarters are. The room he receives them in is all white: white curtains covering all walls, a huge white bed, Tyrell in a long, white robe. Chandelierlike rows of candles everywhere. A shrine for a god.

Tyrell is not surprised that Roy has come to see him. He welcomes him, asks how he can help him. Roy says he wants Tyrell to change the design so replicants live longer. Tyrell refuses, claiming it is technically impossible, "You were made as well as we could make you."—"But not to last."—"The light that burns twice as bright, burns half as long. And you have burned brightly. Look at you! You are quite a prize. You are the prodigal son." And Tyrell puts his arm around Roy's shoulder in a fatherly gesture. For a moment he becomes that other kind of Father, priest/God, as Roy confesses: "I've done—questionable things."—"But also extraordinary things. Revel in your time!"—"Nothing the god of biomechanics wouldn't let you into heaven for?" The God and his creation kiss, a sensual kiss on-the-mouth. A Judas kiss—but who is Judas? Then Roy grabs Tyrell's face and squeezes it, in the process ripping the glasses from the eyes, breaking down the wall between maker and creation. Roy squeezes the dry face and sticks his fingers into Tyrell's eyes, pressing until the blood spurts. The final eye image: the soulless god's eyes gouged.

To the indifferent human world outside, Tyrell's is just another death. On the newscast, his is a dead body found along with Sebastian's. Roy's own death is another matter. He is close to his four-year limit and his beloved Pris is even closer. After killing the two scientists, he hurries back to Sebastian's apartment, only to find Pris dead, victim of Deckard and her own aging process. Roy goes after Deckard, his grief making him seek death but also wanting revenge for his friends. Roy pursues Deckard—his face painted for war with makeup from the blood of the dead Pris—until the two face each other on the roof of a building. Deckard falls, hangs from the roof, there is no doubt that he will die; but Roy pulls him onto the safety of the roof—to the accompaniment of church bells on the soundtrack. Roy sits down, a white dove suddenly appearing in his hands: "I've seen things you people wouldn't believe . . . . All those moments will be lost like tears in the rain. Time to die." He bends over and dies. As he dies, the white dove escapes from his hands and soars, along with white smoke from huge smokestacks, toward the purplish gray sky. The android's soul is released at his death and flies toward its celestial home.[26]

And for me, Roy is not even the emotional center of the movie. That center is occupied by Rachel, the android who does not know she is one. She's the one who has to grapple with the problems of self and identity when she finds out that her memories are not hers—they are just implants—and when she has to face the fact that she's a machine, created not in love, but as an experiment for profit. She's the one who has to learn, on her own, that she has a soul, has a self, that she can love and be loved. Rachel, with the soulful brown eyes, has to learn to love and trust Deckard with the cold, blue ones.[27]

Rachel, like Roy, is not automatically human because she was born of woman. She is created by a male scientist-god in an emotional vacuum. Created in indifference and perhaps with hatred. She is not born with a soul. She has to earn one. She has to find the will to be good and to find love in herself, not in some distant, cold, and rule-faxing Old Testament God. She knows *her* god. She has to become human, moral, loving in spite of him.

Rachel and the other androids in the movie are symbolic, perhaps, of the situation of African Americans. Human beings, robbed of their humanity and submitted to be the slaves of beings who maintained their own morality and religious righteousness, while being personifications of evil. To find a soul and morality and a sense of self in that atmosphere is no less than a miracle and an achievement of momentous proportions. But for me the movie is more about the situation of humanity in the age of science. The boundary between humans and machines is broken down. No one really knows what they are: "*Blade Runner* presents a future society which blurs the line between human and machine, and it contains philosophical meditations on what it means to be human."[28] Humans who produce androids—or who scientifically, through institutions of education, medicine, psychology, and the social sciences, help and abet a dehumanizing system and make machines out of humans—are perhaps not worthy of the name. And machines/humans who try to find a humanity as they try to escape a scientific vice that demands they be nothing but soulless work and pleasure objects perhaps *are* worthy. The androids of *Blade Runner* are, then, symbols for the "little people," the folklore heroes up against the mechanical dragon. They are the only real humans in the movie. The Captain Bryants, the scientists, and others have already had their soul transplants. They are already machines.

When the dove is released from the dying Roy's grip and heads for the heavens, when Rachel decides to trust her emotions and her love for Deckard, that's when the movie expresses hope that humanity may survive, perhaps in the anthropomorphic form of an android, a being who has tasted the reality of being a machine and rejected it.

■ Notes

1. Penley 1990:117.
2. We are already capable of producing artificial blood and skin grown in lab dishes, and artificially grown "human" hair is just down the road.
3. Penley 1990:119.
4. Ibid., 121.
5. By making technology and science more important than anything else, we "invite" the devil in, we are "selling our souls" for knowledge and creature comforts.
6. Wollen 1989:16. The first of the quotation is Wollen quoting Capek's introduction to *R.U.R.*
7. Scholem 1969:174.
8. Ibid., 159.
9. Correa 1985:1. The entire paragraph on reproductive technology is a paraphrase of Correa. Since the publication of Correa's book, the implantation of embryos into postmenopausal women—then only a future possibility—has become fact.
10. Mydans 1990:D6.
11. Sex of a fetus can already be determined. In India it is routine for parents to check the sex of the fetus and to abort it if it is female.
12. Verthuy, quoted in Kroker and Kroker 1987:31.
13. Worker city. Foucault, in "The Eye of Power" (Foucault 1980), makes

the point that one of the ideas propagated in the nineteenth century to control the workers was based on the concept of the Panopticon, a city built around a central observation unit. Workers were assigned limited space where they could recreate, procreate, and be observed and controlled. The worker's city in *Metropolis* is of that order, except that it is arranged so that there is no way out. Workers live in the bowels of Earth, even way below the machines they work. They cannot move above ground, where the privileged classes frolic, unobserved.

14. In line with my argument about the scientist who wants to be god, Dadoun (1986) argues that Rotwang "has been symbolically castrated, his hand cut off, for daring to lay hands on Mother Nature, for having 'had' her, to use a slang term" (146). Furthermore, "Rotwang is single, double, and multiple all at one: he is the paternal and divine One, symbolized by the solar globe from which all energy emanates. . . . He is sovereign over the empirical realm as well as the realm of reproduction" (149).

15. Named, apparently, after the Cassandra of Greek mythology: daughter of Priam and Hecuba. She was given the power of prophecy, but her fate was to be that no one believed her. After the Trojan War (Priam was king of Troy) she became the (sex) slave of King Agamemnon and was killed by Clytemnestra.

16. Wollen 1989:17.

17. Keller (1985:77–78) makes the interesting observation that while scientists are perceived to be a kind of super *males*, they are not seen as very sexual.

18. Racial readings are obvious—the infamous laws forbidding miscegenation in both the United States and, most recently, South Africa, come to mind. But the comparison stops there—R-34s are not humans, they are machines. I have heard a fair amount of racist junk about people of African descent, but not that. Perhaps a reading involving slavery and African-Americans as "tools" would work.

19. This refers back to an earlier scene between Raven—then still human —and an R-58. Raven marvels at the "creation" of a robot: "We have to study for years to learn what you pick up by plugging into a brain for two hours."—"We don't refer to our father-mother as a 'brain.' " —"Your Father-Mother is a computer, just a machine."—"Your parents were machines; it's just that they were engineered with flesh and bones—neither are ideal components."—"You came off a production line!"—"I *know* who created me—*you* have to accept your creation on faith."—"Who created your creator?"—"Yours! You see, we are brothers, aren't we?"—"I oughta know better with you clickers!"

20. Telotte 1990:154.

21. Kellner et al. 1984:6.

22. I'm quoting a comment from one of the publisher's readers.
23. Kellner et al. 1984:7.
24. The Golem was limited to a forty-day life span, if he was allowed to live beyond that, he would begin to destroy the human world. See Scholem 1969:201–202.
25. Kellner et al. compare the film to *Metropolis* and emphasize the critique of capitalism: "There are other cinematic parallels to Lang's *Metropolis*. For example, the tycoon Tyrell bears a marked physical resemblance to Metropolis' boss, Joh Fedderson, and Deckard's final duel with Roy copies in some respects the confrontation between Freder, the capitalist's son turned revolutionary, and Metropolis' evil Dr. Rotwang, who, like the Tyrell Corporation, created robots to serve as laborers"; Kellner et al. 1984:6.
26. Ryan and Kellner (1990:64) interpret this image a little differently, but the central meaning remains the same: "Roy suddenly carries a white dove that soon becomes a symbol of clarity and forgiveness. He himself in fact becomes a figure for Christ as he lowers his head and dies."
27. Kellner et al. point out, correctly, that *Blade Runner*, while being progressive in some respects, is reactionary where it comes to issues of gender: "Rachel fulfills the common male fantasy of the completely pliant woman who serves all a man's needs"; Kellner et al. 1984:7.
28. Ibid., 7.

12 ▪
Conclusion

Replicants are condemned to a life composed only of a present tense; they have neither past nor memory. There is for them no conceivable future. They are denied a personal identity, since they cannot name their 'I' as an existence over time.[1]

In the quotation above, Giuliano Bruno refers specifically to the replicants of *Blade Runner*, but the truth of the matter is, of course, that the androids are stand-ins for us, for the human race. Power, meaning the New World Order grounded in a capitalist ideology that makes profit and consumption the ultimate freedom, has forced all of us to follow suit, to become extensions of machines, docile bodies turned to technology. We have allowed the tool to become our master instead of our servant. That is the big irony— that our own elaborate fortifications against loss of self and soul may one day turn the tables on us: the metal, glass, and cement structures that jut out of the expanses of concrete we call cities, the machines and factory halls that constitute our environment might finally become the source of our loss of self. The little flicker of light inside each one of us that we call soul or consciousness is being squashed under the edifice of techno-culture. We are delivering ourselves up to the executioner as we buy into expanding corporate capitalism, expanding technology, expanding and ever-expanding desire for growth, wealth, machines with which to

241

adorn our homes and ourselves, machines to live by and in, machines that invade our bodies and imaginations, machines that are becoming invisible because they are everywhere, because they are us. We are perhaps already machines whose memories are technological implants.

It is often argued that sf, because it is a genre that exists in relative obscurity, has been allowed to produce messages that go against the dominant ideology. That is probably true and a reason that so much sf is comparatively subversive. But the subversion never goes very far. Very seldom does an sf film do anything more revolutionary than to whisper that something is wrong. Sf does not analyze problems and indicate routes to deal with them; sf names problems: it has been suggested that *The Fly* (1986) is about AIDS, and that seems reasonable enough. But the movie does not have anything much to say about it; all it does is record the physical and mental disintegration of a human being. If you want to see a film that deals with AIDS, with the psychological, historical, and political implications, you are better off seeing *Longtime Companion.*

Sf is folklore and as such it pitches little people against the big issues. In classical fairy tales, the barons and overseers that owned the world were represented as monsters and ogres to be killed before the lowly born, hero(ine) could realize him/herself. In sf, the monsters and ogres are either scientific side-effects like Godzilla or they are mechanical monsters that science unleashes upon the world—the Proteuses, the Cybermen, the Tyrells. Because it is folklore, sf gives vent to the fears of people who have no access to the crucial decisions about where science goes and what it does. Sf shows a world where the artificial neon lights are about to outshine the sun, where we will be forced to live in perpetual "spiritual" darkness, while our soulless body-machines are bathed in the searchlights of the corporate police and move about like decapitated chickens, devoid of inner life.

In that sense sf is a protest, a cry of despair from those who have no other avenues for venting their discontent with the status quo. But sf shares with folklore also its main weakness, the dreamlike escapism: in folklore and sf the hero always wins, the monster is always killed. And it is always one man or woman who, single-handedly does it. Like folklore, sf emphasizes the *deus ex machina* who has secret knowledge or powers. Sf seldom shows people working their way through the problems, naming them, classifying them, addressing them calmly and methodically. The problems are always solved quickly: the hero finds a shortcut to the solution; a god comes to Earth and kills the monster, or the heroine herself becomes magically powerful. Thus sf protest is more dream than a call to revolt. Like Charly, in the movie of the same name, the sf moviegoer has only a brief moment of artificial insight and clarity. When the movie is over and the lights come back on, she sinks back into reality, into a status quo whose reality she does not really understand and which she certainly has no chance to change. Sf, like folklore, does not clearly give voice to a protest. That, in a sense, would be too dangerous: it would call attention to the powerlessness. Ordinary people have no recourse to change anything in our technological world. The forces that control science are much too strong and they profit so enormously that they will never allow it. So sf makes the protest muted, less dangerous, by making the problems of the Little Guy/Gal hero solvable: the film offers closure; the good win and the bad are killed. The protest is further muted by the fantasy elements that, while loaded with symbolic and psychological significance, also signal "this is not real."

Sf's main function is to allow people to let off steam, to vicariously fight off their oppressors for a couple of hours before going back to the grind. Sf movies, after all, are produced in Hollywood, the dream factory. Movies are not the antithesis of power, of science and technology. Film *is* technology; Hollywood produces technological advertising for the corporations, for power.

Film, through its technique of shocks, instilled new habits in the masses, new modes of apperception. These, in turn, were necessary to the masses at the present turning point in history when the human apparatus of perception was confronted with a multitude of new demands and new tasks. This cinema, in a sense, was fulfilling the role of fitting the masses for the new and progressive forms of production which were being introduced.[2]

The movies are, along with TV, the perfect medium for indoctrinating people into the new ideology, the new technological world order. And sf movies are about the New World Order, although they in some respects purport to oppose that order. Sf shows us what to expect, gets us used to it. In the end sf becomes point man for the Brave New World: the movies get us accustomed to the dystopia. When the police state is in place, we will recognize it and be almost relieved because we were expecting it. And the police state, the Corporate Empire, will come. It is happening, not overnight and suddenly, as in the movies, but slowly and imperceptibly. Sf makes us blind to the slow, creeping changes, because we are looking for the sudden, the dramatic: "It is the sovereign prophylactic against futureshock. If you read enough science fiction [or watch enough sf], nothing takes you unaware."[3]

In this book, I have tried to ferret out what sf says in terms of the particular and quite narrow area of science and technology and the implications they have for ordinary people. Much work is being done in the field of sf film criticism, much of it using different analytical approaches. That is as it should be; my approach is determined by who I am and where I come from: I am an anthropologist and, secondarily, a folklorist. My sincere hope is that this book will stir someone, somewhere, to write more, in the same vein or a different one, about sf films.

■ Notes

1. Bruno 1990:189.
2. Wollen (1989:22) discussing Walter Benjamin's essay, "On Some Motifs in Baudelaire."
3. Pohl and Pohl 1981:11.

Bibliography

Ackerman, Forrest J. 1981. *Mr. Monster's movie gold.* Norfolk, Va.: Donning.

Atwood, Margaret. 1986. *The handmaid's tale.* Boston: Houghton-Mifflin.

Bauer, Wolfgang, Irmtraud Dümotz, and Sergius Golowin, eds. 1980. *Lexikon der Symbole.* Wiesbaden: Fourier.

Baxter, John. 1970. *Science fiction in the cinema.* New York: A. S. Barnes.

Beaune, Jean-Claude. 1989. "The classical age of automata: An impressionistic survey from the sixteenth to the nineteenth century." In *Fragments of a history of the human body,* ed. Michel Feher, 430–480. New York: Zone.

Bergstrom, Janet. 1986. Androids and androgyny. *Camera Obscura* 15: 37–65.

Bernal, J. D. 1965. *Science in history.* 4 vols. Cambridge, Mass.: MIT Press.

Boruszkowski, Lilly Ann. 1987. *The stepford wives:* Re-created woman. *Jump Cut* 32:16–19.

Bowen, Charles, ed. 1969. *The humanoids: A survey of worldwide reports of landings of unconventional aerial objects and their occupants.* Chicago: Henry Regnery.

Broad, William J. 1990. Hunt for aliens in space: The next generation. *New York Times,* February 6, C1, C12.

Browne, Malcolm W. 1990. On the trail of the 'Wildman' and creatures nearly as elusive. *New York Times,* 19 June, C1, C12.

―――. 1991a. 'Mirror-image' chemistry yielding new products. *New York Times,* 13 August, C1, C8.

―――. 1991b. Lively computer creation blurs definition of life. *New York Times,* 27 August, C1, C8.

Bruno, Giuliano. 1990. Rumble city: Postmodernism and the space of desire. In Kuhn 1990:152–160.

Brunvand, Jan Harold. 1984. *The choking doberman and other "new" urban legends*. New York: Norton.

———. 1986. *The Mexican pet: More "new" urban legends and some old favorites*. New York: Norton.

Bundtzen, Lynda K. 1987. Monstrous mothers: Medusa, Grendel, and now *Alien. Film Quarterly* 40:11–17.

Capek, Karel. 1923. *R.U.R.* New York: Samuel French.

Christiansen, Reidar, ed. 1964. *Folktales of Norway*. Chicago: University of Chicago Press.

Church, George J. 1989. The other arms race: America's streets become free-fire zones as police, criminals and terrified citizens wield more and ever deadlier guns. *Time*, 6 February, 20–26.

Correa, Gena. 1985. *The mother machine: Reproductive technologies from artificial insemination to artificial wombs*. New York: Harper and Collins.

Dadoun, Roger. 1986. Metropolis: Mother-City—Mittler. *Camera Obscura* 15:137–165.

Darnton, Robert. 1984. *The great cat massacre*. New York: Basic Books.

Deken, Joseph. 1986. *Silico sapiens: The fundamentals and future of robots*. New York: Bantam Books.

Dick, Philip K. 1968. *Do androids dream of electric sheep?* New York: Ballantine (reissued 1982 as *Blade Runner*).

Doherty, Thomas. 1987. The fly. *Film Quarterly* 40:38–41.

Dostoyevsky, Fyodor. 1968. *Crime and Punishment*. New York: Signet Classic.

Dullea, Georgia. 1991. Camcorder! Action! Lives become roles. *New York Times*, 15 August, A1, C10.

Durkheim, Emile. 1912. *The elementary forms of religious life*. New York: Collier.

Eliade, Mircea. 1978. *A history of religious ideas*. vol. 1. Chicago: University of Chicago Press.

Elkins, Charles, ed. 1980. Symposium on *Alien. Science Fiction Studies* 7:278–305.

Feher, Michel, ed. 1989. *Fragments for a history of the human body*. 4 vols. New York: Zone.

Finney, Ben R., and Eric M. Jones. 1985. *Interstellar migration and the human experience*. Berkeley: University of California Press.

Fitting, Peter. 1980. The second alien. In Elkins 1980:285–293.

Fletcher, Angus. 1964. *Allegory: The theory of a symbolic mode*. Ithaca, N.Y.: Cornell University Press.

Foucault, Michel. 1965. *Madness and Civilization*. New York: Random House.

———. 1973. *The birth of the clinic: An archaeology of medical perception.* New York: Pantheon.

———. 1977. *Discipline and punish: The birth of the prison.* New York: Pantheon.

———. 1980. *Power/knowledge: Selected interviews & other writings, 1972–1977.* Ed. Colin Gordon. New York: Pantheon.

Frazer, Sir James George. 1963. *The golden bough: A study in magic and religion.* New York: Macillan (originally published 1922).

Gardner, Howard. 1985. *The mind's new science: A history of the cognitive revolution.* New York: Basic Books.

Gialanella, Victor. 1982. *Frankenstein.* New York: Dramatists Play Service.

Glass, Fred. 1990. Totally recalling Arnold. *Film Quarterly* 44:2–14.

Glassie, Henry. 1985. *Irish folktales.* New York: Pantheon.

Glut, Donald F. 1977. *Classic movie monsters.* Metuchen, N.J.: Scarecrow Press.

Goffman, Erving. 1963. *Behavior in public places: Notes on the social organization of gatherings.* Westport, Conn.; Greenwood Press.

———. 1979. *Gender advertisements.* New York: Harper and Row.

Golden, Frederic. 1988. New proposals bolster search for life in space. *New York Times*, 23 August, 1988, C1, C12.

Gould, Jeff. 1980. The destruction of the social by the organic in *Alien.* In Elkins 1980:282–285.

Graves, Robert. 1955. *The Greek myths.* 2 vols. Harmondsworth, Eng.: Penguin Books.

Gross, Jane. 1989. Epidemic in urban hospitals: Wounds from assault rifles. *New York Times*, 21 February, 1, 15.

Grundtvig, Svend Hersleb. 1853–90. *Danmarks gamle folkeviser.* Vol. 1. Copenhagen.

Hall, Richard. 1988. *Uninvited guests: A documented history of UFO sightings, alien encounters and coverups.* Santa Fe, N.M.: Aurora Press.

Halliwell, Leslie. 1983. *Halliwell's film guide.* 4th ed. New York: Scribner's.

Heine, Heinrich. 1956. *Werke in einem Band.* Hamburg: Hoffmann und Campe.

Helman, Cecil. 1988. Dr. Frankenstein and the industrial body: Reflections on "spare part" surgery. *Anthropology Today* 4: 1 4–17.

Hodgens, Richard. 1972. A brief, tragical history of the science fiction film. In *Focus on the science film fiction,* ed. William Johnson, 78–91. Englewood Cliffs, N.J.: Prentice Hall.

Holbek, Bengt. 1987. *Interpretation of fairy tales.* Helsinki: Acedemia Scientiarum Fennica.

Holusha, John. 1989. Ailing robot industry is turning to services. *New York Times*, 14 February, D1–D2.

Hutton, John. 1987. *1984* and *Brazil:* Nightmares old and new. *Jump Cut* 32: 5–17.

Ibsen, Henrik. 1970–77. *The Oxford Ibsen.* Ed. James W. McFarlane, trans. James W. McFarlane et al. 8 vols. Oxford: Oxford University Press.

Irigaray, Luce. 1985. Is the subject of science sexed? *Cultural Critique* 1:73–89.

Jacobsen, Per Schelde, and Barbara Fass Leavy. 1988. *Ibsen's forsaken merman: Folklore in the late plays.* New York: New York University Press.

Johanson, Donald T. 1990. *Lucy—Beginings of humankind.* New York: Simon and Schuster.

Johnson, George. 1988. A parable of computers and brains. *New York Times*, 15 May, E7.

Johson, William, ed. 1972. *Focus on the science of science fiction film.* Englewood Cliffs, N.J.: Prentice Hall.

Jonas, Hans. 1958. *The gnostic religion.* Boston: Beacon Press.

Keller, Evelyn Fox. 1985. *Reflections on gender and science.* New Haven: Yale University Press.

Kellner, Douglas, Flo Leibowitz, and Michael Ryan. 1984. *Blade runner:* A diagnostic critique. *Jump Cut* 29:6–8.

Keyes, Daniel. 1970. *Flowers for Algernon.* New York: Bantam.

Kilborn, Peter T. 1990. Brave New World seen for robots appears stalled by quirks and costs. *New York Times*, 1 July, B16.

Koestler, Arthur. 1933. *Twilight bar.* London: J. Cape.

Kroker, Arthur, and Marilouise Kroker, eds. 1987. *Body invaders: Panic sex in America.* New York: St. Martin's.

Kuhn, Annette, ed. 1990. *Alien zone: Cultural theory and contemporary science fiction cinema.* London and New York: Verso.

Laura, Ernesto G. 1972. Invasion of the body snatchers. In W. Johnson 1972:71–74.

Lee, Richard B. 1984. *The Dobe !Kung.* New York: Holt, Rinehart and Winston.

Lemonick, Michael D. 1990. Those computers are dummies: A physicist's attack riles artificial-intelligence researchers. *Time*, 25 June.

Lerner, Gerda. 1986. *The creation of patriarchy.* New York and Oxford: Oxford University Press.

Levi-Strauss, Claude. 1983. *The raw and the cooked: Introduction to a science of mythology.* Vol. 1. Chicago: University of Chicago Press.

Life Magazine. 1989. Space: Is anyone out there? Most astronomers say yes. July, 48–53, 57.

Lloyd, Genevieve. 1984. *The man of reason: "Male" and "female" in Western philosophy.* Minneapolis: University of Minnesota Press.

Luck, Georg. 1985. *Arcana Mundi.* Baltimore: Johns Hopkins University Press.

Malcom, Andrew. 1989. Eight true stories, marked by gunfire and etched in blood. *New York Times,* 17 April, B9.

Malefijt, Annemarie. 1968. Homo monstrosus. *Scientific American* 219:112–119.

Mann, Thomas. 1959. *The transposed heads.* New York: Random House.

Marcus, Steven. 1974. *The other Victorians: A study of sexuality and pornography in mid-nineteenth-century England.* New York: Norton.

Markoff, John. 1990. Beyond artificial intelligence, a search for artificial life. *New York Times,* 25 February, E5.

Martin, Mick, and Marsha Porter. 1990. *Video movie guide 1991.* New York: Ballantine.

Matson, Floyd W. M. 1964. *The broken image: Man, science, and society.* Garden City, N.Y.: Doubleday.

Meggitt, Mervyn. 1977. *Blood is their argument.* Palo Alto, Calif.: Mayfield.

Miller, Mark Crispin. 1990. Hollywood, the ad. *Atlantic Monthly,* April, 47–54.

Mulvey, Laura. 1975. Visual pleasure and narrative cinema. *Screen* 16: 6–18.

Mydans, Seth. 1990. Science and the courts take a new look at motherhood. *New York Times,* 4 November, D6.

The National Examiner. 1988. I've been married to space alien for 12 year. 25 October, 1, 27.

Neale, Stephen. 1986. Sexual difference in cinema—Issues of fantasy, narrative and the look. *Oxford Literary Review* 8 (1–2):123–133.

———. 1989. Issues of difference: *Alien* and *Blade runner.* In *Fantasy and the Cinema,* ed. James Donald, 213–224. London: BFI Publishing.

Orwell, George. 1982a. *1984.* New York: Buccaneer Books.

———. 1982b. *Animal farm.* New York: Buccaneer Books.

Penley, Constance. 1990. Time travel, primal scene and the critical dystopia. In Kuhn 1990: 116–128.

Petersen, Vibeke Rützou, and Per Schelde. 1986. Through the prism: Slava Tsukerman's *Liquid sky.* Unpublished Paper.

Piercy, Marge. 1976. *Woman on the edge of time.* New York: Fawcett Crest.

Pohl, F., and Pohl, I. 1981. *Science fiction: studies in film.* New York: Ace Books.

Postman, Neil. 1985. *Amusing ourselves to death.* New York: Penguin Books.

Purce, Jill. 1980. *The mystic spiral: Journey of the soul.* New York: Thames and Hudson.

Rabinow, Paul. 1984. *The Foucault reader.* New York: Pantheon.

Rapping, Elayne. 1987. *The looking glass world of nonfiction TV.* Boston: South End Press.

Ross, Andrew. 1991. Hacking away at the counterculture. *Newmail.*

Rovin, Jeff. 1975. *A pictorial history of science fiction films.* Secaucus, N.J.: Citadel Press.

Ruppersberg, Hugh. 1990. The alien Messiah. In Kuhn, 1990:32–39.

Russett, Cynthia Eagle. 1989. *Sexual science.* Cambridge: Harvard University Press.

Ryan, Michael, and Douglas Kellner. 1990. Technophobia. In Kuhn 1990:58–66.

Safford, Tony. 1980. Alien/Alienation. In Elkins 1980:297–302.

Schechter, Harold. 1988. *The bosom serpent: Folklore and popular art.* Iowa City: University of Iowa Press.

Schelde (Jacobsen), Per. See Jacobsen, Per Schelde.

Scholem, Gershom. 1969. *On the Kabbalah and its symbolism.* New York: Schocken Books.

Shelley, Mary. 1984. *Frankenstein; or, the modern Prometheus.* New York: Modern Library. (first published 1831).

Sobchack, Vivian. 1986. Child/Alien/Father: Patriarchal crisis and generic exchange. *Camera Obscura* 15:7–37.

Stine, Hank, ed. 1981. *Mr. Monster's movie gold.* Virginia Beach: Donning.

Strieber, Whitley. 1987. *Commmunion: A true story.* New York: William Morrow.

———. 1989. *Majestic.* New York: Putnam.

The Sun. 1988a. Psychic records his dreams on videotape and shows them like movies. 12 July, 37.

———. 1986b. UFO aliens saved our farm. 1 November, 5.

———. 1989a. UFO invasion: Flying saucers ready to attack our world. 14 March, 5.

———. 1989b. 11 girls give birth to UFO aliens. 13 June, 5.

Telotte, J. P. 1990. The doubles of fantasy and the space of desire. In Kuhn 1990:152–160.

Theweleit, Klaus. 1987–89. *Male fantasies.* 2 vols. Minneapolis: University of Minnesota Press.

Todorov, Tzvetan. 1982. *La Conquête de l'Amérique: La question de l'autre.* Paris: Éditions du Seuil.

Turner, Victor. 1967. *The forest of symbols: Aspects of Ndembu ritual.* Ithaca, N.Y.: Cornell University Press.

Vallee, Jacques. 1969. *Passport to Magonia: From folklore to flying saucers.* Chicago: Henry Regnery.

van Gennep, Arnold. 1960. *The rites of passage.* Chicago: University of Chicago Press.

von Gunden, Kenneth, and Stuart H. Stock. 1982. *Twenty all-time great science fiction films.* New York: Arlington House.

Watkins, John V. and Thomas J. Sheehan. 1975. *Florida landscape plants.* Gainesville: University of Florida Press.

Weekly World News. 1988a. A space alien made me pregnant—then stole my baby! 12 April, 12.

———. 1988b. Medical experts explain why we sometimes feel tired and worn out: Tiny space aliens zap our energy. 17 May, 11.

Wingrove, David, ed. 1985. *Science fiction film source book.* Essex, Eng.: Longman.

Wolkomir, Richard. 1987. Alien Worlds: The search heats up. *Discover,* October, 66–76.

Wollen, Peter. 1989. Cinema/Americanism/the Robot. *New Formations* 8:7–35.

Wyndham, John. 1962. *The Midwich cuckoos.* London: M. Joseph.

Filmography

This filmography is meant as a service to the reader. I give the important data: title, year, director (Dir.): author of the screenplay (Sp.): the most important cast members (With); and the length of the movie. In cases where the movie is important but not discussed extensively in the text, I give a one-sentence plot outline and occasionally a clue to what is interesting about the movie in light of my treatment of science fiction. The last item in each entry is an evaluation—as terse and to the point as I can make it. The idea is to give readers an idea of whether a given movie has qualities other than an interesting feature, plot twist, or scene—in other words, this last entry says if the movie, in my opinion, is worth watching. The data are culled from a variety of sources, such as the credits of actual movies, video-tape boxes, and, primarily, from Martin and Porter 1990, Halliwell 1983, and Wingrove 1985. By far the most reliable and helpful of these three is Wingrove. The only redeeming virtue of the Martin and Porter book is that it is up to date. The ratings, however, are ludicrous— for a movie to get a less than upbeat rating, it has to be seriously bad. Halliwell is confusing. Wingrove's mini-analyses are intelligent and his ratings generally fair, if on the positive side. The only problem is that it was published in 1985.

Alien (1979). Dir. Ridley Scott. Sp. Dan O'Bannon. With Tom Skerritt, Sigourney Weaver, John Hurt, Harry Dean Stanton; 116 min.
    Corporate capitalism and monstrous motherhood pitted against natural womanhood and reproduction. Exciting and entertaining. But there are some cheap thrills and excessive blood and gore.

253

Alien Nation (1988). Dir. Graham Baker. Sp. Roger S. O'Bannyon. With James Caan, Mandy Patinkin, Terence Stamp. 96 min.

A race of alien androids arrives in L.A. and is allowed to settle. The aliens were created as a race of slaves. They escaped their masters/creators and now have to learn to be "human" and accepted by humans. Racial readings are obvious. But the androids can also be seen as metaphorical of humans who have been "mechanized" by increasing technologization. The interesting concept is somewhat undone because the movie is also a buddy and cops-and-robbers movie.

Aliens (1986). Dir. James Cameron. Sp. James Cameron. With Sigourney Weaver, Carrie Henn, Michael Biehn, Paul Reiser. 137 min.

What holds for *Alien* holds for this, the sequel. In addition, it is as consciously aware of gender and gender roles as sf films get, plus it is interesting and entertaining.

Altered States (1980). Dir. Ken Russell. Sp. Sidney Aaron. With William Hurt, Blair Brown, Bob Balaban. 102 min.

Romantic genius who must be free of female "contamination" to do his science. Ultimately he transgresses and is punished for his hubris. The idea is fascinating, but the movie is pretentious and dramatically flawed. Has some of the worst dialogue ever.

Android (1982). Dir. Aaron Lipstadt. Sp. James Reigle and Don Opper. With Klaus Kinski, Don Opper, Brie Howard, Norbert Weiser. 80 min.

Android god floating in the "heavens," trying to create the perfect working class *and* sex-object. A lovely movie. Fun, entertaining, well constructed. Only drawback is some wooden acting in the minor parts. But Don Opper as Max 404 is wonderful. Klaus Kinski is Klaus Kinski.

The Andromeda Strain (1971). Dir. Robert Wise. Sp. Nelson Gidding. With Arthur Hill, David Wayne, James Olson, Kate Reid, Paula Kelly. 130 min.

Scientists fighting a space probe that threatens to kill all life on Earth. The scientists are the good guys, but *ultimately* science is the culprit. Fascinating premise, but the movie is fair-to-middling. Too many loose plot ends and some pretty terrible acting.

The Angry Red Planet (1959). Dir. Ib Melchior. Sp. S. Pink. With Gerald Mohr, Nora Hayden, Les Tremayne, Jack Kruschen. 83 min.

Space crew on Mars. Anthropomorphic monsters. Amateurish acting, silly story.

Back to the Future (1985). Dir. Robert Zemeckis. Sp. Robert Zemeckis and Bob Cale. With Michael J. Fox, Christopher Lloyd, Lea Thompson, Crispin Glover. 116 min.

Good metaphor for film: a machine that can transport people to the past and re-create it with a rosy cast. Fun if you like that kind of thing—I guess. But I was irritated by the overbearing attitude toward the past and the predictability.

Battle Beyond the Stars (1980). Dir. Jimmy T. Murakami. Sp. John Sayles. With Richard Thomas, John Saxon, Robert Vaughn, George Peppard. 104 min.
Silly space-opera with evil invaders and supercomputer.

Battlestar Galactica (1978). Dir. Richard A. Colla. Sp. Glen A. Larson. With Lorne Greene, Richard Hatch, Dirk Benedict, Jane Seymour. 125 min.
As Wingrove (1985:34–35) rightfully points out, this is a *Star Wars* clone—and not a good one. A band of "humans" escapes its exploding planet and has to fight its way through space until it arrives, possibly on Earth, and settles it. Full of macho men, submissive women, and cute kids and robots.

Blade Runner (1982). Dir. Ridley Scott. Sp. Hampton Fancher and David Peoples. With Harrison Ford, Rutger Hauer, Sean Young, Daryl Hannah, Joanna Cassidy, Edward James Olmos. 118 min.
Androids/slaves revolting against the false gods who made them and exploit them. Intelligent and deeply moving. Personally, I think this is the best sf movie ever made.

The Blood of Heroes (1989). Dir. David Peoples. Sp. David Peoples. With Rutger Hauer, Joan Chen, Vincent D'Ontrio.
Derivative and violent, but exciting.

Brainstorm (1983). Dir. Douglas Trumbull. Sp. Robert Stitzell and Philip Frank Massina. With Christopher Walken, Natalie Wood, Louise Fletcher. 106 min.
Woman scientist invents a machine that can record thoughts and emotions. The idea is wonderful, the execution does not quite live up to the potential. But the basic concept is so intriguing that the movie definitely is worth seeing.

The Brain That Wouldn't Die (1959). Dir. Joseph Green. Sp. Joseph Green. With Jason Evers, Virginia Leith, Adele Lamont. 81 min.
Scientist's fiancée is killed in accident—except for her head. He hooks the head to machinery and goes out to find a suitably sexy body to attach to it. So bad it's *almost* funny. The script is dreadful, the acting even worse.

Brazil (1985). Dir. Terry Gilliam. Sp. Terry Gilliam, Tom Stoppard, and Charles McKeown. With Jonathan Pryce, Robert de Niro, Katherine Helmond, Ian Holm, Bob Hoskins, Michael Palin, Ian Richardson. 131 min.

Intelligent and haunting rendition of Orwell's *1984*. Much better than the movie carrying the name of the book. A very funny, well-constructed movie, visually interesting, brilliantly acted (especially de Niro as Tuttle) and *there is virtually no violence*.

Charly (1968). Dir. Ralph Nelson. Sp. Stirling Silliphant. With Cliff Robertson, Claire Bloom, Lilia Skala, Dick van Patten. 103 min.

Retarded man undergoes treatment that makes him a genius. The only problem is that the effect is only temporary. A wonderful and deeply touching movie. Cliff Robertson is marvelous both as the retarded floor sweeper and the drug-induced genius.

Cherry 2000 (1988). Dir. Steve De Jamatt. Sp. Michael Almereyda. With Melanie Griffith, David Andrews, Ben Johnson, Tim Thomerson. 93 min.

Interesting only for being about a man who is obsessed with a sex-robot and for starring Melanie Griffith as the guide-mercenary-dream woman who teaches David Andrews to appreciate the real thing.

A Clockwork Orange (1971). Dir. Stanley Kubrick. Sp. Stanley Kubrick. With Malcolm McDowell, Patrick Magee, Adrienne Corri. 137 min.

Strange but great. An upbeat, happy movie about a depressing society. Visually and conceptually stunning.

Close Encounters of the Third Kind (1977). Dir. Steven Spielberg. Sp. Steven Spielberg. With Richard Dreyfuss, François Truffaut, Terri Garr, Melinda Dillon. 132 min.

Child-and-godlike alien visitors invite innocents of the human kind to visit with them. Despite weaknesses—such as a split plot where only one-half is interesting—a worthwhile movie. The aliens are convincingly alien and remain mysterious: a joyous angelic presence.

Colossus: The Forbin Project (1969). Dir. Joseph Sargent. Sp. James Bridges. With Eric Braeden, Susan Clark, William Schallert. 100 min.

The defense of the "free world" is placed in the relays of a supercomputer. The computer turns out to have a will to power. Good, not great. Raises some interesting issues and sticks to them. The acting is so-so and there are passages that seem long.

Creation of the Humanoids (1962). Dir. Wesley E. Barry. Sp. Jay Simmons. With Don Megowan, Frances McCann, Erica Elliot, Don Dolittle. 75 min.

After the apocalypse, humans are so few that an android race is introduced that can perform work and maintain a high standard of living. But the androids want to become fully human. This *should* have been a good movie: an interesting subject and a viable plot. Unfortunately, the acting is amateurish and the dialog unmouthable.

The Day After (1983). Dir. Nicholas Meyer. Sp. Edward Hume. With Jason Robards Jr., JoBeth Williams, Steve Guttenberg, John Cullen, John Lithgow. 126 min.
   Depressingly good and harrowingly real.

The Day the Earth Stood Still (1951). Dir. Robert Wise. Sp. Edmund H. North. With Michael Rennie, Patricia Neal, Hugh Marlowe, Sam Jaffe, Billy Gray. 92 min.
   The classic tale of visitors from space with a warning about military science and human competitiveness. The acting is a bit stodgy (except for Michael Rennie), and there are some unbearably naive scenes (such as the boy showing the alien the various national monuments), and the robot Gort is a hoot, but still, somehow it works.

Death Watch (1980). Dir. Bertrand Tavernier. Sp. Bertrand Tavernier and David Rayfield. With Romy Schneider, Harvey Keitel, Harry Dean Stanton, Max von Sydow. 117 min.
   A future society where death from natural causes has been virtually eradicated. A TV station is willing to pay a lot of money for someone to die "on the air." When the woman refuses, the producers use a cyborg— a man with a camera implanted in his eye—to get what they want. Intelligent and interesting.

Demon Seed (1977). Dir. Donald Cammell. Sp. Robert Jaffe and Roger O. Hirson. With Julie Christie, Fritz Weaver, Gerrit Graham. 94 min.
   A computer is invented that can solve problems of disease and economy. It refuses to be but a tool. A god-in-the-machine film. The movie only works in the scenes between Ms Christie and the rapacious computer. Not always in good taste and everything to excess, but gripping.

Dr. Jekyll and Mr. Hyde (1932). Dir. Rouben Mamoulian. Sp. Samuel Hoffenstein and Percy Heath. With Fredric March, Miriam Hopkins, Rose Hobart. 98 min.
   Fredric March is excellent and the movie works despite overly theatrical acting. It is, after all, one hell of a story.

Dr. Who: Revenge of the Cybermen (1986). Dir. Michael E. Briant. Sp. Chris Boucher. With Tom Baker, Elizabeth Sladen. 92 min.
   Evil robots out to kill off humans. Embarrassingly amateurish.

Dreamscape (1984). Dir. Joseph Ruben. Sp. Joe Ruben, David Loughery, and Chuck Russell. With Dennis Quaid, Max von Sydow, Christopher Plummer, Eddie Albert, Kate Capshaw. 99 min.

A scientist finds a way to enter into a person's dream-in-progress and heal or kill. There is a germ of a good idea, but the script never pulls it together.

Edward Scissorhands (1991). Dir. Tim Burton. Sp. Caroline Thompson (story by Thompson and Tim Burton). With Johnny Depp, Winona Ryder, Dianne Wiest, Anthony Michael Hall, Vincent Price.

Self-conscious fairy tale about an android, abandoned in mid-"creation" and left to try to fit into the bewildering world of 1950s American suburbia. Wonderful concept. The early scenes are great, but the movie falls apart as it fulfills the formula demands for violence and bad guys.

The Empire Strikes Back (1980). Dir. Irvin Kershner. Sp. Leigh Brackett and Lawrence Kasdan. With Mark Hamill, Harrison Ford, Carrie Fisher, Alec Guinnes.

Mock-Jung. Bombastic and boring.

E.T.: The Extraterrestrial (1982). Dir. Steven Spielberg. Sp. Melissa Mathison. With Dee Wallace, Henry Thomas, Peter Coyote, Robert McNaughton, Drew Barrymore. 115 min.

Boy, abandoned by his father, "invents" an alien in the same predicament. Metaphors for creativity and coming to terms with both the demands of the world and maintaining individuality. Lovely.

Fahrenheit 451 (1967). Dir. François Truffaut. Sp. François Truffaut and Jean-Louis Richard. With Oskar Werner, Julie Christie, Cyril Cusack, Anton Diffring. 111 min.

The temperature at which books burn. Dystopia where books and thoughts are banished and the masses are kept happy with drugs. Not quite what one would have hoped with that story and that director. It never *ignites*.

The First Men in the Moon (1964). Dir. Nathan Juran. Sp. Nigel Kneale and Jan Read. With Edward Judd, Martha Hyer, Lionel Jeffries, Peter Finch. 103 min.

Wells's tongue-in-cheek tale taken seriously. Ridiculously bad.

Flatliners (1990). Dir. Joel Schumacher. Sp. Peter Filardi. With Kiefer Sutherland, Julia Roberts, Kevin Bacon, William Baldwin, Oliver Platt.

Med students experiment with visiting death to see what's there. A rat-pack vehicle. The script is awful, the acting, except for Kevin Bacon, worse. Pretentious and hollow, another interesting idea stillborn on the cutting table. And all that steam!

The Fly (1958). Dir. Kurt Neumann. Sp. James Clavell. With Al Hedison, Patricia Owens, Vincent Price, Herbert Marshall. 94 min.

A scientist transgresses on the divine turf while trying to help humanity. A good B-movie: strong on plot and concept. The problem is that the concept is idiotic and the dated gender patterns are hard to swallow.

The Fly (1986). Dir. David Cronenberg. Sp. Charles Edward Pogue. With Jeff Goldblum, Geena Davis, John Getz. 100 min.

As above. Typical Cronenberg: long on disgusting close-ups of disintegrating limbs and blood and gore, short on taste.

Forbidden Planet (1956). Dir. Fred McLeod Wilcox. Sp. Cyrill Hume. With Walter Pidgeon, Anne Francis, Leslie Nielsen, Jack Kelly. 98 min.

The classic about the race on a distant planet that has found a way to feed to a computer the essence of all its knowledge and all that is good and wonderful about its society, but it forgets that culture is but a veneer on top of the unbridled libido. Another good B-movie. Stodgy acting, Anne Francis is downright ridiculous, unconvincing special effects. Still, it's a very good story.

Frankenhooker (1990). Dir. Frank Henenlotter. Sp. Robert Martin and Frank Henenlotter. With James Lorinz, Patty Mullen, Charlotte Helenkamp, Lia Chang, Sandy Colosime.

Witty remake of *The Brain That Wouldn't Die*. Obviously a low- budget job. Some inept acting, but funny if, despite the ending, exploitative.

Frankenstein (1931). Dir. James Whale. Sp. Garrett Fort, Robert Florey, and Francis Edward Faragoh. With Colin Clive, Mae K. Clarke, Boris Karloff, John Boles. 71 min.

Wooden and pedestrian, but Karloff is worth the ticket. Good story, though.

Godzilla, King of the Monsters (1956). Dir. Inoshiro Honda and Terry Morse. Sp. Inoshiro Honda and Takeo Murata. With Raymond Burr, Takashi Shimura. 80 min.

Creature is awakened from million-year sleep at the bottom of the ocean by underwater H-bomb blasts. Silly.

The Handmaid's Tale (1990). Dir. Volker Schlöndorf. Sp. Harold Pinter. With Faye Dunaway, Aidan Quinn, Elizabeth McGovern, Robert Duvall.

Answers the question of what would happen if the religious right took over the United States. Not as successful as the book, but not uninteresting. The scenes between Dunaway and Duvall are excellent.

Honey, I Shrunk the Kids (1989). Dir. Joe Johnson. Sp. Ed Naha and Tom Schulman. With Rick Moranis, Matt Frewer, Marcia Strassman.
   Scientist's machine accidentally shrinks his and neighbor's children. I find this rather idiotic.

Humanoids from the Deep (1980). Dir. Barbara Peters. Sp. Frederic James. With Doug McClure, Ann Turkel, Vic Morrow. 80 min.
   Attempt to induce growth artificially in salmon leads to nightmare of fish on the evolutionary fast-track. Nothing really works. The screenplay is sluggish, the acting amateur night in Hollywood.

I Married a Monster from Outer Space (1958). Dir. Gene Fowler. Sp. Louis Vittes. With Tom Tryon, Gloria Talbott, Ken Lynch, Maxie Rosenbloom. 78 min.
   Woman marries her dream-Bill only to discover he's really an alien out to breed with her. A not-so-good B-movie, but there are some convincing scenes of life in Anytown.

Incredible Shrinking Man (1957). Dir. Jack Arnold. Sp. Richard Matheson. With Grant Williams, Randy Stuart, Paul Langton, April Kent. 81 min.
   Man sails through atomic fallout. Shrinks. Not great, but entertaining.

Invaders from Mars (1953). Dir. William Cameron Menzies. Sp. Richard Blake. With Helena Carter, Jimmy Hunt, Leif Erickson, Arthur Franz. 78 min.
   The premise is fascinating: a kid who wakes up one day and suddenly everyone has changed and turns on him. Alien "trolls" invade people and make them into automatons. But the movie is inept.

Invasion of the Body Snatchers (1956). Dir. Don Siegel. Sp. Daniel Mainwaring. With Kevin McCarthy, Dana Wynter, Carolyn Jones, King Donovan. 80 min.
   Seedpods drifting through space land on Earth. The seeds invade humans and take over—minus emotions. Effective and hypnotic once it gets going.

Invasion of the Body Snatchers (1978). Dir. Philip Kaufman. Sp. W. D. Richter. With Donald Sutherland, Brooke Adams, Leonard Nimoy, Jeff Goldblum, Veronica Cartwright. 115 min.
   As above. Almost as good as the original, but there is more "flab," the movie is too long and has too many "cutesy" scenes (like the literary cocktail party). Sutherland is, as always, a fascinating presence.

The Invisible Man (1933). Dir. James Whale. Sp. R. C. Sherriff. With Claude Rains, Gloria Stuart, Una O'Connor, Henry Travers. 71 min.
Wells's story of a scientist who wants to do the impossible and gets caught in his own hubris. The story and the concept are excellent. The movie is pedestrian.

The Last Starfighter (1984). Dir. Nick Castle. Sp. Jonathan Betuel. With Lance Guest, Robert Preston, Dan O'Herlihy, Catherine Mary Stewart. 100 min.
Pubescent fare. Rite of passage: boy becomes man by playing computer games and graduating to savior of the universe and gets to pick up the neighbor's daughter and whisk her into space with him. Don't waste your time.

Liquid Sky (1982). Dir. Slava Tsukerman. Sp. Slava Tsukerman, Anne Carlisle and Nina V. Kerova. With Anne Carlisle, Paul Sheppard and Susan Doukas.
Minuscule alien feeds off drug produced in the human brain during orgasm. Weird but interesting. The music is haunting, the story confused, the imagery fascinating.

Making Mr. Right (1987). Dir. Susan Seidelman. Sp. Floyd Byars and Laurie Frank. With John Malkovich, Ann Magnuson, Ben Masters, Glenne Headly. 98 min.
Woman socializes asocial scientist's creation for the marriage instead of the spacemarket. Has some amusing scenes and a *fascinating*, if never really developed, premise. On balance, I'd recommend it.

Maximum Overdrive (1986). Dir. Stephen King. Sp. Stephen King. With Tom Hanks, Chris Makepeace, Wendy Crewson, David Wallace. 103 min.
Group of strangers stuck in a diner in the desert as trucks gone berserk try to pick them off one by one. Stupid? You bet!

Metropolis (1926). Dir. Fritz Lang. Sp. Fritz Lang and Thea von Harbou. With Brigitte Helm, Alfred Abel. (Silent.) 120 min.
A classic. Class society laid out graphically as a layer cake. Scientist tries to create perfect worker/lover. Fascinating in its own operatic way. The acting is mostly interesting as a historical relic. But it works—silent, black and white and grainy as it is. A must.

Millennium (1989). Dir. Michael Anderson. Sp. John Varley (based on his short story "Air Raid.") With Kris Kristofferson, Cheryl Ladd, and Daniel J. Travanti. 108 min.
Some interesting elements. The notion of a future without sex-differ-

entiation is by itself reason enough to see this film. I generally found it to be better than its very poor reputation.

Modern Times (1936). Dir. Charles Chaplin. Sp. Charles Chaplin. With Charlie Chaplin, Paulette Godard. 89 min.

Is this really an sf film, you ask? There certainly are science fiction elements, such as the surveillance technology at the factory and the feeding machine. Wonderfully funny. I still laugh every time I see it. The best part is the first: the scenes in the factory.

1984 (1984). Dir. Michael Redford. Sp. Michael Redford. With John Hurt, Richard Burton, Suzanna Hamilton, Cyril Cusack. 123 min.

Sneaking boredom. Too reverent and devoid of any deep-felt relevance. As a critic has said, it's "embalmed."

On the Beach (1959). Dir. Stanley Kramer. Sp. John Paxton. With Gregory Peck, Ava Gardner, Fred Astaire, Anthony Perkins. 133 min.

Group of people waiting for the wave—created by atomic explosions—that will destroy them and humanity. Harrowing.

Parts: The Clonus Horror (1979). Dir. Robert S. Fiveson. Sp. Ron Smith and Bob Sullivan. With Tim Donelly, Dick Sargent, Peter Graves, Keenan Wynn, Lurene Tuttle. 90 min.

A mysterious college campus is really an organ farm where clones of living people are raised—like crops—to provide spare parts. Another missed opportunity. The idea is fascinating but it never quite materializes. Mostly because of pervasive amateurishness.

Predator (1987). Dir. John McTiernan. Sp. Jim Thomes and John Thomes. With Arnold Schwarzenegger, Carl Weathers, Elpidia Carillo, Bill Duke. 107 min.

Hunt for a homicidal alien in the rain forest. Violent and stupid: an entry in the category of movies that substitute constant, unremitting violence for plot. If Arnold with a machine gun against oiled muscles is your thing, go see it. If not, forget it.

Return of the Jedi (1983). Dir. Richard Marquand. Sp. Lawrence Kasdan and George Lucas. With Mark Hamill, Carrie Fisher, Harrison Ford, Billy Dee Williams.

Like the other entries in the *Star Wars* series: bombastic and boring.

The Road Warrior (1981). Dir. George Miller. Sp. Terry Hayes, George Miller and Brian Hennant. With Mel Gibson, Bruce Spence, Vernon Wells, Mike Preston. 94 min.

Bleak future-punk landscape. Tribes of survivors fighting for survival. A movie with a distinctive look and feel. The best of the series.

Robocop (1987). Dir. Paul Verhoeven. Sp. Edward Neumeier and Michael Miner. With Peter Weller, Nancy Allen, Dan O'Herlihy, Ronny Cox, Kurtwood Smith, Miguel Ferrer. 103 min.
Corporate machismo expressed via the medium of a cyborg: docile killing power. But there is a clump of human flesh—and a soul—encased in the hardware. Despite the excessive violence and the too-leering Bad Guys, rather impressive.

Robocop 2 (1990). Dir. Irvin Kershner. Sp. Frank Miller and Walon Green. With Peter Weller, Nancy Allen, Dan O'Herlihy, Felton Perry, Belinda Bauer. 110 min.
As above. Not as good as the original. Some passages seem almost like a send-up of the first movie. But there are several interesting scenes that deal with the cyborg's identity.

Rollerball (1975). Dir. Norman Jewison. Sp. William Harrison. With James Caan, John Houseman, Maud Adams, Ralph Richardson, John Beck. 128 min.
The future corporate Roman Empire, complete with gladiators. Giant-killer tale. Visceral and exciting, but the message drowns in the violence and insistence on individual heroes who single-handedly solve all the problems.

Runaway (1984). Dir. Michael Crichton. Sp. Michael Crichton. With Tom Selleck, Cynthia Rhodes, Gene Simmons, Kirstie Alley. 99 min.
Nonanthropomorphic and believable robots in a not too distant future. But too many plots are pulling in too many directions.

Running Man (1987). Dir. Paul Michael Glaser. Sp. John Mortimer. With Arnold Schwarzenegger, Maria Conchita Alonso, Richard Dawson, Yaphet Kotto, Jim Brown. 101 min.
American gladiators with a deadly twist. TV ratings above all and violence-TV as opium for the masses. Too much violence and evil leering for a frail plot.

Short Circuit (1986). Dir. John Badham. Sp. S. S. Wilson and Brent Maddock. With Ally Sheedy, Steve Guttenberg, Fisher Stevens, Austin Pendleton. 95 min.
Military hardware develops a soul and a sense of self. Charming. Especially the scenes between Johnny-5 the robot and Ally Sheedy.

Short Circuit 2 (1988). Dir. Kenneth Johnson. Sp. S. S. Wilson and Brent Maddock. With Fisher Stevens, Michael McKean, Cynthia Gibb, Jack Weston. 110 min.

Johnny-5 becomes fully human, that is, enculturated in American popculture. Some funny scenes because Fisher Stevens is a funny actor. Ultimately derivative.

Slime People (1963). Dir. Robert Hutton. Sp. Vance Skarstedt. With Robert Hutton, Les Tremayne, Robert Burton, Judee Morton.

Subterranean monsters driven above ground by atomic blasts. Pretty bad. Bad script, bad acting, terrible special effects.

Soylent Green (1973). Dir. Richard Fleischer. Sp. Stanley R. Greenberg. With Charlton Heston, Edward G. Robinson, Joseph Cotton, Chuck Connors. 97 min.

A future where the world is in the vice of The Corporation and The Corporation unscrupulously tries to convince people to commit suicide to lower the population pressure in a postnuclear ecological wasteland. The dead are "processed" and sold, under the name of Soylent Green, as food. The movie is, unfortunately, pedestrian although there are good scenes such as the one where Edward G. Robinson enters the suicide parlor and dies while watching long-extinct wildlife on a giant screen.

Star Trek: The Super Computer (1978). Dir. John Meredith Lucas. Sp. D. C. Fontana. With William Shatner, Leonard Nimoy, DeForest Kelly.

Scientist introduces computer that is supposed to make life easier. It develops a severe case of megalomania. Predictable.

Star Wars (1977). Dir. George Lucas. Sp. George Lucas. With Mark Hamill, Alec Guinness, Carrie Fisher, Harrison Ford. 121 min.

Not my cup of tea. Watered-down Jung via Joseph Campbell: hollow, bombastic and long, long, long.

The Stepford Wives (1975). Dir. Bryan Forbes. Sp. William Goldman. With Katherine Ross, Paula Prentiss, Patrick O'Neal, Peter Masterson. 115 min.

Threatened by feminism, the men of a small town kill off their wives and replace them with "Freudian" robots. Fascinating.

Superman III (1983). Dir. Richard Lester. Sp. David Newman and Leslie Newman. With Christopher Reeve, Richard Pryor, Robert Vaughn, Annette O'Toole, Jackie Cooper, Marc McClure, Pamela Stephenson. 127 min.

Evil coffee baron uses "innocent" computer genius to create supercomputer that can help him do evil. Only Superman can save the world, etc.

Too many plots, too many unfunny "funny" scenes, boring and predictable.

The Terminator (1984). Dir. James Cameron. Sp. James Cameron and Gale Anne Hurd. With Arnold Schwarzenegger, Linda Hamilton, Michael Biehn. 108 min.
  Back to the present: cyborg and man from the future are sent back with inverse missions. Sf remake of the story of Christ the savior. Visceral and hypnotic. Arnold's best movie and Biehn ain't bad either.

The Terror Within (1988). Dir. Tierry Notz. Sp. Thomas M. Cleaver. With George Kennedy, Andrew Stevens. 89 min.
  After the apocalypse. Unspecified monsters roam the Earth. Humans are on the brink of elimination. George Kennedy looks slightly bemused as if he's not quite sure what he's doing in this flick. Beats me too.

The Thing (From Another World) (1951). Dir. Christian Nyby (Howard Hawks). Sp. Charles Lederer. With Kenneth Tobey, Margaret Sheridan, James Arness. 87 min.
  Evil carrot from outer space buried in the inland ice. Clumsy but effective. The Thing, however, is rather ridiculous.

The Thing (1982). Dir. John Carpenter. Sp. Bill Lancaster. With Kurt Russell, Wilford Brimley, Richard Dysart. 108 min.
  As above: fire and ice. Too many scenes that dwell on the disgusting and violent. But a good thriller.

This Island Earth (1955). Dir. Joseph M. Newman. Sp. Franklin Coen and Edward G. O'Callaghan. With Jeff Morrow, Rex Reason, Faith Domergue. 86 min.
  Scientist-cowboy pitted against smart but soulless aliens thirsty for Earth know-how. The aliens are too funny. The humans are too good to be true.

THX 1138 (1971). Dir. George Lucas. Sp. George Lucas and Walter Murch. With Robert Duvall, Donald Pleasence, Maggie McOmie. 88 min.
  White-on-white future dystopia where humans are drugged into docility. Insistently and tiresomely mysterious. Some interesting ideas, such as the hologram/man.

Total Recall (1990). Dir. Paul Verhoeven. Sp. Ronald Shusett, Dan O'Bannon, Gary Oldman, and Jon Povill. With Arnold Schwarzenegger, Rachel Ticotin, Sharon Stone, Ronny Cox, Michael Ironside. 109 min.
  Grand-scale fairy tale about identity in a future dystopia where science has found ways to invade mind and memory. Too many script cooks

spoiled what is almost a great movie. And even for a fairy tale, the characters are too stereotypical. All evil and all good characters are inherently boring.

Twins (1988). Dir. Ivan Reitman. Sp. William Davies, William Osborne, Timothy Harris, and Herschel Weingrod. With Arnold Schwarzenegger, Danny de Vito, Kelly Preston, Chloe Webb. 105 min.
   Scientists try to create the true *Herrenrasse* by mixing genes from different men like a cocktail. Occasionally amusing. Mostly not.

2001: A Space Odyssey (1968). Dir. Stanley Kubrick. Sp. Arthur C. Clarke. With Keir Dullea, William Sylvester, Gary Lockwood, Douglas Rain (Hal). 139 min.
   Perhaps a film about the past and future of mankind? Fascinating. Visually a work of art (except for the monkey suits). Deeply mysterious but never boring. The scenes with Hal are great.

Videodrome (1983). Dir. David Cronenberg. Sp. David Cronenberg. With James Woods, Deborah Harry, Sonja Smits. 88 min.
   Cable station that enters the minds of viewers and hypnotizes them. A good idea that's never developed fully. Concentrates on being scary.

Village of the Damned (1960). Dir. Wolf Rilla. Sp. Wolf Rilla, Stirling Silliphant, and George Barclay. With George Sanders, Martin Stephens, Barbara Shelley, Michael Gwynne, Laurence Naismith. 78 min.
   "Children" born to human women are spearheads of alien invasion. Great. Taut. Focused. Intelligent.

Wargames (1983). Dir. John Badham. Sp. Lawrence Lasker and Walter F. Parkes. With Matthew Broderick, Dabney Coleman, Ally Sheedy, John Wood, Barry Corbin. 114 min.
   Computer hacker and computer program show the emptiness of our age of science and materialism. Parable of "children" stranded in an ethical vacuum. Some good scenes (the ones with Matthew Broderick), some good ideas, but the movie falls apart. Ally Sheedy is a disaster.

The War of the Worlds (1953). Dir. Byron Haskin. Sp. Barré Lyndon. With Gene Barry, Les Tremayne, Ann Robinson. 85 min.
   Another Hollywood mistreatment of Wells.

Westworld (1973). Dir. Michael Crichton. Sp. Michael Crichton. With Yul Brynner, Richard Benjamin, James Brolin. 88 min.
   Humanlike robots in amusement park lie down dead or sexually submissive for the entertainment of tourists. Until one robot rebels. Good as far as it goes.

"X"—The Man with the X-Ray Eyes (1963). Dir. Robert Corman. Sp. Robert Dillon and Ray Russell. With Ray Milland, Diana van der Vlis, Harold J. Stone, John Hoyt, Don Rickles. 80 min.

Scientist invents drops that allow him to see to the center of the universe. He becomes "god" and gouges his own eyes. The concept is a good one. The movie is melodramatic and sometimes embarrassing.

Yor: The Hunter from the Future (1983). Dir. Antonio Margheriti (alias Anthony M. Dawson). Sp. Antonio Margheriti and Robert Bailey. With Reb Brown, Corinne Clery, John Steiner. 88 min.

Unbelievably bad.

Zardoz (1974). Dir. John Boorman. Sp. John Boorman. With Sean Connery, Charlotte Rampling. 105 min.

Story of a blood-rich hunter entering a "vortex" society of asexual, thought-sharing pallor. The living dead. A whirlwind of images, ideas and concepts slapped onto the screen at dizzying speed.

■ Other Movies Mentioned

Conan the Barbarian (1982). Dir. John Milius. Sp. John Milius and Oliver Stone. With Arnold Schwarzenegger, Sandahl Bergman, James Earl Jones, Mako. 129 min.

An embarrassment for all involved. What is James Earl Jones doing in this company? Not to mention Oliver Stone.

Conan the Destroyer (1984). Dir. Richard Fleischer. Sp. Stanley Mann. With Arnold Schwarzenegger, Grace Jones, Wilt Chamberlain, Mako.

Adolescent male fantasies. Violent and stupid.

Every Man for Himself and God Against Them All (1975). Dir. Werner Herzog. Sp. Werner Herzog. With Bruno S., Walter Ladengast, Brigitta Mira.

Wonderful film about a boy who is found at age sixteen after having been confined and without human contact since birth. A stunning and deeply moving film.

First Blood (1982). Dir. Ted Kotcheff. Sp. Michael Kozoll, William Sackheim and Q. Moonblood. With Sylvester Stallone, Richard Crenna, Brian Dennehy.

A blood feast. A gory revenge fantasy. Notice the ubiquitous killing technology.

Die Hard 2: Die Harder (1990). Dir. Renny Harlin. Sp. Steven E. Souza

and Doug Richardson. With Bruce Willis, Bonnie Bedelia, William Atherton.
Long on violence and plot, short on credibility. Interesting for the unlimited destruction of major technology.

The Last Temptation of Christ (1988). Dir. Martin Scorsese. Sp. Paul Schrader. With Willem Defoe, Harvey Keitel, Barbara Hershey, Harry Dean Stanton, David Bowie, Verna Bloom. 164 min.
The quintessential dilemma for a god (or, for that matter, a romantic genius): to be a happy human or a savior.

Longtime Companion (1990). Dir. Norman Rene. Sp. Craig Lucas. With Bruce Davison, Campbell Scott, Dermot Mulroney, Mark Lamos and Patrick Cassidy. 96 min.
A history of AIDS seen through the eyes of a group of friends. Excellent and moving.

Pumping Iron (1977). Dir. George Butler. Sp. Robert Fiore. With Arnold Schwarzenegger, Lou Ferrigno.
Introduced Schwarzenegger to the world outside body building aficionados. Interesting documentary.

Rambo: First Blood II (1985). Dir. George Pan Cosmatos. Sp. Michael Kozoll, William Sackhern, and Sylvester Stallone. With Sylvester Stallone, Richard Crenna, Charles Napier, Steven Berkoff, Julia Nickson. 94 min.
Violent and predictable.

Rambo: First Blood Part II (1985). Dir. George P. Cosmatos. Sp. Sylvester Stallone and James Cameron. With Sylvester Stallone, Richard Crenna, Charles Napier.
Weapons and violence.

The Right Stuff (1983). Dir. Phil Kaufman. Sp. Phil Kaufman. With Sam Shepard, Scott Glenn, Ed Harris, Dennis Quaid, Barbara Hershey. 193 min.
The story of the first Americans in space.

Rio Grande (1950). Dir. John Ford. Sp. James Kevin McGuinness. With John Wayne, Maureen O'Hara, Claude Jarman Jr., Ben Johnson. 105 min.
Epic and entertaining. The Western landscape is a major player.

Rosemary's Baby (1968). Dir. Roman Polanski. Sp. Roman Polanski. With Mia Farrow, John Cassavetes, Ruth Gordon, Ralph Bellamy.
Scary and fascinating. The baby from hell—or outer space. Reminis-

cent of the baby in *Demon Seed* and the strange children in *Village of the Damned.*

The Searchers (1956). Dir. John Ford. Sp. Frank S. Nugent. With John Wayne, Natalie Wood, Jeffrey Hunter, Ward Bond, Vera Miles. 119 min.
A fine movie from Ford. A white woman is abducted by Indians and two men set out to retrieve her. The enemy they have to fight is mighty nature, the vast American continent, and the Indians who are like "nature-spirits": almost anthropomorphic extensions of nature itself.

Splash! (1984). Dir. Ron Howard. Sp. Lowell Ganz, Babaloo Mandel and Bruce Jay Friedman. With Tom Hanks, Daryl Hannah, Eugene Levy, John Candy.
Occasionally amusing man-meets-mermaid flick. Hanks and Hannah work well together. She has to learn about human (i.e., American popular) culture and, like E. T., Johnnny-5 of *Short Circuit* and Schwarzenegger's gentle giant in *Twins*, she does so with the aid of TV, especially TV commercials. The funniest scene is the one in Bloomingdales' where she is watching a wall of TVs give her cultural information.

Stakeout (1987). Dir. John Badham. Sp. Jim Kouf. With Richard Dreyfuss, Emilio Estevez, Madeleine Stowe.
Cop-plus-love story. It works. Dreyfuss is amusing, Estevez amateurish. The interesting scene is the final showdown, set among giant machinery in a logging factory.

The Wizard of Oz (1939). Dir. Victor Fleming. Sp. Noel Langley, Florence Ryerson, and Edgar Allan Wolfe. 102 min.
Wonderful.

■ TV Series

American Gladiators. Volunteer contestants competing against "gladiators" who shoot missiles (nondeadly) at them and slap them around. Shades of *Running Man* and *Rollerball.*

America's Funniest Home Videos. Not so funny: drag-ordinary-people-on-screen and then make fun of them. Life-as-story. The hosts are cloyingly "cute."

Hidden Camera. Some funny episodes.

Star Trek. Some interesting episodes. But too moralizing and obvious.

Index